LIFE OF
BRINE

LIFE OF BRINE

A SURFER'S JOURNEY

PHIL JARRATT

hardie grant books

Published in 2017 by Hardie Grant Books,
an imprint of Hardie Grant Publishing

Hardie Grant Books (Melbourne)
Building 1, 658 Church Street
Richmond, Victoria 3121

Hardie Grant Books (London)
5th & 6th Floors
52–54 Southwark Street
London SE1 1UN

hardiegrantbooks.com

 A catalogue record for this
book is available from the
National Library of Australia

Life of Brine
ISBN 978 1 74379 232 2

Cover and text design by Philip Campbell Design
Typeset by Cannon Typesetting
Printed in Australia by Griffin Press, part of Ovato, an Accredited
ISO AS/NZS 14001 Environmental Management System printer.

 The paper this book is printed on is certified against the
Forest Stewardship Council® Standards. Griffin Press holds
FSC® chain of custody certification SGS-COC-005088. FSC®
promotes environmentally responsible, socially beneficial and
economically viable management of the world's forests.

To Jackie, for better or for worse.

CONTENTS

At 65. (Photo Jason Mccallum)

INTRODUCTION

The wave that took my breath away, and almost took my life with it, was the one I didn't see coming. It smacked me down from behind, like a coward punch, just as I broke the surface and gasped hungrily for air.

I should have been expecting that second wave. The wave that nailed me initially had been the first of a multiple-wave set, and surfers are supposed to know these things, but in my struggle to find the surface, I'd lost all the planning and logic that a good surfer usually employs.

I was gripped by something a little bit scary, but it was less than panic. As far as I can recall, I didn't really think I was fighting for survival, if indeed I thought about anything at all. It was simply that moment that every surfer becomes acquainted with sooner or later, that moment when you think that maybe, just maybe, you have bitten off more than you can chew.

And then the ocean was smashing me again, driving me down, not in the easy arc of a diver, but the frenzied rinse of a washing machine, shaking, shuddering, gripping me like some horrible thrill ride. When the force of the wave finally passed I burst to the surface again, taking in air in shallow, raspy breaths. I clambered onto my surfboard and lay, spread across it, while smaller sets of waves washed me, and it, closer to the inshore reef. It was then that I had the scariest realisation. My breathing was still laboured, not returning to normal as it should, as it had every other time the ocean had given me a hiding. I was gasping and wheezing, powerless to do anything other than allow the force of the waves to push me into the shore.

The fin of my board scraped across the last rock shelf and somehow I managed to pick myself up, negotiate three or four awkward steps through the shallows and drop to the black sand, exhausted, anxious, and yet at some deeper level, weirdly calm.

I lay there on the tideline next to my board for a long time—perhaps twenty minutes—while my friends surfed on, oblivious to my plight. Early morning joggers, power walkers and dog walkers just ignored me, some old stumble-bum surfer sleeping off a big one perhaps, or maybe a '60s casualty peaking on acid. I can't remember everything that went through my mind that morning, but I know that what frightened me more than anything was the stream of thoughts and memories that punctuated my more rational thinking. The random thoughts—waves, good times in exotic places, bad times in shitholes, kids, grandkids, family crises, share prices, the wife, old loves, bad jokes, good wine, god knows what else—or rather, the fact that I was having them, made me consider the old clichés about a man's life appearing before him, like some lame musical comedy in the moments before the final curtain. Was this what I was experiencing? Would my final words be, 'Is that all there is?' Or 'I wish I'd spent more time at the office'?

And then I started to feel better. I was still short of breath, but the pain in my back and shoulders, which I'd put down to the wrenching of tired old muscles during the hold-downs, began to recede. I sat up, checked my pulse (still there), slowly stood, then picked up my board and even more slowly began the walk along the beach, up the temple steps, across the bay, through the creek and to the cafe where my wife and friends would be waiting for me to join them for breakfast.

As I walked, I tried to piece the morning together—it was not yet nine, but it seemed it had been a long day already. It had begun for me soon after first light, when I strapped my Bali longboard onto the side rack of my scooter and puttered down Jalan Pantai Pererenan to Pondok Nyoman, where our friends were staying. The ocean was clean and inviting, but the tide was too low and the swell too big for the rivermouth break in front of Nyoman's, so Rusty, John and I had made the quick decision to walk a kilometre along the beach to Old Man's, a reasonably user-friendly wave that worked better in these conditions.

The paddle out at Old Man's was easy enough between sets but the swell was hitting it very straight. We paddled around for ages looking for a place to take off where we'd have a reasonable chance of

Pererenan, Bali, 2014.

completing the wave. Rusty took the lead, of course—over seventy and still the hungriest. Half a century ago, Rusty Miller's photo, a study of concentration sliding down a meaty wave at Sunset Beach, became a billboard for a popular beer brand, seen all over America's burgeoning freeway system. He still paddles and drops down the face with that steely glare of concentration etched on his wrinkled face. It's only when he leans into a graceful turn and races along the green wall that his expression lights up, and he appears to drop twenty, maybe thirty years.

But Old Man's wasn't cooperating with us. So when the young Californian longboarder Jared Mell knee-paddled through our group and said, 'Have you guys been watching the bommie?' we glanced at the set of big waves breaking in deeper water way out to sea and promptly fell in behind him.

Medewi, Bali, 2013.

I had already taken a couple of set waves on the head at Old Man's, and felt like I might have been coming down with some kind of tropical virus. I just seemed to be lacking energy. So I watched another large set break as the others approached the impact zone of the outer break, then paddled quickly to the inside, planning to find my feet on something smaller.

I let two waves go because I hadn't yet paddled deep enough, then saw another large set looming wider on the outside. Damn, I'd missed my window. I turned and paddled hard for deeper water, but the first wave broke just in front of me. I put my trust in the Velcro strip around my ankle and dived for the depths.

Look, this was no day for heroes and fools. It was just another slightly-larger-than-average, late dry-season day on the Canggu coast of South Bali, a strip of beach and reef better known for its Russian-owned surf schools and hordes of Eurotrash beginners than for death-defying surf sessions. Those of us who surf there regularly do so for convenience rather than quality. Although there are certainly some memorable days, this particular morning wasn't one of them. It was just a few old guys having fun, until one of them wasn't.

More than a dozen Australian men aged over fifty died in the surf in Bali that season and the next. I was extremely lucky not to be one of them, although I didn't know that at the time.

'How was your surf?' my wife asked. She was checking her Facebook, having swum a few lengths of the rooftop pool, finished a watermelon juice and ordered a coffee. It was the way we liked to start the day in Bali. I tried to smile.

'Okay,' I lied. 'Jesus I'm getting old. Everything aches.'

Everything continued to ache that spring. I found myself gasping for breath in the surf after almost every wave, and the pain in my neck and shoulders often got so bad I had to paddle in. On the steamy October morning I was to launch my book, *Bali Heaven and Hell*, at the Ubud Writers & Readers Festival, I lugged a wheelie-bag full of books a few blocks to the courtesy bus stop. I sat in the bus breathless and sweating, unable to talk. In the writers' green room I slumped on a couch and drank bottles of water. My first gig of the day was a chat show with Rusty Miller. Rusty arrived, took one look at me and said, 'You look like shit.'

I got through the session and the book launch, and the celebratory dinner that followed, with a little help from alcohol, which seemed to

Signing session with Rusty Miller, Ubud Writers Festival, 2014.

keep me calm and focused. I related all of this—or most of it—to my GP at home in Noosa a couple of days later. She looked at me in disbelief, arching her eyebrows when I explained my self-medication program. Finally, she said, 'I think you've had a heart attack.'

I have enormous respect for this doctor but her diagnosis was so absurd that I almost laughed in her face. 'I think I'd know if I'd had a heart attack, Sylvia,' I smirked.

'Well, why don't I book you in to see a cardiologist today and then we'll both know.' It wasn't a question—she was already on the phone.

And so it began, the long, scary, boring, commonplace, life-changing sequence of hospital corridors and concerned faces and false laughter and cannulas and angiograms and endless public ward nights of farts and gurgles that combine to take you on the journey from being invincible to being a heart patient. And there are no return tickets. However lucky you may have been (and with a ninety-five per cent blockage in my major descending artery, I was pretty lucky), however normal your resumed life might seem, you are a heart patient for the rest of your days.

I was feeling somewhat pissed off about this prospect until I went to one of those post-heart attack counselling sessions that are more or less compulsory. We were mostly men, and mostly around my age, except for one exceptionally fit-looking younger man who couldn't sit still. He was angry, very angry. He couldn't listen to the mostly sensible advice that was being dispensed. He kept interrupting with bursts of anger and directionless abuse. I wanted to tell him to shut the fuck up, but I realised that if I was him I would probably be just as angry, maybe more so. The more abusive he became, the more I felt for him. He was in the prime of life—I'd already had sixty-three good years. (Make that sixty—I'm not sure the initial mewling and puking bit was all that much fun.)

That poor whining bastard in the counselling sessions did me a huge favour. He made me realise I'd already been blessed with a good and eventful life and a wonderful family, then blessed again with a second chance. Every day from here on in was a bonus, and should be treated as such. I know, I know, leave no cliché unturned, but try having a heart attack first, then come back and tell me it's a cliché. Of course, I often forget all this and fall into the old patterns that could damage or even kill me, but the realities of my second life always return before too long, and hopefully before I've caused too much damage.

One of the deals I cut with myself while being wheeled around the corridors by people in blue coats and caps, or while lying awake listening to the snorers and farters in the public ward, was to stop putting things off. Like writing this memoir. For years I'd been stockpiling my old articles and diaries for that leisurely period of life in the fairly distant future (let's call them the golden years) when I would have the time and inclination to share the stories and characters and passions collected over a lifetime of close and abiding association with the ocean, and more particularly with the ocean's waves. Whatever I've done in my life, it's always come back to that, and while I'm no different to any other journeyman surfer who forgot to grow up, I feel I at least have the basic skills needed to write about it. And the time is now.

This, then, is no apologia for the wasted, waxy years. It's just one surfer's story, one life of brine.

CHAPTER ONE

FIRST WAVE

The first wave. It's where a life in surfing should start, isn't it? But I can't remember my first one. First kiss, yes. First full-blown sexual experience, yes, of course. More about that later. First wave? Mmm.

Surfers have been remembering their first waves and writing about them for centuries now, for better or worse. Consider the following from Mark Twain (Samuel Clemens), who reported for the *Sacramento Union* from the Hawaiian Islands in 1866:

> In one place we came upon a large company of naked natives, of both sexes and all ages, amusing themselves with the national pastime of surf-bathing. Each heathen would paddle three or four hundred yards out to sea, (taking a short board with him), then face the shore and wait for a particularly prodigious billow to come along: at the right moment he would fling his board upon its foamy crest and himself upon the board, and here he would come whizzing by like a bombshell! It did not seem that a lightning express train could shoot along at a more hair-lifting speed. I tried surf-bathing once, subsequently, but made a failure of it. I got the board placed right, and at the right moment, too; but missed the connection myself. The board struck the shore in three-quarters of a second, without any cargo, and I struck the bottom at about the same time, with a couple of barrels of water in me. None but natives ever master the art of surf-bathing thoroughly.

I'm rather glad I never read old Sam on 'none but natives' before my own saltwater journey began, but maybe I would have taken heart from this, written by Jack London, the adventure novelist and travel writer, in 1907:

> I shall never forget the first big wave I caught out there in the deep water. I saw it coming, turned my back on it and paddled for dear life. Faster and faster my board went, till it seemed my arms would drop off. What was happening behind me I could not tell. One cannot look behind and paddle the windmill stroke. I heard the crest of the wave hissing and churning, and then my board was lifted and flung forward. I scarcely knew what happened the first half-minute. Though I kept my eyes open, I could not see anything, for I was buried in the rushing white of the crest. But I did not mind. I was chiefly conscious of ecstatic bliss at having caught the wave.

The 'ecstatic bliss' was short-lived. London got shockingly sunburnt that day at Waikiki and was rarely seen on a surfboard again. On the other hand, and more than a century later, Pulitzer Prize winner William Finnegan's captivating account of his first wave, ridden at San Onofre, California, at age ten, describes the beginning of a lifelong quest:

> I wobbled to my feet. I remember looking to the side and seeing that the wave was not weakening, and looking ahead and seeing that my path was clear for a very long way, and then looking down and being transfixed by the rocky sea bottom streaming under my feet. The water was clear, slightly turquoise, shallow. But there was room for me to pass over safely. And so I did, again and again, that first day.

I know so well that feeling, that moment of sheer amazement that you are skating across gorgeous coral reef with just a thin column of clear water and a plastic-coated plank between you, but for me that all came later. The memory of my first time is a blur spanning a couple of early '60s summers, during Australian surfing's general transition from balsa to foam surfboards and my personal transition from a Narm rubber surfoplane to other people's surfboards and then, finally to my very own, presented to me on my thirteenth birthday.

It may seem strange to surfers of subsequent generations that I got my first surfboard at the ripe old age of thirteen, having already squandered half a dozen good years that might have been used to develop my skills.

This can be explained in part by the fact that surfboards were so heavy back then that small children simply couldn't manipulate them. But it also has to be remembered that there was no such thing as a surf school. Despite the growing number of surfboard riding clubs up and down the coast, few had embraced such ideas as junior training and development.

The boardriding clubs were more inclined towards surfing's answer to military bastardry, known as 'grom torture', in which fledgling surfers of my generation were subjected to humiliating and often painful pranks, such as having their heads flushed in the toilet bowl, or being buried up to the neck in sand as the tide advanced. At my home beach, older surfers would occasionally pelt us with 'brown elephants', or human excrement, to call a turd a turd. Whenever we noticed a couple of our surfing heroes drop silently off their boards and start to wriggle out of their shorts, we knew to paddle like crazy, away from the barrage of disgusting missiles that was about to be unleashed.

Perhaps understandably, many parents—my own included—were deeply suspicious (maybe even fearful) of the 'blossoming surfie cult' (to quote an ABC *Four Corners* program of the time), and did everything they could to steer their offspring towards more wholesome pursuits, such as soccer or stamp collecting, both of which I had a fling at. But in my case, persistence paid off. It probably helped that I was the youngest surviving child, more indulged than my older sisters.

The birthday board was a dog of a thing, a purple polyurethane foam Barry Bennett pig shape, one of the earliest foam surfboards produced in Australia. It had been pigment-coated by one of its previous owners to cover up the waterlogged sections and the general yellowing of the inferior foam.

Having heard that a neighbour had a full-sized foam surfboard for sale at a price my parents might consider affordable, I didn't think to inspect it, I just dropped a few hints as my birthday approached. My father purchased it for nine pounds, having haggled it down from the ten quid asking price, as was Dad's way.

Dad knew nothing about surfboards, but nor did I, so we were both pretty chuffed when he led me down to the garage, where the waterlogged Bennett had been artfully displayed on a couple of sawhorses, the family's Wolseley sedan and the workhorse Commer van having been backed up a few metres to heighten the dramatic impact.

'Well, what do you think?' he asked.

I paraded around the hideous thing, pretending to admire its contours, running my fingers across the rough and waxy surface. As I recall it, the Bennett was about nine feet three inches long, with a slightly tilted wooden D-shaped fin that extended just beyond the rounded tail. It seemed to have been dropped on its tail during delivery, and through the smashed fibreglass I could see the splintered ends of a thick balsa centre stringer bordered by thinner redwood ones.

I really didn't know what to look for in a surfboard, but I knew it was none of the above. My dream board did not feature a purple pigment disguising a waterlogged and rotting core. My dream board was brightly coloured like a rainbow, and it shone and glistened in the sun. But this was a surfboard nonetheless, and it was mine.

I said to Dad, 'It's beautiful. It's grouse. It's a gas. I love it!'

My dream board was in fact a composite of the kinds of boards that had been loaned to me over the summer of 1963–64, when I had decided it was time I learned to ride a proper surfboard. Several of the surfers who frequented my home beach were prepared, if somewhat reluctantly at first, to let me struggle with their heavy boards down to the shore and try to catch a broken wave without decapitating myself. But one of the older boys who would arrive in packs in their station wagons and utility trucks on weekends and summer evenings, would not only loan me his board at the end of his surf session, but would also show me what to do with it. He was the most skilled of the surfers who visited our beach, and his name was Bobby Brown.

I loved to watch Bobby Brown surf. He would flick his head and shoulder in the direction he wanted to go, and his heavy board would obediently follow. Other surfers used the same dramatic flourish, but it looked like a pose. When Bobby flicked, it seemed like the most natural thing in the world. He was a teenager who had just reached driving age and was a carpentry apprentice near Cronulla, on Sydney's southside. In midsummer there was plenty of daylight left after knock-off time, so if the swell and the wind were favourable, Bobby and his mates would drive the hour south to my beach.

Bobby Brown probably only loaned me his surfboard three or four times, but on each occasion he gave me a piece of advice to take into the water with the board. One time he waded out into the water with me and showed me how to paddle hard seaward and then jump up on the board

Bobby Brown at Sandon Point, 1963. (Photo Bob Weeks)

in a parallel stance and let the momentum push me through the breaking wave. It was the coolest thing in the world, and I mastered it long before I could actually ride a wave with any conviction.

A few months after teaching me the basics, Bobby beat the great Midget Farrelly in the New South Wales titles, and went on to surf in the first world championships at Manly. Bobby was my first surfing idol. I never saw him hurl a turd in anger, or humiliate a grom in any other way. But less than four years after I attempted to stumble to my feet on his board, he was dead at twenty-one, the innocent victim of a vicious glassing in a Cronulla pub.

Which brings us back to that first wave. Certainly, I caught waves and stood up on borrowed boards over that summer break, but I doubt it was pretty, and none of those rides has survived in my memory bank. For me, the first real experience of the thrill of the glide came at the end of that summer, on a board borrowed not from the older visiting surfers but from one of my new friends at Corrimal High School, where I had begun my secondary education at the end of January.

These surfing buddies were almost exclusively the children of European immigrants who had settled with their large, loud families and strange cooking smells in low-cost fibro cottages a block or two back from the beach. They had odd names like Jurek and Piet and Gunther, and many were in the lowest classes of their form because their command of English was hampered by the fact that they spoke another language at home. The beach and the surf were new to them, but they learnt quickly, usually with a quiet intensity that my own approach was sadly lacking.

On one of those February or March evenings on the Coal Coast when the hot, dry wind from the escarpment backs off and the ocean develops the texture of golden glass, on one of those special evenings that even now, more than half a century on, I can still feel and smell, I paddled into a small wave and got to my feet in one swift movement, then turned the board slowly and deliberately and trimmed along the face of the wave, the heavy board beating a rhythm as it slapped the swell under my feet. My confidence grew with every metre I travelled, and when finally the wave petered out on the shore, I knew I could do this, I knew I could become a surfer. It wasn't the first wave, but it was the first one that mattered.

On surfari to the Coal Coast, 1962. (Photo Bob Weeks)

I also knew, as I pedalled my Speedwell Special Sports up the darkening hills towards home, that I would be late for dinner and there would be all hell to pay. And that in the new scheme of things, this didn't matter a damn. I was a surfer now. I ran to my own set of rules, danced to the beat of a different drum.

CHAPTER TWO

Paddling with Dad, 1957.

HOME

Corrimal, where we lived, was a working-class town a few miles north of Wollongong. Although there were collieries dotted along the hillside, and the giant smoke stacks of the Port Kembla Steelworks could be seen belching black carbon clouds into the atmosphere just to the south, through young eyes my hometown felt almost Arcadian in those years, a friendly and newly multicultural village bounded by endless golden beaches on one side and the thick rainforests and jutting peaks of the Illawarra Escarpment on the other. The sun rose over the blue Pacific and set (too early for an after-school surfer) between Brokers Nose and the Corrimal Colliery, where half the town worked 'down the pit'.

My parents spent almost their entire married lives in this town, yet neither was from the area. My father, Lewis Walter Jarratt, known as Lew, was born in Perth in 1916, but grew up mostly in the remote Pilbara coastal port of Onslow, where his father, Walter, was the town butcher. Walter dropped dead at forty-nine from unknown causes, most likely a heart attack. My father was just fourteen at the time. Although he had older sisters already in the workforce, butchering was men's work, so he left school to ply his father's trade.

I don't know how good a butcher Dad was. He apparently had no training, other than watching Walter at work, but in my childhood years I remember the flourish with which he slapped the carving knife across the steel before attacking the Sunday roast, building a perfect stack of pork or lamb slices just begging for Mum's gravy. But it was not Dad's butchery skills (or lack of them) that brought the shop undone. It was the cyclone of 28 March, 1934, which ripped across Beadon Bay, taking half of Onslow with it.

Post-cyclone there was no rebuilding of the Jarratt butcher shop. Instead, my dad went off to work as a clerk at the Onslow Harbour and Light while he studied wireless operating by correspondence. My elder sister Wyverne (the true historian of the family) has collected and scanned precious photo albums, including Dad's sepia Kodak snaps of old Onslow, the wide sandy streets, the long pier lined with luggers, the diving bells, the dark, smiling faces of the Malay pearlers. When I look at them now I am immediately transported back to my earliest memories of family, when my father used to tell me stories rather than read to me at bedtime. There were many good yarns, but the ones I liked best were about Onslow, a wild place of improbable characters and unlikely adventures.

But by 1938 Dad was apparently over the rough-hewn charms of Onslow, judging by the slew of professional references he sought and got from leading politicians, public servants and clergy of the north-west, all of which depict him as a straightforward, honest, polite and hardworking young man who would be an asset to any company. But it seems none of these helped him move on—he remained at the Department of Harbour and Light until war was declared in September 1939. As soon as he could, Dad and a few mates drove to Perth in a borrowed car to enlist in the RAAF.

I'm not sure how the young Airman Jarratt ended up in barracks at Ultimo in Sydney in 1941. But I do know that soon after arriving, he met eighteen-year-old Margaret Parry, a pretty dental nurse from Penshurst on Sydney's southern line who was waiting to be accepted into the newly formed Women's Australian Auxiliary Air Force. Margie was born in Hurstville in 1923, the second child to Robert and Alice Parry, who had both emigrated from Wales as teenagers and had married in Sydney in 1919.

At the start of the Great War, Bob Parry had enlisted in the Australian Imperial Force, but his service was short-lived. He was medically discharged after little more than a year, following an accident at Central Station where he fell from a platform. The injury plagued him for the rest of his life, particularly after he became a Christian Scientist and would accept no medical intervention.

My first memories of him—he was 'Gampi' to us, in the Welsh tradition—are from when he was about the age I am now. He seemed ancient, a tall but stooped man who used a cane and made hard work of the short walk from the Penshurst railway station to the family home, 'Pen-y-lan', in Penshurst Avenue. When he sat down in his lounge chair he wou[ld] remove his heavy leather shoes to reveal an enormously swollen left foot, light his pipe, close his eyes and wait for the pain to subside.

The young Alice Parry was rather plain, but with a kind smile. My first memories of her are from the mid-'50s, when I was frightened by the prospect of having to enter the dark and malodorous spare bedroom where her mother, Ma Ma Smith, lay dying. Duty done, Alice would lead me quietly away and soothe me by dropping light globes from the back verandah and squealing with delight as they exploded on the concrete below. It was our favourite guilty pleasure.

Margie was a sweet kid, but as the middle child was sometimes over-looked at home in favour of the firstborn, David, and the baby, Doreen. At fifteen she graduated from Hurstville Central Domestic Science School and two and a half years later was engaged to be married to the short but dashing airman from the boondocks of Western Australia.

They were married at St Johns Church of England, Penshurst, on 11 December, 1943. After a reception at Margie's family home, the bride and groom spent their wedding night at the plush Hotel Sydney, the sixteen pound tariff a gift from Margie's dad. The following morning they caught a Government Tourist Bureau bus to the small seaside town of Narooma, where they checked in to the Ocean House private hotel, from which their first floor room afforded a view across the Princes Highway to the bay.

Sydney's beaches at the time were barricaded with barbed wire to help repel a feared Japanese naval invasion, but the Narooma coast looks wild and empty and beautiful in the Box Brownie snaps they took of each other, frolicking in the sand and the rocky headlands, Lew looking buff in woollen bathers with contrasting belt, Margie impossibly glamorous in a daring one-piece.

My parents would sometimes speak of those times, usually when we were on a family camp-ing holiday on the South Coast, and Margie would smile at her

Lew and Margie sunbaking, 1943.

wheel, and slip her hand onto his knee as the old Commer ... er the strain of towing a primitive caravan up a hill. But it ... ten.

... closest my father got to seeing active service was a couple ... vin, and on Melville Island when a Japanese invasion was considered likely, the war seemed to leave him in a hurry to get on with life. Fifteen months after Lew and Margie were married, my sister Wyverne was born in Sydney. Lew, still stationed in Darwin, read about the birth in Margie's excited letters, but his firstborn would be a year old before he was discharged, in February 1946.

By the time their second daughter, Robyn, was born in October 1946, the Jarratts had relocated to the South Coast. Lew and Margie had spent the war dreaming of a life together in a small town where they could raise a family and build a business. In the winter of 1946 Dad took the plunge. He travelled down the coast alone, rented a room in a boarding house and obtained a lease on a cream-tiled shop on the Princes Highway at Corrimal. He used his discharge payout to make a down payment on a rundown cottage less than a kilometre from the shop.

So Lew and Margie had a house (of sorts) for their young family, a shop, and a potential market in the fast-growing population of postwar European immigrants. But what were they going to sell? Few families had cars, so selling and repairing bicycles seemed to make sense, particularly as

Mum, Dad and sister Robyn in the shop at Corrimal, 1949.

Dad had always repaired his and his friends' bikes in Onslow. And before the arrival of Japanese-made transistor radios and television sets, every family had a big old mantle wireless that needed frequent repairs, for which he was also qualified.

Lew hung up a shingle that said 'LW Jarratt—Radios, Electrical Appliances and Cycles', but he had no credit and only enough cash to buy a couple of each, so he filled his store with whatever he could beg, borrow or make, including plants potted from the garden of the cottage, bunches of flowers, Margie's homemade jam and wooden toys that Lew had made. If the shop looked sparse, it was nothing compared to home. Wyverne remembers that apart from beds, the only furniture consisted of tables and cupboards that Mum knocked up from packing cases and fruit boxes. There being no refrigerator, the ice man delivered two or three times a week, and Margie put out the billy every night for the milko to fill, a sixpence underneath its blackened base.

Less than two years Wyverne's junior, Robyn was apparently the exact opposite of her sister—a problem baby, whereas the firstborn had been perfect. She howled at will, sometimes all day and all night. Our parents found the solution in the chook run in the backyard, where they deposited her, perhaps only once or twice, but the family legend has grown to become all night and often. My mother always claimed, with no apparent irony, that ten minutes in the chook pen was long enough to quieten Rob down.

The lifestyle of our family in the years before my arrival seems harsh, but I'm sure it was no worse than many Australian families endured in the immediate postwar period. And things started to look up pretty quickly. As soon as he could afford to buy more stock, Lew made a corridor down the middle of the shop from entrance to counter, and filled one side with Speedwell cycles, the other with whitegoods and electrical appliances. He hired a jack-of-all-trades mechanic to run the repair shop out the back while he ran the business from a tiny office off the side, and a succession of pretty European migrant girls served behind the heavy wooden counter.

Much to the surprise of the rest of the Corrimal business community, LW Jarratt's began to thrive. Early in 1951, Lew came home to his heavily pregnant wife and declared that he had negotiated a 2000 pound loan from the Bank of NSW and bought an even more rundown house on the highway just down the hill from the shop. It turned out to be an astute investment, but Margie loathed it from day one.

CHAPTER THREE

188 Main Road, Corrimal, dressed up for the Queen, 1954.

THE PARK RANGER

Number 188 Princes Highway (or Main Road, as it was locally known) was conveniently located down the hill from Dad's store, next door but one to the Princess Theatre and the Memorial Park, and directly opposite the Methodist Church. Close to Dr Foy's surgery and Mrs McCrohan's general store and veg, and just across the street from Guest's cake shop and bakery and the co-op, our house was the absolute last word in convenience and sociability—you couldn't walk out the front door without striking up a conversation with one of the local characters.

But Mum was not happy. She felt she deserved better. The house was mouldy, falling down and often smelly, with a thunderbox pan dunny miles down the unlit backyard. I spent the first eight years of my life in that house. It was where my father ran his doomed campaign for state parliament, where the Queen passed us in the royal cavalcade of 1954, and where we helped Dad unpack television sets for delivery around the town, although we were allowed no such luxury ourselves—we had to hike up the hill in our dressing gowns and slippers to sit on folding chairs on the footpath and watch *I Love Lucy* through the window of our own shop.

Mum dubbed it 'the house from hell', and in later years wrote a damning description of it: 'Between the kitchen and the third bedroom was the lobby of leaks, where the floor bent like a bath tub and it took nine buckets to catch the leaks when it rained. There was no drainage from the kitchen: everything just dropped into a muddy drain that fed into the driveway. No wonder the girls got hepatitis.'

But it was big, and the backyard went on forever, even if the fallen branches of the coral tree could make a mess of a bare foot, and the convolvuli housed a million ticks. I can't say when my earliest memories here date from, but it must have been after Mum had conceived again and my younger brother, Paul, was stillborn in Bulli Hospital in September 1953. It would be normal now for a family to grieve such a tragedy and tend a tiny grave with flowers on each anniversary, but our family shelved it completely. It was only in adulthood that I had any inkling I'd lost a brother, and only in the course of writing this memoir that I learned any of the detail.

Not that there's much to learn about a sibling who never really was, and only slightly more about how the tragedy affects those surrounding it. Margie fell into a deep depression that even the procession of the new Queen of England, right past our front door, if you please, couldn't bring her out of. I was too young to notice, but apparently there were frequent overnight absences, when it was explained she was 'seeing Sister'.

Queen Elizabeth II and her relatively new husband, Prince Philip (for whom I had been named), were to head north along the Princes Highway in a motorcade, having spent all of two and a half hours in Wollongong. Paint, bunting and flags were not cheap, and Lew reasoned that since royalty never looks back, only the southern façade needed to be painted and adorned. Mum rallied, and took us out to the front fence to wave Union Jacks and cheer the monarch, along with the 120,000 other residents who lined the road, but I don't remember any of it.

Having made a success of his small business in a relatively short time, Lew Jarratt had attracted the attention of the Liberal Party flacks, who were (then as now) constantly on the lookout for cannon fodder in unwinnable seats. Here was a disciple of the doctrine of free enterprise, a Menzies man to his bootstraps. Come on down! To say the seat of Bulli was unwinnable is a gross understatement. It was the safest Labor seat in the NSW Parliament, contested by the Liberal Party (unsuccessfully) only three times in twenty-three years. Following the death of the sitting member, Dad was contesting it in a by-election against a twenty-seven-year-old printing company rep and unionist named Rex Jackson—later known as 'Buckets', and thoroughly discredited. Buckets might have turned out to be a crook, but in 1955 he was the miners' mate, and he romped in with a two to one majority over Dad, who finished just ahead of the detested Communist candidate.

At home I liked to amuse myself in the enormous garage, which housed all kinds of interesting stuff from the shop, like dilapidated radios

YOUR LOCAL MAN

1 **LEW JARRATT**

"It's time for a change"

Dad's election poster, 1955.

and record players that had been traded in on new ones and were waiting to be repaired before being put back on the shelves. I became particularly attached to a huge wooden radiogram, an original His Master's Voice that I knew as George. I would talk to George for hours, even though he couldn't talk back—not even if I'd known how to switch the thing on, put a record on the turntable and apply the needle to it.

I was also becoming friendly with a real person, Theo Tsakalos, an older boy whose family's equally ramshackle home stood between ours and the Princess Theatre. Theo's parents were Greek and Egyptian and they smoked cigarettes and laughed loudly as strange smells emanated from their kitchen and the adjoining porch. They seemed to enjoy life.

Theo and I really only had one thing in common—our fascination with the enormous and crumbling Princess Theatre, a cinema that had once been a boxing stadium. The part that interested us probably dated back to the boxing era—a dilapidated back wall with a sheet of corrugated iron concealing a boy-sized hole, which led to a walkway behind the cinema screen. Keeping low, to avoid our silhouettes appearing on screen, we spent many a Saturday afternoon watching the reverse image of the Tarzan serial and Western matinee. We were so close to the screen that Johnny Weissmuller seemed in danger of landing in our laps as he swung from vine to vine, his jungle cry ringing in our ears.

My other downtown friends were the Vangelovich twins, Tommy and Chrissy, who lived above their parents' fish and chip shop at the other end of town, a couple of doors beyond the pub. The twins were budding soccer stars, so occasionally we would take our ball down to the Memorial Park, midway between their place and mine, but I wouldn't let the twins kick it anywhere near the flower beds. I'd become quite proprietorial about the park since making friends with Reg, the park ranger. Because I was such a good helper, Reg had made me a park ranger badge like his own, but I ordered so many kids around that my parents eventually confiscated it.

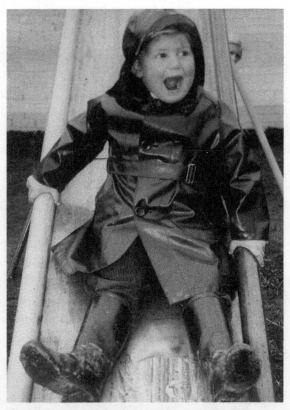

The Park Ranger, 1954. (Photo *South Coast Times*)

I must have been an obnoxious brat, with or without the badge, because one day after I'd read some offenders the park riot act, they dragged me behind the toilet block and smeared shit over me. I ran home crying and my father took me by the shoulders and held me at arm's length (I'm not sure if this was for gravitas or to avoid the stink) while he spoke.

'Who did this to you?' His voice was soft, but I could tell he was enraged—far angrier than he'd ever been with me. I told him they were boys I didn't know and he marched me back down to the park, still covered in shit, and asked if I could see them anywhere. I pointed out the culprits on the far side, swinging above the creek on a rope tied to a tree. Dad told me to wait, then sprinted across the park like Dave Power, our local bank johnny who'd just won a bronze medal at the Cardiff Empire Games.

I'd never seen my father run before and I was frightened that something might break, but he covered the distance in record time, grabbed the boys and pinned one against a tree with his leg while he smacked the butt of the other. You could do that without consequences in the '50s. The boys ran off bawling, but when Dad returned he had his stern face on and I felt the force of his open palm across the seat of my crap-coated pants. 'They told me what you said to them,' was the only explanation given.

CHAPTER FOUR

Margie in 1941.

HOLY STOKE

Perhaps in retaliation for having to live in the house from hell, Mum decided to buy a ticket to heaven, via the Billy Graham Crusade in Sydney. By the time the handsome and enigmatic preacher from the Deep South reached Australia in 1959 he was already a rock star of religion, his brilliantly choreographed and highly emotional rallies having inspired millions to accept Jesus Christ as their saviour.

My two older sisters had already found their way to the Lord, and were getting more serious about it by the day, but once the euphoria and the happy clapping of her Sydney Showground conversion wore off, Mum found that befriending the family of the local parson was a more convenient way to serve God. This was how I made my first best friend, Derek Brand, the younger son of the firebrand Methodist preacher Allan Brand, who Dad said was a communist because he'd been to Moscow and had marched in a Ban the Bomb protest in London.

Even though it was just across the street, Dad rarely came to church with the rest of us. He worshipped his own gods, particularly a father and son tag wrestling team named Gino and Leo Garibaldi, whom he took me to see perform (or fight, as he insisted) at the Pioneer Hall in Wollongong. A sceptic by nature, Dad was inexplicably a sucker for World Championship Wrestling. He also took me to see Killer Kowalski, Mark Lewin and Mario Milano, as well as a bunch of less colourful punch pullers and canvas acrobats whose names have left me.

Often he would take me to the shop on Saturday afternoons. He was supposed to be repairing bikes or doing the books, but work would stop when he flicked the display TV on in time for World Championship

Dad outside the shop, 1949.

Wrestling. The tag-team bouts were our favourites. I can still see and hear my dad willing the good guy to get off the ropes before the other guy smashed a chair over his head. I never heard my father swear, but as the chair came crashing down on Mario Milano or Leo Garibaldi he would shout 'Aaaaaark!' This was like the well-known crow call without the 'f'. It was the same thing he'd scream if he hit his finger with a hammer.

I suppose I remember the wrestling so well because as a father and son we didn't do much else together. We lived very close to the beach, but we never went there as a family. I wasn't allowed to play club soccer on Saturdays because I would be letting my team down when we went away, but we only ever went away for a week or so in January (which wasn't even the football season), usually to a beach campground up or down the coast. Those brief summer holidays were the only occasions I ever shared beach time with my father, either ill-fated attempts at casting a fishing line beyond the breakers or only slightly more successful body-surfing sessions. I know my inability to cast frustrated the hell out of Dad ('Aaaaark!'), but his inability to surf a wave to the beach was profoundly disappointing for me. I loved the surf from my very first encounters, and I wanted to share that with him.

But back to the Brands. The Reverend may have been too far left of the political spectrum for my father's liking, but he was such an open, unfiltered presence it was impossible not to like him. Quick to anger, quick to forgive, he bellowed his pronouncements of tough love as though he were forever in an invisible pulpit.

As it was, Derek and I, a year apart, were inseparable. He was the opposite of his father, a mellow cruiser of a guy who was a gifted artist and a born waterman, although the term was unknown to us at the time. We both loved the thrill of the surf, but Derek's passion for all things aquatic rubbed off on me in other ways, although I never managed to master a spear gun.

Me with my best friend Derek.

It was at the Brands' dining table that I first witnessed what may have been a near-religious experience (it certainly rivalled Billy Graham for colour and movement), or perhaps demonic possession. It was brought on by the idea of surfing and what we have come to know as 'the stoke'. When overexcited surfers compare the surfing experience with sex, drugs or finding their god at the 'church of the open sky', the high they are describing is the stoke, a euphoric condition usually reached through the actual riding of waves, although sometimes achieved through the remembrance or anticipation of same.

When the Brands left the Corrimal parsonage for Chatswood in Sydney's north, I was so devastated that my parents arranged for me to spend a weekend with Derek. We were having dinner at the Reverend's table when the stoke began to take over Derek's older brother, Graham. I'd never seen anything quite like it.

Through the archway that separated the dining room from the lounge room in this middle-class suburban home, a black and white television set flickered. A man was reading the evening news in a faintly American accent, and he was up to the bit about the weather: '... and weekend beachgoers should watch out for big dumpers as heavy seas pound Sydney's coastline ...'

Graham's ear cocked involuntarily in the direction of the television. He was seventeen, pimply and very excitable. Something struck a nerve in him. Peas and gravy went flying as he jumped out of his chair and in one swift movement propelled himself onto the table, crouching between the bread board and the salad bowl before launching into an arching bottom turn that ripped the checkered tablecloth from beneath the groaning plates of Friday night roast. Oblivious, Graham cross-stepped along the table, singing tunelessly but enthusiastically, 'Now the time is growing near, you're movin' down the wall ...' He planted a calloused foot over the end of the table as the Reverend rose up in fury. 'As steady as she goes, you got your toes upon the nose ...'

'For the love of God, boy, get off the table and compose yourself!' shrieked the Rev, his face as red as the beetroot in the salad.

'... and now you're hangin' five, hangin' five toes ... upon the Malibu!'

'Have you completely taken leave of your senses, boy? Get down from the table this minute before I knock you down!' The Reverend had picked up a wooden serving spoon. Although he had a shocking temper, I'd never seen him use a weapon on one of his own—but nor had I seen him so provoked. Graham was in a world of his own, jiving to the sound of his own voice, wiping the non-existent spray from his brow as he rode his imaginary wave through the middle of dinner.

Eventually the possession passed and, slightly embarrassed, Graham climbed down from the table. The Reverend clipped him over the ear, then grabbed him in a massive hug, patting his matted hair and sighing. 'Good Lord, but you put us through some trials, lovey.'

CHAPTER FIVE

OUR JAPANESE SISTER

At the end of the summer of 1960–61, Dad sold the house from hell to the Rural Bank for a vast profit and the family moved to a recently developed estate on the foothills below the Illawarra Escarpment, in the afternoon shadow of Brokers Nose, with a distant view of the ocean and the smokestacks of the Port Kembla Steelworks.

Our modest two-bedroom cream brick bungalow was my parents' dream. It had air conditioning, a stereophonic radiogram and even a tiny black and white television in the 'sun' room (which was on the western side of the house, closest to the mountain, and got virtually no sun). But it was my nightmare, being the furthest possible distance from my newly discovered playground—the beach.

I was resentful of the move as soon as I saw the block of land—I couldn't understand how distant views of the ocean could trump actual proximity to it—and my resentment only grew as I was dragged around the display villages full of project homes that were beginning to proliferate around the western perimeter of Sydney. While my sisters were at church, or church choir practice, or teaching Sunday school, or at church youth fellowship activities, I spent weekends with my parents looking at bathroom tiles in Baulkham Hills or carpets and underfelt at Cobbity Farm.

But my resentment reached new heights when we went to the block to inspect the work in progress and I worked out that there was no bedroom for me. What were they thinking? We saw the master bedroom, which looked huge compared to the small space my sisters would share.

And then we saw the sunroom. I was very young, and not very bright, but I figured it out.

'Wait a minute,' I said, 'where's my room?'

Dad took me to the far end of the sunless sunroom and said, 'This is where your bed will go ... but only until we build your proper room.' Tears were welling up as he took me by the hand and led me through the workmen's rubble of the backyard and under the house to a dim and musty space next to the double garage. Dad had to almost double over to fit. We crouched and looked at the mound of clay and broken bricks.

'This is where we're going to build your bedroom, you and me, mate.' (I was often 'mate' or 'my little mate' if he wanted me to stop crying.)

We moved into the cream brick house at 6 Powell Avenue and every Sunday Dad would take the shovel and hand me the spade and down we'd go to dig my cell. Meanwhile, I slept in the sunroom with the TV and the sofa bed, where guests were supposed to sleep. After dinner Mum would fall asleep in her chair while watching television and knitting. Luckily, there was a wardrobe between me and the rest of the room, and I had a set of headphones for my crystal set so I could lie in bed at night and listen to the cricket from England.

When he realised he wasn't going to make it as a politician, Dad became more active in community organisations and service clubs,

Powell Avenue, Corrimal.

joining Bulli Rotary Club in 1957 and helping found Corrimal Rotary in 1959. We were pretty much a white-bread family, despite the fact that Lew had grown up around Malay and Japanese pearlers in Onslow before the war and counted them among his closest friends. In the '50s we were surrounded by European immigrants, who generally found easy acceptance, but the scars from Kokoda, Changi and the Burma Railway were too fresh for the Japanese to be afforded the same welcome.

So it came a little bit from left field when Dad began to play a leading role in the recently established Rotary International Student Exchange Program, pushing heavily for his own club to host Japanese students. I was too young to understand the wartime bitterness that lingered well into the '60s, but years later, when we met for a drink at the Marble Bar in the Sydney Hilton, we talked about it briefly. He and Mum were off to Japan, and I asked him why he had been so keen on bringing Japanese kids to Australia in those days. He sipped his small whisky and said, 'Because they were the future of Japan, and the memories of the war were the past. It was important that we realised that the Japanese were human, just like us.'

My parents were going to Japan to see Toshiko Kojima, who had become our Japanese sister and daughter in early 1962 and remained a lifelong family friend. I remember being completely enchanted when she came through the gates at the old Sydney Kingsford Smith Airport to meet us, then almost swooning when she presented us with a sukiyaki dinner at home, dressed in her traditional kimono, all alabaster skin and flowing grace. To a little boy, she was an impossibly exotic creature from a faraway land.

If Dad was intending to bring the world into our home in 1962, he was also intent on seeing a bit of it for himself. After Toshiko had moved on to another host family, he and Mum announced that they were going to take their first overseas trip. It was about time—Dad was forty-six, Mum thirty-nine.

On the steps with Toshiko, 1962.

Our Japanese sister

The bad news was that I was to spend the four months with my grand-parents in their recently acquired retirement home unit at Sans Souci, opposite the Taren Point ferry. Although we'd finally dug a hole under the house big enough for me to sleep in, and I'd more or less forgiven Dad for making me live in a dungeon, this seemed to me seriously deranged behaviour all over again. I'd seen the retirement unit and it was a box. Gampi had a big high bed for his bad leg in one tiny room and Nanny had a single bed in the other room. Where was I supposed to sleep?

'Nanny will fix something up in her room,' Mum said, to which the appropriate answer would have been 'over my dead body'. I decided not to risk the clip over the ear and started howling instead.

Next, there was the matter of school. I was supposed to start a new school, learn new stuff and make new friends, just because they were going on a holiday? It was too much! I stormed off to my boy-cave and slammed the door so hard you could hear the dry clay rearranging itself on the other side of the thin wall.

But my brief time at Sans Souci turned out to be an excellent adventure. I was about to turn eleven, and I was curious about many areas of pre-pubescent interest in which my new friends at Sans Souci Public seemed quite expert. Neither of my parents smoked, but my aunt did, and I thought she looked terrific, holding the cigarette just so and filling the room with her clouds of blue smoke.

My new mates taught me how to smoke bamboo. It tasted horrible and burnt your throat, but we sat in a patch of it halfway between school and home and had a smoko most afternoons. On the weekends there were bigger fish to fry. Across the road from my grandparents' unit was a park that extended from the public baths to the ferry landing, where folks gathered to stroll, let their kids use the swings, picnic by the Georges River and, well, smoke.

There were butts strewn everywhere. My little gang of coughing puffers would first find an empty cigarette pack, then fill it with the longest butts we could find. Lipstick butts were usually the best because women didn't smoke hungrily down to the filter like most men. When we'd filled our pack, we'd climb one of the big trees, find a comfort-able nook and smoke while we gazed out at the boats on the river and Botany Bay.

Sex was becoming quite important too. We weren't sure how it worked but one of our gang, a kid called Louie who had helped me master long division, reckoned he'd seen his parents at it. He described the bizarre spectacle in some detail as we sat in the tree and smoked. The question was, how would you possibly get a normal girl to even consider taking part in such a thing? It was a question we had a few years still to ponder.

The other thing I learnt while at Sans Souci was that my grandfather was not a well man. He was in agony just getting from his high bed to his smoking chair, where he smoked either a pipe or a Champion Ruby rollie in an elegant holder, and wheezed and coughed frequently. He rarely left the house, other than to take the bus to the Church of Christ, Scientist, but every day he would struggle out of bed and put on a white shirt and tie, tailored slacks and a cardigan, and huge tartan slippers, one cut down the middle to accommodate his bad foot. When I came home from school, redolent of our bamboo bungers, he would always greet me from his chair in his soft Welsh, untarnished by half a century in the Antipodes, 'Come here, my little mannikin, and tell me about your day.'

I never felt I knew or understood him, but I still remember his ways, and the things he said have stayed with me. When they returned from their travels my parents gave me an autograph book half-filled with the signatures and lame one-liners of supposedly famous people they'd met. Before I left my grandparents' care, I asked my Gampi to sign a page in my new book. He wrote, in beautiful flowing hand, his favourite quote from Shakespeare: 'This above all, to thine own self be true.'

He was dead from pancreatic cancer within two years.

CHAPTER SIX

Cronulla, 1964. (Photo Bob Weeks)

LIFE'S A BEACH

In my final year at Corrimal Public School, the beach began to take over my consciousness, despite our increased distance from it—particularly after I received a brand new Speedwell Special Sports bicycle with three-speed Sturmey Archer gears for my twelfth birthday. This enabled me to speed from home to the beach and back, my Narm rubber surfoplane tied around me and resting on the luggage rack behind.

Getting the bike was the good part about turning twelve. The bad part was that Mum and Dad decided it was time I was told about the birds and the bees. Dad had to go to Sydney on some matter concerning his new hearing-aid business, and Mum's plot was that I should have the day off school and drive with him. Along the way he could explain about the business—not the hearing-aid business, the other kind.

It took him all the way to the Appin turnoff to pluck up the courage to start, and then he was pathetic. Clearly I knew more about it than him, having picked up an encyclopaedic knowledge of the old in-out game since Louie had alerted me to the caper a year earlier.

'You're twelve now, mate,' Dad began, 'and I want you to know that if there's anything you're not sure about, anything at all, you can just ask me. All right?'

'Yes, Dad. Thanks.'

That was it. Fortunately I'd recently graduated from Cubs to Boy Scouts, where my patrol leader Max proved to be an outstanding sexual educationist. Maxie lived just down the road from us, so we would walk home together from Scouts. One memorable evening we stopped at a fibro house next to the soccer ground, not far from the recently

33

South Coast surfers, early 1960s. (Photo David Milnes)

demolished house from hell. We peered over a paling fence into the back-yard, where several heavily made-up women were smoking cigarettes on a wooden deck.

'See them sheilas?' Max whispered. 'They do it for money. They're called prostitutes.' I nodded. 'How much money ya got?' He giggled, and then we watched in silence as they came and went through a screen door, presumably called to attend to customers. I was excited by the whole idea of it, but also worried that we would be caught watching them, or worse, that the cops would roll up and arrest the prostitutes, their customers and the two young perverts watching them.

Continuing our journey of discovery, we wandered past Luigi's Royal Cafe, next to the Princess Theatre, where Max said you could generally spot beautiful Italian tarts. With none visible from the footpath, we continued on to the Corrimal Community Hall, where the Friday night rock and roll dance was in progress. Heading the bill was the beautiful Bandstand songstress Laurel Lee.

'You want to meet Laurel Lee?' Max asked.

Two years older than me, his voice more or less broken, and already shaving at least once a week, Max was bold, brash and fearless, but this was never going to work. He grabbed me by my epaulette and hauled me through the crowd of bodgies and widgies smoking out the front. We stood out like Arabs at a bar mitzvah in our shorts and silly hats. The suited doorman greeted us with something approaching affection.

'Hello boys, looking for someone?'

Max said, 'We want to meet Laurel Lee.' Just like that. As it happened, the band was on a break, and the singer was within eyesight, chatting just inside the main door. The doorman laughed, disappeared inside for a moment and emerged with the most beautiful woman I'd ever seen. The grainy black-and-white image on the television set didn't do her justice.

'Couple of good-looking young blokes wanted to say hello,' the doorman said. Laurel Lee shook our hands warmly and made some small talk about how she'd been in the Brownies when she was young and it had helped shape her character, or something like that. Max and I weren't listening. We were looking. Her low-cut top and tight-waisted dress amplified the impact of her bosoms, which were almost close enough to touch. And then she smiled again, waved her dainty painted fingers and was gone.

Max's sexual education of our patrol also became more hands on, so to speak, when circumstances allowed. The hills behind our house led to a bush track that meandered around the edge of the Corrimal Colliery and on up to Brokers Nose. Along the way there were many glades where a hiking Boy Scout patrol could stop and spend a hidden half hour learning things that weren't necessarily in Lord Baden-Powell's manual.

'Righto,' said Max, 'let's stop for a drink of water in here.' He led the way through the ferns to a grassy spot where shafts of sunlight were just penetrating the tree canopy. Max told us to take off our shorts and underpants and sit on them. 'Do youse know how to spunk up?' he asked. We looked at him blankly, so he took his own impressive shaft in one hand and began stroking it up and down. 'Go like this and think about a naked sheila. Think about her titties and what she's got between her legs and what you're gonna do to her.'

By the time us rookies had mastered the stroke and conjured up a suitably erotic image to be going on with, Max was grunting and groaning and nearly ripping his penis from its base. Then he let out an anguished cry and we watched in amazement as an opaque, creamy liquid spurted from his cock and landed on his inner thigh. He rolled back and laughed in big, deranged guffaws, then looked around at our pathetic efforts. 'Come on you blokes, spunk up!'

I don't think I rose to the occasion that day, but it was only a matter of weeks before I was masturbating at every opportunity, even once or twice at Max's bush clinics, although mostly I preferred the more solitary pleasure.

I liked Max's no-nonsense style, but he wasn't a surfer, and I was increasingly drawn to boys who were. (There were no girls who surfed that I had seen.) When I moved up to Corrimal High School the following year I was suddenly surrounded by surf-mad 'gremmies'. This was the first summer of the surf boom, when a new kind of youth culture imported from California came booming out of our transistor radios, cinema and television screens. Kids up and down the coast used peroxide or lemon juice to help achieve the stompy-wompy blonde-haired look of the surfer boy. But as I mentioned earlier, my first surfing buddies were not like this at all. They had funny names, funny haircuts, funny teeth, and often struggled with English. Beach life was new to them and they frequently wore inappropriate clothes for it.

Surfing didn't come naturally to them either, but they were game for anything and they were fast learners. In the schoolyard they were often 'wogs' or 'dagoes' or 'wops' or 'Ities' to us WASP kids, and we sometimes made fun of the strange smells that emanated from their lunch boxes, and the smell of garlic on their breath. But at the beach we were all equals. We were all branded 'kooks' by the older surfers, who had already mastered the art of riding the relatively new Malibu-style surfboard, that we called 'mals', and we soon formed a multiracial gang of kooks who aspired to be better.

Most of my new friends had come from austere new-world beginnings in the Nissen huts of the Balgownie Migrant Hostel, where assisted passage migrants lived in each other's pockets while establishing a new life, working in the coal mines and the steelworks. The crowded huts were basic at best, but many of the families had come from far worse situations in postwar Europe. The 'New Australians', as the politicians and the media had dubbed them, worked hard, saved their money and soon bought humble cottages in East Corrimal next to the beach, a part of town not yet considered desirable. The Polish, Dutch, French, German, Italian and Eastern European families and their surfing sons became my other world.

Patrick and Jurek (Steve) Olejniczak were my first best friends out of this group, and Thys Bronneberg followed soon after. The Olejniczak boys were half Polish, half French, both fast developing into good surfers. Pat was academically bright but the class clown, Steve was, ah, not so academically bright, but also the class clown. Their dad was a dour Pole

The Balgownie Migrant Hostel.

who didn't say much, but I loved everything about their French mum, from the smells that issued from her kitchen to her lusty laughter at the bawdy jokes she shared with her boys in a patois that was not always clear to me, though her gestures told enough of the story.

The Bronneberg household was more austere, Thys's mother having been a judge in Batavia before Sukarno's long and bloody creation of Indonesia caused the Bronnebergs and many other Dutch families to flee. This was what I loved about the beachside ghetto of East Corrimal. Behind every garishly painted, neat-as-a-pin façade, between every planted row of the backyard vege patch, there was a story to be told.

There was one thing I couldn't help but admire about my New Aussie surfing mates: they had balls. Even their mums had balls. It showed in the way these kids approached their surfing and in the way their family stories only emerged when you were considered near enough to family yourself. There was no self-pity, nor self-aggrandisement. They were what they were, and they were getting on with their new lives in Australia.

But my parents weren't so sure about my new circle of friends. Dad was committed to creating world peace through the Rotary International Student Exchange Program, and by now we'd had European kids living with us as well as Japanese, but somehow me spending all my leisure hours in what they perceived as a migrant ghetto was a different saucepan of spaghetti.

Although most of our gang lived within a few blocks of East Corrimal Beach (also known, inexplicably, as 'Brandy's'), we all kept our boards in Dino's Shed, a second garage in Dino's backyard, which was about the closest you could be to the beach without having your feet in the sand. Dino, like me, was a white Anglo-Saxon in the midst of a European clusterfuck, but he was the elder of our tribe, a quiet, softly spoken goofy foot who surfed better than any of us, and was revered by all.

We left our boards in Dino's Shed because we needed to gather there so Dino could tell us where we would surf that day. In the days before surfcams and swell forecasts, Dino was our *kahuna* (leader), and Kahuna always made the call. Coming from the furthest away, up in the hills away to the west, I would pedal as fast as I could to get to Dino's just after first light, and be absolutely gutted if the crew had left without me, boards on heads, a towel packed between skull and mal to soften the impact, bound for whichever of the six walking-distance surf spots Dino had decreed.

Although we were all mates, there was a pecking order. Being the least accomplished surfer, I was probably at the bottom. But if I had been left behind, I was not about to be left out. I would place my towel on my head, balance the Barry Bennett purple pig on top of it, and trek from break to break until I found them. It wasn't rocket science. Even with my elementary knowledge of surf science, I knew that if the wind was south it was Bellambi (a long walk), and if the swell was up it was the bommie or the pier, and if it was small it was the point.

But a much better and closer option was Brandy's itself, which offered a variety of breaks in standard morning offshore conditions. First were the shifting peaks between the car park and the big sandhill, most notably where the creek ran out; next was a scattering of reef and rock that we called 'The Point', but was a fat, soft lefthander that was barely worthy of the name; and last was an offshore clump of reef in a direct seaward line from the Bellambi sewerage outlet that we knew alternately as the 'Shithole' or the 'Sharkhole'.

I only surfed this last break a few times, but I can attest that it stank to high heaven. The water was murky and not a pleasure to dangle your feet in. No-one but our gang surfed the Shithole, and no-one surfed it better than a boy named Piet, who consistently made the drop down the black face of the wave, his feet wide apart in a survival stance. It wasn't pretty, but it was effective.

Quite a few of the Europeans adopted the wide-legged survival stance popularised by the Californian surfer Greg Noll, whose heroics at Waimea Bay and Mākaha usually featured in the climactic big wave sequences that finished every early surf movie. One of our gang even earned the nickname 'Makaha' for using it on every wave he caught.

I liked to think my surfing was more stylish, like my original mentor, Bobby Brown, in reverse, since I was a goofy foot. I practised my moves in front of Mum's full-length mirror at home when no-one was around, keeping my hands flat and palms down in front of me and my feet close together, except when I pushed my left foot back and twisted my knee inwards to sweep into a glorious drop-knee cutback, sometimes throwing both hands in the air for extra flourish. I couldn't do a drop-knee in the surf, of course, but in front of the mirror I was a wizard.

Apart from Bobby Brown, and a couple of good local surfers, our gang at Brandy's didn't have much to compare ourselves with. But when the southerly changes came through and blew out the beach breaks, we would head for the better-known point break at Bellambi, where all the style masters were on parade, including the very best local surfer, a boy in 3F at school named Kevin Parkinson.

CHAPTER SEVEN

Kevin Parkinson, Bellambi, 1964. (Photo David Milnes)

KEVY

Kevy Parkinson was in 3F—the lowest grade in which normal subjects were taught—not because he was stupid but because he so rarely attended school. We all understood why Kevy didn't go very often. What was the point? Clearly he was going to be a champion surfer.

Bobby Brown remained my surfing idol but Kevy was a close second, even though he rarely gave us the time of day. When you're that good, why would you? I'll tell you how cool Kevy Parkinson was. One day at Bellambi we were sitting by the wall of the toilet block, sheltering from the wind. Kevy waxed up his board, lit a cigarette, jumped in off the rocks outside the baths wall, knee-paddled out to the break, turned and caught his first wave, bottom-turned beautifully, then lay into a delicate cutback, ashing his cigarette into the green face of the wave as he changed direction. We gasped in unison.

Kevy's mother made boardshorts for him and all of the cool crew, which of course didn't include our little league of nations. But my mum was pretty handy at the Singer sewing machine too, and whenever Kevy showed up at the beach in a bold new fashion statement (long shorts, short shorts, high waists, hip huggers, floral patterns or block colours with contrasting waistband, arrows down one leg, you name it) I would commit the design to memory, sketch it out for Mum and appear a week later in exactly the same boardies.

Kevy never seemed to appreciate that imitation was the sincerest form of flattery.

I had but one slim chance of creating a blip on Kevy's radar and that was through my friend Peter Tweedle, whose older brother Billy was in the Kevy cool crew. A year younger than me, Peter was still in primary school. Ordinarily, that would mean I couldn't be seen hanging out with him, but his connections won out. We started surfing together, and when he graduated to high school the following year we became fast friends, particularly after we both smashed our front teeth out on the same challenging day on the Bellambi lefts.

I still remember vividly how I lost my front teeth, although I'm not sure what happened to Peter's. I took off on a long-lining left, heading straight for the wall of the rock pool, at which point it was essential to steer or flick your heavy board over the back of the wave to avoid a collision. I must have left my flick a second or two too late, because my board was picked up by the cascading curl and the triple-cloth, double-glassed, fat rail smashed into my lip with great force. I was thirteen now, a teenager, but I was stunned and in tears as I clambered over the urchin-infested rocks to rescue my Bennett pig from the battering it was taking against the rock wall.

There were more tears later when I got home. I was mostly upset about the dings and scratches all over my board, but when I walked into the kitchen and smiled, Mum burst into tears. Once I had examined the damage in the bathroom mirror, I joined her. When Dad got home he didn't cry but he did say 'Aaaaark!' a lot, presumably thinking about the dental bills.

'Well, that's it for surfing then,' he said with finality, heading off to tend to the intricate series of ponds and water features he was constructing in the backyard.

It wasn't, of course. The end of surfing, I mean. That unstoppable force was only just beginning.

I eventually received two false teeth on a fibreglass plate, but for several weeks beforehand, Peter Tweedle and I paraded around heroically with our gappy smiles, always ready to tell the story about the huge waves that had claimed our teeth. The incident may have given us a little more cred at the beach, and Peter and I now hung out like Tweedledum and Tweedledee, but none of this got me any closer to Kevy Parkinson.

It did, however, have another positive outcome. Dad decided to build me a surfboard buggy out of bike parts, so I could attach it behind my Speedwell and be less dependent on others for transport. Presumably this was because he believed that hanging out with my migrant gang had somehow contributed to the reckless behaviour that led to our dentist

'60s board buggy. (Photo Jeff Carter Archive)

being able to order a new Holden and book a holiday on the Gold Coast. Again, this was misguided logic because it pushed me into a closer friendship with the only other boy I knew who had a surfboard buggy, Neil 'Thommo' Thomson. We immediately began plotting an Easter bicycle safari to the distant surfing mecca south of Shellharbour known as 'The Farm', which was immediately vetoed by Dad.

Many lies were told during the preparations for this adventure. When Thommo and I set off at dawn on a rainy Good Friday, my parents had somehow formed the impression that I was spending the holiday weekend with the Thomson family, so Neil and I could go surfing with his older brother in his panel van.

We pedalled for hours through the puddles at the unmade edge of the road while cars whizzed by, dangerously close. (Maybe this was why Dad had said no to the trek.) Soon after the rain stopped and the sky began to brighten, I hit a huge pothole on a back road, puncturing a tyre on my bike and buckling the back wheel of the buggy beyond repair. When I finished cursing I looked at Thommo and said, 'You go on, mate. It's all over for me.'

Our plan had been to camp under a lean-to made up of a tarp slung over our buggies, and to buy sausages and grill them over a campfire. Not much fun alone. 'Me too,' said Thommo.

We walked our rigs to a corner shop with a phone box outside. I put sixpence in the slot and called Mum, who went into hysterics and then told Dad, who eventually picked us up in the Commer van. Not a word was spoken all the way home, which turned out to be not very far at all if you weren't cycling and towing a massive weight. I was grounded until Anzac Day.

During my first year at Corrimal High a massively built surfer and surf lifesaver (or 'clubbie', as we derisively called them) named Darrell Eastlake had started hanging out at our beach. In spring he opened the South Coast Surf Hut on Railway Street, just a couple of hundred yards from the school. This was the first surf shop I had ever seen, and I was endlessly fascinated by everything in it, including Darrell, who had a deep, laconic drawl and the easy walk of a surfer, despite his size.

On surfless days I liked to drop into the Surf Hut on my way home, to look at the rack of glistening new boards from such legendary manufacturers as Gordon Woods, Bill Wallace, Norm Casey and Brian Jackson.

Darrell Eastlake (left) outside his South Coast Surf Hut, 1964.

There wasn't much in the way of surfwear, just a few T-shirts with surf-board builder logos on the front or back, and a couple of pairs of Platts boardshorts. But Darrell always had a pile of the latest surfing magazines, including the amazing *Surfer* magazine, all the way from California.

I loved sitting in the Surf Hut, listening to Darrell and flipping through surf magazines, but it soon became a hangout for Kevy Parkinson's cool crew, with the prettiest girls in school not far behind. The only kid in first form still in short pants, I became a figure of fun. Soon, I would ride past on my Speedwell Special Sports and only go in if Darrell was there by himself. He knew what was going on, and was sympathetic. 'Don't take any notice of those idiots, matey. There's plenty of blokes in offices wishin' they had a pair of shorts on, I can tell ya.' But Darrell was easily distracted, especially when surrounded by pretty schoolgirls, and his support was sporadic at best.

It seems ludicrous to me now, because as Darrell indicated all those years ago, wearing less is good, but at the time I truly believed that the parental edict that saw me in grey serge shorts when virtually every other boy in my year was wearing long trousers was a particularly evil form of cruelty. Both my parents were inflexible on this pointless law, but there

Kevy Parkinson at Bellambi, 1966. (Photo David Milnes)

was one exception. I was allowed to wear my long trousers to the end of year school social, at which there was to be live music provided by the Del-Re-Echoes, a local band in which my guitar teacher played rhythm guitar. This was to be where the laughing and the snide remarks stopped. This was the night when the school would see me for what I was—a super cool surf guy wearing grown-up tapered-leg sports slacks, and who knew the band, for chrissake!

I was allowed to wear the slacks, but the unruly hair had to go. The afternoon before the social I was given five shillings and sent to Col the barber, who actually had a striped red pole out the front—and an SP bookie shop out the back. There was one barber's chair, and a waiting bench that seated five or six. The small room stank of Craven As, which Col and his clients obsessively smoked, and 2KY, the racing station, bellowed from a mantle radio, but I didn't mind waiting. If you flipped through the stack of race forms on the little table where the ashtrays lived, you could usually find a dog-eared copy of *Man* magazine, with risqué swimsuit model pictorials and bawdy cartoons. Col himself was a particularly ugly man with stained teeth and a heavily Brylcreemed black comb-over.

I waited patiently for my turn, furtively checking the *Man* pictorials. 'Next! Come on, sonny, haven't got all bloody day.' Col was standing next to his chair with a newly lit cigarette hanging from his pursed lips and a white neck cloth in his hands. I climbed into the chair and said, 'Square back and sides, please.'

The Beatles had toured Australia during the previous winter and virtually overnight, hair had crept over collars and fringes approached eyebrows. The next best thing to scruffy collar-length hair was a square back and sides, particularly if it was left long enough on top that you could throw it around a little. This is the look I had asked Col to create.

After his first run with the razor I knew I was in trouble. After the second, I was sobbing. My hair was all over the floor and Col was ashing his cigarette on it. 'What's the matter, sonny? I haven't cut you,' he muttered.

'I asked for a square back and sides.'

'You asked for a *short* back and sides and that's what you're getting.'

Like the difference between short pants and long, a couple of inches of shaved skull seems so inconsequential now, but it mattered so much then. I looked at my ridiculous haircut in the mirror, my big ears now accentuated, and knew I was ruined. Even the migrant kids whose dads slapped a pudding bowl on their heads and cut around it had a better look than me. The tapered slacks, the button-down collar shirt and the thin woollen tie couldn't disguise the fact that I looked like a dork. No-one would talk to me. No girl would dance with me.

In the progressive barn dance, I put my sweaty arm around Tanya Lightfoot's back and tried not to trip her as we spun around. 'You've had a haircut,' she giggled. 'It's a bit funny, but kind of nice.'

I smiled back at her. I was in love.

CHAPTER EIGHT

Surfers at Midway, 1962. (Photo Bob Weeks)

DINO'S SHACK

The world began to spin faster. It was 1965. I was in long pants at last. I had kissed a girl. I was becoming obsessive about surfing. I had a job selling newspapers every morning to supplement my pocket money. Life was good.

Now that both my big sisters had left school and were almost out of their teens, the parental rules seemed to relax a little. That said, when Darrell Eastlake started the Corrimal Boardriders Club I still wasn't allowed to join, because it wasn't the right kind of environment for me, mixing it up with older boys who drank, smoke and used foul language. I was mildly disappointed, although most of the guys at Dino's Shed chose not to join anyway, presumably because over the summer Dino and the older boys had built a fairly sophisticated construction of stolen wood and corrugated iron that soon became known as Dino's Shack, where there was no shortage of the aforementioned sins.

Dino's Shack was hidden from view behind the first line of tussocky sandhills that separated the beach from Bellambi Lagoon. It was nestled so deeply into the sand valley that you could squat on the slope above it and check the surf without being seen. The only telltale sign was the smoke from a campfire that burnt whenever Dino and his gang were in residence, which was almost every weekend. The biggest room could sleep about a dozen in sleeping bags or blankets on the sand—more if drink had been taken, and it usually had. There was a second room off to one side where members of the gang could take guests of the opposite sex, unless they preferred the complete privacy of the other dunes, of which there were many.

I'm pretty sure none of us had read Frederick Kohner's 1957 surf-lit bestseller *Gidget: The Little Girl With Big Ideas*, nor seen the surf-ploitation Hollywood movie that followed, but if we had, or if we'd known anything about Tubesteak Tracy's Malibu shack and the raffish beach culture that grew up around it, we wouldn't have had to modify Dino's Shack very much at all to fit the mould.

Of course, my parents knew nothing of the cultural anthropology I was studying hidden from prying eyes behind the tussocks—they were not relaxed enough for that yet. I always claimed to be sleeping over at a friend's house, and surprisingly, they never seemed to check, freeing me to lug my board over to the dunes at dark on Friday, pay my share for the pub run, lay out my sleeping gear and often stay until Sunday afternoon.

Sometimes I'd be turned away from the shack and have to make alternative arrangements. This was usually because of an expected visit by a girl or girls who were believed to be willing to entertain several of the gang. Dino and some of the other older surfers, like Steve Olejniczak, had a surprisingly strong moral streak. While this did not necessarily modify their own behaviour, it made them protective of the 'grems' in the group.

Gidget and Miki, Malibu, 1957.

But we saw enough, and participated in enough, to fast-track our sex education, skipping the niceties. My problem was that I didn't like the taste of beer, which arrived in boxes of tall bottles and was shared around, soon becoming warm from the fire and the saliva of a dozen overexcited surfers. Occasionally there were bottles of spirits, but I tried rum and gin and didn't like them much either. Then one night someone brought a bottle of cheap port and a bottle of lemonade 'for the girls'. There were no glasses for mixing, but I took a slug of port and washed it down with lemonade. I had found my tipple.

(When I was fourteen I looked old enough to get into the Friday night sessions at the Bellambi Hotel. Decimal currency had just been introduced, and I found I could walk into the bar with a brand new dollar note, order eight port and lemonades over a couple of hours, and leave with a considerable buzz going and four cents change. One night the elderly barmaid took me aside—she obviously knew I was well underage—and whispered, 'See any old blokes in here drinking that?' I shook my head. 'That's because if you drink that rotgut you won't live long enough to get old.')

Slowly I came around to beer, which was just as well because the scene at Dino's Shack was getting so big that the older surfers were bringing kegs. It was also getting messy. I have a vivid memory of waking one morning and seeing bodies passed out all over the sandy valley floor, interspersed with surfboards and pieces of clothing. Nothing particularly bad had happened, but I felt guilty being there, and I came less often after that.

My first local, the Bellambi pub.

That's why I wasn't there the night the police raided the shack and took several people away for questioning about underage drinking, moral dangers and the like. The next morning they came back and knocked the place down, taking away most of the materials.

Dino and some of the gang rebuilt the shack further into the dunes, but the parties and campfires were less frequent, and they stopped altogether after Dino was called up in the first National Service ballot. His apprenticeship completed, he had no grounds for deferment, though he went quite happily, seeming to relish the adventure. But when he came back from his tour in Vietnam, he seemed distant and smiled infrequently, and often he would walk right past our group and surf alone in the murky waters of the Shithole. And then we didn't see him anymore.

Somewhere around this time—it must have been Easter 1966—I finally managed to lose my virginity, although the evidence for this was so feeble that I may merely have misplaced it. Thommo and I were on the Sydney train, bound for sideshow alley at the Royal Easter Show. There was a boisterous group of girls from another school sharing our carriage. I sat next to one and we began 'pashing' almost immediately. The courtship proceeded at breakneck pace, and by the time we entered the long darkness of the Coalcliff tunnel, we were braced over the cistern in the toilet, our undies around our ankles and our sex organs vaguely locked together long enough for me to, in the immortal words of Patrol Leader Max, 'spunk up' over the porcelain. I'm not sure how the girl enjoyed it. I didn't ask. We hurriedly cleaned up with toilet paper and went our own separate ways.

I recounted the experience (with considerable pride) to Thommo later as we made our way between the fat lady and the snake charmer. It seemed that he had run into difficulties and had only managed to achieve an 'upstairs inside', which he had found memorable nonetheless. I'd like to say that having broken the drought, my sexual encounters then came thick and fast, so to speak, but in fact it was to be quite a while before I discovered that horizontal sexual pleasures could be far more gratifying for both parties.

Although they had forbidden me to join Darrell Eastlake's Corrimal Boardriders, my parents raised no strenuous objections when a rebel group of surfers formed Bellambi Boardriders and I was asked to join the junior ranks. By now I had moved on from the waterlogged purple Barry Bennett pig in favour of a near-new lime green Norm Casey nine-foot-eight with a nylon pintail fin. The older surfer who sold it to me drove a matching lime green Morris Mini Minor, but apparently the board was such a dog that he was prepared to forfeit the colour coordination to get rid of it.

'This'll straighten out your surfing,' he told me. And indeed it did, since I could hardly turn the board. But oddly enough it provided a stable platform on which I was able to walk the board, ride the nose, perform spinners and crouch up front in a Paul Strauch stretch—named after a famous Hawaiian surfer and used to great effect by a new hero, seventeen-year-old Jeff Hakman, a diminutive Californian transplant who had just won the inaugural Duke Kahanamoku Invitational at Sunset Beach.

I read all about this in the latest *Surfer* magazine in the pile at the South Coast Surf Hut, but it was the last time I went there. Darrell wasn't particularly happy about surfers defecting to the Bellambi club, and in a short while the Corrimal club, the Surf Hut and Darrell himself had gone. (The next time I saw Darrell Eastlake, about twenty years later, he'd reinvented himself as a television sportscaster and I was writing his scripts.)

I loved being in the Bellambi Boardriders from the start. Every couple of weeks we bundled into cars owned by the older surfers and travelled to exotic locations like Sandon Point or Port Kembla Oil Piers or Windang Island for our club contests, known as point-scores. Several times a year we would compete against other South Coast clubs, such as Wollongong, Port Kembla and Warilla. Because the very best surfers, like Kevy Parkinson, Ken Middleton, Mick Carabine and Paul 'Dirtyface' Brooks, had been

South Coast Championships at Bellambi, 1965. (Photo David Milnes)

Dino's Shack

poached by the Windansea Club, a Sydney-based invitation-only outfit, it was a relatively even playing field and our club held its own.

Through the more senior members I also got to meet the surfboard builders of our region, including John Skipp and Mick Carabine. John and Mick had been running a South Coast factory for Cronulla-based Brian Jackson Surfboards, just along the highway from Dad's shop, but were about to go out on their own. The local board-builders were friendly enough, and good surfers, but when I had saved up enough for a new board I went not to them but to the new Mecca of surfboards—Brookvale.

Brookvale was a relatively new industrial estate on Sydney's northside, tucked in behind Manly and Freshwater beaches. It had been a market garden bounded by swamps and a creek, but its proximity to the beach and low real estate prices had made it a magnet for the surfboard manufacturers who had enjoyed a boom since the introduction of lightweight and durable foam blanks to replace balsa at the core of surfboards. Surfing's popularity had also grown at warp speed on the back of the surf-stomp craze that was sweeping the country, making stars out of teenage surfie chicks like Little Pattie, Beach Boys wannabe vocal groups like The Delltones, and guitar bands such as The Atlantics.

My friend Thommo was also in the market for a new board, so his older brother John, soon to join the growing ranks of National Service inductees, drove us up to Brookvale early one Saturday, which was the day the manufacturers tried to clear out shop stock by lining up discounted boards in front of their showrooms. We did a drive-by of the leading shops—Barry Bennett and Gordon Woods on Harbord Road, and Scott Dillon and Bill Wallace on Winbourne Road—before parking centrally and setting out on foot. Bennett's was the first stop. The price seemed right but nothing took my fancy. Down the hill at Gordon Woods, John Thomson leaned into us as we approached the lawn. 'That's him,' he whispered. 'Gordon Woods.'

Gordon Woods was old like my dad, but what distinguished him was his country club attire. He wore a golf shirt, Bermuda shorts, long socks and brogues. He reminded me of my Uncle John, who usually teamed a cravat with his golf ensemble. Gordon Woods seemed more relaxed, although he didn't strike me as a surfer. He finally came over and shook John's hand. He said, 'Young chaps looking for a board?' He mussed Thommo's curly hair and gave me a pat on the shoulder. 'Let's see what we've got.'

My first impression of Gordon Woods was that he was a thorough gentleman, and I still feel the same way about the man, now in his nineties, who has become a legend in surfing and a personal friend. I just knew I could trust him, and when he pointed to a poo-brown Nat Young model, I knew it was the board for me. We completed the round of the factories and then went back to Gordon Woods, where he gave me a fair trade-in on the Norm Casey, and then dropped a little more off the price to meet the cash I had in an envelope.

I couldn't wait to get my Nat model Woodsie into the water, but a new board had to be properly waxed first—a monumental job in those days—so once Thommo had selected his board (a Woodsie as well, from memory, although my self-absorption was such that I can't really be sure) we made the long drive home, set the boards up on sawhorses in the Thomson backyard and spent a long hour heating our hardware-store blocks of paraffin wax and applying it to the deck.

It was almost dark when we eventually knee-paddled out at Bellambi, but I knew from my first wave on the new board that I had taken a giant step forward. As the beach grew golden with the sunset I carried my board on my head up to the car park, where John Thomson helped me get it onto the roof rack.

'Seems to suit you,' he said.

I glowed all the way home.

Gordon Woods (far right) and staff, Brookvale, 1966.

Dino's Shack

CHAPTER NINE

Bellambi Reef, 1965. (Photo David Milnes)

BELLAMBI BOARDRIDERS

Slowly but surely, surfing was taking me away from my family, and it felt good. It wasn't so much rebellion on my part, more a mutual realisation that my teen years needn't be a burden to my parents if they just cut me some slack.

Not that my school performance was all that bad: I remained in the A class, although I was a middling academic performer when I probably could have been near the top, and I played soccer for the school but soon slipped to the B-grade team. Any optional activity that might interfere with my surf time had to go. In first form I had won a literary award for my contributions to the school magazine, but those skills were not to re-emerge until I started contributing to surfing magazines. Sadly, my fascination with the guitar went, too. I had taken lessons for several years after my parents picked up a cheap guitar for me on the dock at Genoa in 1962, and slowly mastered the basic chords and a few leads—the 'Peter Gunn Theme' was my go-to piece.

If I had known that just around the corner every man and his dog would be heading up the coast in a Kombi van with a girl, a surfboard and a guitar, maybe I would have stuck at it. If I had known that the rich list would soon be made up almost exclusively of boys who had graduated from private schools, then maybe I would have gone to the grammar school my parents had chosen for me. But I went surfing, and I have never regretted that.

The Bellambi Boardriders Club was my fast-track to juvenile delinquency. By the time I was fifteen there were enough older guys with cars

57

to get me wherever I wanted to go, and enough guys with panel vans with mattresses in the back to provide relative discretion for sexual adventures. At first I was only allowed out on Saturday night, and had to be home by midnight, but I found you could fit a lot into that window. Typically, our gang would get together at the quaint old Bellambi Pub soon after dark, wearing our surf dude uniform of blue sneakers, Lee jeans and Pendleton striped shirts. Apart from its heritage façade, the Bellambi Pub was best known for its slackness in identifying underage drinkers, so we would consume a pie or a couple of sausage rolls and wash them down with as much beer as we could afford (I'd moved on from port and lemonade). The object was to arrive at the Wonderland dance hall, a short wobbly drive away, full of Dutch courage—an expression that was somewhat lost on my beach gang, half of whom were Dutch.

Wonderland had live bands on the weekends and it was a magnet for girls from as far afield as Bulli to the north and Wollongong to the south. The surfers' stomp had almost had its day, but girls still danced in a pack, and with a head of steam on, you could pick your target and just start dancing with her, no questions asked. If the girl liked you, she would smile and you would pair off from the pack.

I can't remember how many dances, attempts at conversation and 'pashes' were considered necessary before asking a girl to adjourn to somewhere more comfortable, but I do remember the procedure, because it required a degree of forward planning, no matter how much of a booze buzz you had on. It involved asking at least two, preferably three friends with panel vans if you could borrow the mattress in the back should you get lucky. Since we were all there with the same objective, and older boys with cars seemed to do better than us, it paid to have back-up. It also paid to know what your mate's 'shaggin' wagon' looked like and where it was parked, since keys didn't make the lights go on in those days.

The encounters weren't always memorable but they were always quick. Premature ejaculation was a constant companion, but the loan of the mattress in the back was usually only good for half an hour at most anyway. Hell, you could talk before and after, although I often had to screw and run in order to beat the parental curfew.

My association with older surfers in the club also meant there were more frequent weekend trips away to other surf spots, either as a club excursion or in smaller informal groups. Ulladulla was a popular destination because we could surf Green Island in a northerly or Golf Course

Reef on a southerly, drink without ID at the Marlin Hotel and sleep it off without fear of interruption on the verandah of the Mollymook surf club.

The official club trips were usually for a regional contest or an inter-club meet, such as the time we hired a bus to transport us all to the Central Coast to take on the Norah Head club and a couple of clubs from Newcastle. I don't remember much about getting there or getting home, other than that we drank all the way up. I don't remember the quality of the surf or who won the contest, but what happened on Saturday night at The Entrance stayed with me for decades.

The Bellambi Boardriders Club didn't exactly cover itself with glory that weekend, and as an individual, nor did I. It's a bit sketchy now, but there was a rough pub with a loud band and we all drank far too much. And there were some rough girls, including one who had recently enjoyed fleeting tabloid fame after stowing away on a Navy ship rather than leave her sailor boyfriend. Having been detected, she apparently sorted things out by spending a couple of hours in the captain's cabin. We didn't score her, but her friend accompanied half the club back to the bus, parked in a dark lot behind the pub.

I found myself towards the back of the queue that had formed along the aisle of the bus, and passed out long before it was my turn to receive the girl's favours. When I came to some hours later I swished my tongue around my dry mouth and made the alarming discovery that my partial denture was no longer a part of me. I staggered out of the bus and found my teeth staring up at me from a puddle of vomit, popped them straight back in and fell asleep again in the foul air of the bus that had become a bordello.

At the time I excused myself from any blame because as far as I was concerned, nothing had happened. But I was there, I more or less knew why, and I may have been a willing participant in a sexual assault, had I been just slightly less drunk. My passing out was a huge joke among my clubmates. To keep up appearances, I went along with it, laughing and pretending to enjoy the notoriety. But I felt guilty and ashamed, and I wanted the trip to be over.

CHAPTER TEN

Kevin Parkinson, Bellambi Pier, 1963. (Photo David Milnes)

SURGING TOWARDS COMPETENCE

Schooldays were coming to an end, and the surfer ranks at school had thinned out. With graduation age now eighteen, this was a bridge too far for many of my surfer mates, who left at Year 10 regardless of how qualified they were for further education.

My friend Patrick Olejniczak was one of them. He was soon an apprentice at the Steelworks, with his own car and a lucrative sideline fixing dings and experimenting with surfboard shaping in his dad's shed. Pat's entry into the workforce couldn't have come at a better time for me. Surfboards had suddenly started to evolve so quickly that my pocket money couldn't keep up. It was no longer enough to work after-school jobs and save enough to trade in your board every year or so. Now you needed a new board every couple of months, and they were getting shorter and more radical in design.

Pat had taught me how to fix my own dings, so I thought I knew enough about surfboard production to strip the glass off the poo-brown Gordon Woods Nat Young model and remodel it into a new shape known as a 'tracker'. A little knowledge can be a dangerous thing, and in no time at all I had sanded the recycled blank down to almost nothing while trying to achieve symmetry. I now had no board, but this didn't matter because in the time it took me to realise I would never be a shaper, the tracker design had already become outdated. I bought a second-hand, absolutely flat-bottomed Jackson pintail, similar to the board Kevy Parkinson was now riding, and cut the Greenough fin down to almost nothing so I could side-slip it down the face of the wave like Kevy.

Kevy Parkinson at Bellambi. (Photo David Milnes)

Fortunately, before too much damage was done, Pat and I worked out a deal where I could pay off a board by working at his new factory after school. In this way I came to play a small part in designing my first custom surfboard, which became known as My Pretty Pink Pintail (stolen from a free-form Bob McTavish article in *Surf International*).

God how I loved that board! I'd completely missed the vee-bottom phase, which had been pioneered by McTavish in 1967, but I loved the new trend towards completely flat-bottom boards, despite my false start with them. The pink pintail was flat as a tack, but it had more rocker than the Jacko and slightly softer rails, and it surfed like a dream. All around me the good surfers I looked up to were still on the McTavish vee program— Ken Middleton, Dick Perese, Paul Brooks, even Kevy Parkinson himself from time to time, throwing wide-legged spanner cutbacks with their arms in the air, but I just couldn't surf like that. On a relatively short but flat-bottomed board, however, I felt the progression from the old-style boards to the new was almost seamless.

If this makes me sound like the Next Big Thing in South Coast surfing, let me assure you that my surge towards competence went largely unnoticed, while local peers like Phil Byrne, Graham Swann, Cronulla's

Eddie Conlan, and Baddy Treloar, Butch Cooney and Mark Warren on Sydney's northside were becoming recognised as the surfers of tomorrow. This point was driven home to me when I somehow managed to qualify for the final round of the 1968 New South Wales Schoolboys Titles held at Manly, and was absolutely smashed by just about all of them.

As summer kicked in, our group started driving south to surf The Farm or Windang Island on a Sunday morning, partly because the waves were often good, but also so we could stop off for a few cold ones at the Warilla pub on the way home and catch the hot band *du jour*, Reverend Black and the Rocking Vicars. Led by Blackpool's Dave Rossall, the Vicars were basically a reincarnation of a slightly notable British blues/pop outfit that had folded. Rossall simply stole their act and headed for the Antipodes, but we didn't know or care. They were great!

The real action, however, was not on the stage or on the dance floor. It was in the toilets and the car park, where it was very easy to score a matchbox of weed or a blotter of acid.

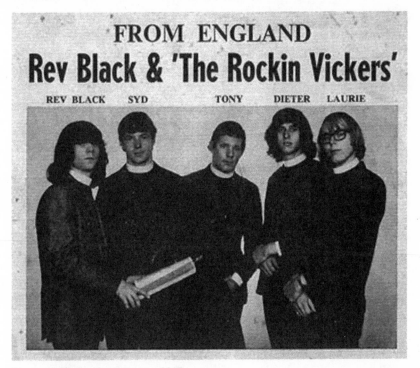

Reverend Black concert poster, 1967.

Kirra carpark, 1960s. (Photo Mal Sutherland)

It was amazing to see how fast the drug culture took hold. Although I'd been a precocious early adopter when it came to alcohol, the idea of losing control on something else seemed faintly abhorrent. So I held back and watched while others stumbled and fell. I toked but barely inhaled, to paraphrase a certain president. I split a blotter of acid with friends once, and as far as I can remember the effects were minimal. My fascination with that drug would come later ...

To my great surprise my parents agreed to let me go on a surf trip to Queensland with a group of school friends over the May school holidays. I suppose at sixteen and seventeen we were considered old enough to have some degree of responsibility, but this trip, by train and thumb, offered limitless opportunity for delinquent behaviour. Five or six of us caught the train to Sydney with our backpacks and surfboards, then jumped onto the North Coast Mail to Byron Bay. Our parents thought we were heading straight for Kirra, on the Gold Coast, where an uncle of one of the gang had a holiday apartment we could use, but first we made nuisances of ourselves in Byron, surfing The Pass all day then sleeping off our beer binge in the sandhills of Clark's Beach. It was Dino's Shack without Dino or the shack, and we had a ball until the police moved us on.

The flat at Kirra was a linoleum-floored dump behind the pub, but we didn't care. We had a choice of surfing the long rights or the pounding beach break left out in front—this was pre-groynes—and we could drink and play pool at the local, or walk ten minutes to the fleshpots of Coolangatta. I had been to the Gold Coast only once before since I'd been a surfer, but that had been with my parents back in 1964 when I wouldn't have known what to look for. Now I saw endless peeling point breaks that were still relatively uncrowded. The other end of the coast bore the name, but this was the real surfer's paradise. I remember being astounded by the length of ride afforded by the points, and the speed with which we found ourselves skating over shallow sandbar sections of the paper-thin waves, so different from anything we had at home. At first I found it tricky to ride the points on my backhand, but by the end of our stay I had mastered the grab-rail, top-turn take-off, which wasn't pretty, but saved a lot of swims.

At the end our week at Kirra, the plan was to catch the train home, but Gary Fletcher and I had other ideas. 'Fletch' was a quietly spoken guy, but he had an adventurous spirit. We decided to give Byron Bay another go, figuring that we could still get home at the same time as the others by cashing in our return train tickets and hitchhiking through the night.

The first part of the plan worked brilliantly—we scored great waves again at The Pass. The ticket office at the Byron Bay railway station wouldn't refund our tickets, so we found ourselves sitting by the Pacific Highway at dusk, waiting for a ride with about $3 between us. The only people who seemed willing to pick us up were farmers with filthy utes or tray-back trucks. It was bitterly cold sitting up there in the night air, and no-one seemed to be going more than a few miles. By morning—the morning we were supposed to be home—we were sitting by the highway somewhere north of Coffs Harbour when our saviour crested a hill in the distance and slowed as he saw us.

I can't remember his name, but he was a teacher at Keira Boys High and a regular in the surf at Brandy's and Bellambi. His wife seemed a little uncertain about us as we strapped our boards onto the roof and piled into the back of the Mini Minor, but over the next twelve hours she came around. Our teacher mate paid for all our pit-stops and dropped us each at our front door, only a day late.

I was immediately grounded for a month.

CHAPTER ELEVEN

DISGRACE

Although I remained friends with most of the surfers who left school early to join the workforce (including my part-time employer, Pat Olejniczak), there was a distinct gang realignment. It was just easier to hang out with the guys I saw every day. My posse was almost exclusively surfers, but I did make an exception for Peter 'Jose' Anderson, who was the singer in a band called the Justin Arthur Group. Jose, who landed at our school after being kicked out of his last one for some long-forgotten indiscretion, was smart, creative, brash and lazy. He was a good friend but a bad influence. The Justin Arthur Group actually had paid gigs, so in my eyes he was a sixteen-year-old rock star. Although I was a few months older, I followed him around like a puppy, and often ended up outside the headmaster's office waiting for a caning.

I haven't mentioned our headmaster up to this point, perhaps because I've managed to expunge much of the memory of 'The Boss'. His name was Clem Skevington, which conjures up Dickensian images that are one hundred per cent correct. He liked to make a point by bruising your breastbone with his dirty-nailed index finger. The teaching staff hated him as much as we did.

In 2001 I was invited to speak at Corrimal High's fiftieth anniversary dinner, and before launching into some Skevington horror stories, I said, 'I'm sure he's long dead, so I can tell this ...' Two women down the front stood up and cried out, 'No, no, he's not dead!' They looked truly frightened, so I quickly changed the subject. Fear of The Boss lived on.

My classmates and I had reached the stage of schooling when teachers, sometimes only a few years older than us, occasionally became friends.

I'm sure this happens more now than it did half a century ago, when the generation gap seemed so much wider, but even then it was not uncommon. I moved closer to that line the first time Glenda appeared at our beach and stripped down to a white one-piece to walk into the sandhills. Our new French teacher, she was beautiful, full-figured, with long dark hair, long lashes and huge eyes. After the Dino's Shack summers, the sandhills had something of a reputation. I desperately wanted to follow her into them ...

My schoolboy crush might have passed quickly, and without incident, except that she seemed (to my young eyes at least) to encourage it. She always had a seductive smile (again, this is subjective) and an encouraging word for me, despite my tortured pronunciation and abysmal vocabulary, and we became friends. I lost interest in girlfriends my own age and lived for the occasions, like Bastille Day, when she cooked us a French dinner at her apartment, or invented other excuses to treat us, her students, as equals.

While there was little opportunity for physical contact, or even privacy, if she was arched in a doorway smoking a Gitane (as she often was), I would make a beeline for it so I could brush past her, or put my hands lightly on her waist as I apologised for squeezing past. It was pathetic, but neither of us tired of it. Student/teacher relationships hadn't been put under the same kind of microscope back then, but it was a dangerous game nonetheless, which was probably part of the attraction.

Final exams were approaching but my mind was on so many things. Academically, I continued to fall behind, but I was proving to be a good organiser. I'm sure I didn't do it alone but I remember becoming heavily involved in the Bellambi Boardriders' presentation night, arranging the purchase and delivery of an absurd number of kegs, and booking the La De Das, a bunch of dissolute Kiwis who were one of the hottest bands in Sydney at the time.

Meanwhile I had become the Justin Arthur Group's biggest groupie, scoring the wine, beer and dope for the weekends and following the band around from one seedy after-gig party to the next. It was a no-brainer that Jose Anderson and I would be the ones to organise the end-of-school party, scheduled for the night after we began 'stu-vac', the week prior to final exams that was set aside for final swotting, or in mine and Jose's case, to begin studying.

The party planning quickly got out of control. The hall and the band had been booked, the booze and drugs ordered, and we were hanging out in the common room collecting ticket money when the shit hit the fan. The sixth form home teacher (an attractive young woman, but no Glenda) walked in and dropped her papers onto a desk with a thud. She cut straight to the chase. 'Anderson, Jarratt, principal's office now!' As we sashayed past her, she shook her head sadly and said, 'What the hell were you thinking?'

It didn't look good, but it was actually far worse. Skevington circled us menacingly, occasionally stopping to prod our chests with his finger. There was no six of the best—we were expelled.

'You can't do this!' I blurted, somewhere between tears and hysteria. 'It hasn't happened yet!'

But apparently he could. There was a fairly thick dossier involving underaged drinking, sexual misbehaviour and drugs—just the normal stuff. We were dead meat and we knew it.

Our parents were called to a meeting and Skevington read them the riot act. Dad had been quiet and measured up to this point, like a jug of cold water on a slow boil. But now he blew up. Parents didn't seem to like Skevington either, and Dad took umbrage at being blamed for the man's inability to run a tight ship. For a moment I thought I might come out of it okay, but then I remembered the day in the park when the bullies smeared shit on me, and I got what they got. No-one was going to win this one.

No longer students of Corrimal High, Jose and I sat our Higher School Certificate as external students in the annexe of the assembly hall with a dozen or so mature-age students, mostly migrants.

My shameful departure from high school was a black cloud that hovered above our house that summer, but of greater concern to my parents was what my immediate future held. If my pass was high enough to qualify, they expected me to enter university, whereas I wanted to get into the workforce as soon as possible. The compromise was that I would seek a management cadetship that would enable me to complete a degree part-time. But a cadetship in what? And where?

Dad had been banging on about the Diplomatic Corps, but after my expulsion even he began to see that this was futile. In the years since they had sailed the seas on the next-to-last voyage of the *Johan van Oldenbarnevelt*, Dad had become somewhat obsessed with international travel, obtaining a travel agent's licence and opening an agency in one of his shops. So it wasn't a complete surprise when he presented me with an

Disgrace

application form for a marketing cadetship with Qantas. Having made the shortlist and been granted an interview, I donned the new suit, bought from Slack's Menswear for the occasion.

I gave the Qantas interview my best shot, but the truth was I had a different plan. Towards the end of 1968 I had received notification from *Surfer* magazine in California that a short article I had written about ocean pollution in Australia had been accepted for publication and I should expect a cheque for $25 'any day'. In the time-honoured tradition of surf mags, the money took a year or two to arrive, but that didn't matter. What mattered was that I was not only going to be published in a real magazine for the first time, I was going to be published internationally! Fame would surely follow, and fortune would be not far behind it.

This more than made up for my disappointment that two unsolicited contributions to a new Australian magazine, *Surf International*, had gone unacknowledged, and it convinced me that my future lay in journalism. I knew next to nothing about it, but I imagined that if I had newspaper training, many doors in surf journalism would open. And I was convinced that journalists got to go wherever they wanted, filing front-page stories from exotic places, pulling chicks at will, making huge bucks and getting plenty of time off to surf.

The new outfit for the Qantas interview.

Surfer magazine cover, 1968.

My father was none too happy about me working in the newspaper trade. He'd had dealings with advertising salesmen from a fishwrap called the *South Coast Times* and found them to be an unsavoury lot. (When I started in the trade I saw what he meant. Newspaper people *were* an unsavoury lot, and I loved them.) But he became resigned to the idea, particularly after the publication of our Higher School Certificate results revealed that I had exceeded my expectations (though fallen far short, of course, of those of my parents and teachers) and my middling pass was enough to get me into an arts degree at the University of New South Wales, which I promised I would pursue once I had got a job at a newspaper.

I made the final cut for a cadetship at the *Sydney Morning Herald* and would know in a matter of weeks if I was to be one of six selected. But I couldn't wait to get out of home and Wollongong. I applied for a job as a copy boy at the rival *Daily Telegraph* and was accepted, so on a steamy night in January a couple of surfing buddies drove me the hour or so up the highway, an overnight bag in the back of the van along with my only surfboard, an egg-railed rounded pin that Pat Olejniczak had made and sold me on a payment plan.

I had made arrangements to stay with my Uncle David and his family at Roseville on the north side of the city, and my mates would drop me at Central Station to take the train. But we didn't go there straight away. We smoked joints all the way up the Princes Highway and arrived at the Mandala Theatre in Paddington totally stoned and just in time for the start of a very cool concert and surf movie. The movie was *Evolution*, which we'd already seen, but having had its first theatrical release, it was now relegated to a background blur behind a band called Leo De Castro and Friends.

This was the era of the 'supergroup', when heavyweight rock stars like Eric Clapton and Michael Bloomfield were putting together pickup bands to record under-rehearsed and interminably long live versions of songs they had already recorded. Leo and Friends was a provincial version of that, with musicians from bands such as Tamam Shud (who had performed the original *Evolution* soundtrack) and Tully, the house band from the Sydney production of the musical *Hair* casually appearing, if they weren't too stoned.

Speaking of which, I was whacked. We sat there, me, Billy and Thys, and I remember feeling on top of the world. I was eighteen, stoned, and free in the big, bad world.

CHAPTER TWELVE

Terry Fitzgerald, Brookvale, 1970. (Photo Albert Falzon)

ROCKIN' IN THE FREE WORLD

The job at the *Telegraph* paid just under ten bucks a week and involved sitting in a dingy room until someone bellowed, 'Copy boy!' Then you had to run, not walk, to the space from which the sound emanated and perform some menial task, ranging from rolling sheets of copy paper into a hard plastic tube and hurling it down a chute to the composing room (mildly interesting) to running to the Lebanese takeaway on Park Street to get some grumpy bastard's lunch (not interesting at all).

The copy boy room at the *Telegraph* was gloomy and paint-peeling and always smelled musty, but it had history. Scratched into the woodwork were the initials of dozens of boys who had once worked here before fleeing the building—and journalism—to find fame and fortune elsewhere. One scrawled signature I recognised was that of Doug Parkinson, the rock singer who had recently hit number one on the charts with a version of The Beatles' song 'Dear Prudence'.

Like Doug, I imagined my future in the copy boy room in terms of weeks rather than months, although I actually didn't mind the job. I became a favourite errand boy of the columnist Ron Saw, said to be the wittiest man in Sydney, and of the editor-in-chief, David McNicoll. In fact, Mr Saw invited me to join him in the pub once or twice. We might have become friends then, instead of later in life, but Dad phoned from home with news from behind enemy lines: I had been granted the cadetship at the *Herald*. I'd cracked the big time!

Fairfax headquarters, where the *Herald* and its afternoon stable-mate *The Sun* were published and printed, was a sprawling precinct just off

Broadway, not far from Central Station. Unlike the narrow corridors and cramped offices of the *Telegraph* in the heart of the city, the *Herald* newsroom was a vast open space filled with rows of desks separated only by the occasional pillar. Sitting behind one of these pillars, if you lined it up correctly, was the only way to avoid the glare of the chief of staff.

Sometime between one in the morning, when the night police rounds staff went home, and the sub-editors were supposed to, and four in the morning, when the *Sun* staff clocked on, a large team of cleaners moved in with buckets and mops. I know they turned up—I saw them often enough—but it made no difference. The newsroom was always filthy, with six-ply copy paper crumpled into angry balls of false starts and hopeless intros strewn across the floor, stained coffee mugs and pie wrappers on desks, and bins and ashtrays overflowing.

Reporters were required to dress appropriately for work, which meant sensible-length dresses and stockings for the women and a coat and tie for the men. It being 1970, however, there were many bizarre interpretations of the dress code. The rock music writer, for example, wore a grey serge suit that might have been his school uniform, but teamed it with Cuban-heeled Beatle boots and a thin leather tie. The religious affairs correspondent, newly arrived from the Old Country, wore an ill-fitting blue suit with a loud Hawaiian shirt (the same one all week) whose busy patterns made it difficult to see if he was wearing a tie. I had two button-down collar business shirts, one tie and one suit. Somehow I made the shirts last until Aunty Judy's weekly wash.

Because I was planning to attend university by day, I was initially given the night police rounds, which meant starting work at six pm and finishing at one in the morning. While this shift was not particularly conducive to a social life, it had other advantages. With the help of a $100 loan from Dad, I had bought a dark blue 1960 Volkswagen Beetle, so until uni started in mid-March, I was free to search the northern beaches for surf, which I did on a daily basis, unless my hangover was too severe. Very early on I was introduced to the peculiar after-hours world of the Sydney Journalists' Club by older sub-editors, who would head there once the paper had been 'put to bed'. In this nondescript third-floor bar, the journos of the city would drink and smoke and debate politics and sport and settle old scores until long after the sun had come up, an event that was never witnessed from the shuttered bar.

But I didn't scramble my brains at the Journo's Club every night. I had started a casual relationship with one of my cousins' friends, a willowy blonde called Carole, who lived with her parents in a beautiful old stone house in harbourside Mosman. Her room was underneath the house, rather like a more salubrious version of my dungeon at Powell Avenue. Carole went out with other boys too, but a couple of nights a week I would park the Beetle up the street, sneak down the side of the house and rap on her window.

This had been going on quite amicably for a while when one night in bed she mentioned that perhaps I would like to take her out, as opposed to climbing in. I didn't immediately see the point, but after discussing it at length with my elders and betters at the Journo's Club, and being advised that a big gesture was required in order to keep the cosy arrangement alive, I spent a small fortune on two supper session tickets to see José Feliciano at the Chevron Hotel in Kings Cross. The extremely adult venue was the idea of my journo mates, but the Feliciano performance was my masterstroke. The Doors' hit song 'Light My Fire' had been a favourite sexual anthem for a few years, but the blind Puerto Rican singer's sensuous cover version was one that Carole often played (very softly) on her record player when I came to visit.

When it came to the actual date, I was totally out of my depth. She wore a shawl over a long and somewhat transparent hippie dress. She looked gorgeous. I wore my work suit. We were shown to a table for two near the back of the smoky room. When the waiter delivered our cheese platter (included in the ticket) I ordered a tall bottle of Reschs Pilsener and two glasses. It had to last the whole show. When José sang our song, I reached under the table and squeezed Carole's thigh. She didn't reciprocate.

While police rounds was not the sexiest department in the newsroom, it was a good place to learn the ropes quickly. It also had its own small office off the main newsroom so the constant monitoring of police radio frequencies didn't interfere with the clatter of typewriters and the barked orders of the chief of staff outside. The room was shared with the *Herald* drivers, a group of men who knew everything about the murky nocturnal life of the paper and its staff, and kept most of it secret. A lowly copy boy sat in front of the radios and kept a time log on any police activity that might be newsworthy. As police rounds cadet, my job was to check the log from time to time and either follow up by phoning around the stations myself, or if it looked like a big story, passing the information on to the roundsman.

The doyen of police roundsmen was a mild, bespectacled, middle-aged man named Basil Sweeney, who had been with the *Herald* for years. Basil was justly famous for his scoops on such stories as the arrest of the notorious escapees Newcombe and Simmonds in 1959, and the mysterious deaths of Dr Gilbert Bogle and Margaret Chandler in salacious circumstances in 1963. Basil was rarely seen in the office. If I felt a situation warranted contacting him via the two-way radio in the staff cars, I would either get an abrupt 'You handle it', or more likely the driver would pass on a message and get back to me later with, 'Baz says you handle it'.

I didn't mind handling it. I was soon filing so many stories each night that a couple had to make it into the paper. I proudly kept a scrapbook of my published works. I am looking at the tiny, yellowed clips now: 'Youth leaps to death', 'Girl, 15, stabbed on train', 'Pop singer hurt in fall'. (This last was Russell Morris, who had slipped over while doing publicity photos at the zoo and suffered a bruise. Even Granny *Herald* was slipping into the trivia pit.)

Sometimes Basil would be so busy doing whatever it was he did to get his scoops that he would send his driver back to the office to pick me up so I could cover the ten-car pile-up or suburban brawl that was newsworthy, but not quite Basil-worthy. In this way I increasingly found myself out and about in the Sydney night, jotting down notes while our photographer shot the bleeding victims or the crumpled cars. If we were on deadline I would dictate a few cogent paragraphs to one of the copytakers over the two-way radio as we sped back so the photographer could hurriedly process his film and make the first edition. An exciting assignment like this would almost certainly result in an all-nighter at the Journo's.

One such story, covered in Basil's absence, concerned an Italian family whose home in the inner western suburbs had been almost destroyed by an out-of-control semi-trailer, the occupants lucky to survive. Although cadets were only given 'by-lines' under exceptional circumstances, I thought that my article, cleverly combining pathos and humour with the facts, might warrant my name on it. Instead, when I arrived at work the next night, the chief of staff bellowed my name. 'Jarratt! See me now!'

The chief of staff was a bulbous-eyed, treble-chinned former seminarian named Brian Johns. We called him 'The Bullfrog'. On warm evenings Johns would often sprawl in his chair at the front of the news-room, feet up on his desk, a cigarette smoking in the ashtray beside him. He'd put his hands behind his head, revealing dark sweat patches under the arms of the blue business shirts he favoured, and scan the reporters' floor. He was a repulsive figure.

I stood in front of him, as anxious as I'd been since coming to the paper. He motioned for me to sit.

'Jarratt, do you speak Italian?'

'No, sir.'

'But if you did, you would no doubt speak it perfectly, with no mistakes of grammar or pronunciation?'

'I don't know, sir.'

'Would you expect to be ridiculed in public, if you made a small mistake?'

I suddenly knew where he was going with this. My story about the semi-trailer crashing into the house had quoted the owner pretty much verbatim, things like: 'Ana all of a suddena, it'sa lika thisa big explosion ...' I thought it was hilarious, but Johns did not agree. He finished his tirade, saying, 'If you ever again use this newspaper as a vehicle for your racist humour, or for ridiculing anyone, you'll be looking for another job. Is that clear?'

I was shattered, but I could also see his point. I'd taken a cheap shot. It wouldn't be the last, but it was a lesson well learnt.

It was customary for the night reporters and sub-editors to gather at the Australian Hotel across Broadway for a couple of schooners before the pub closed. Brian Johns was holding court at one end of the bar with the sports editor, the political editor, the features editor and the arts editor, covering both ends of his broad spectrum of interest. That night as I walked in he motioned for me to join his group, handing me a foamy beer and introducing me to his peers. He said, 'This is young Jarratt. Not a bad hand, you'll be hearing more of him.'

From that night on, Johns, who himself was only at the beginning of a storied career in government, broadcasting and publishing, became my mentor at the *Sydney Morning Herald*. He was an enigma to me, but I came to trust his journalistic instinct, and to admire his deep sense of social justice and the generosity of spirit that he hid behind those bullfrog eyes.

As for Basil Sweeney, there was a feeling among the cadets and other reporters who worked in police rounds that he was far too close to the police to be objective. Nothing was ever said—Basil was a law unto himself—but the following year we were proven wrong when he put public interest ahead of his own and published damaging statistics, leaked by Sergeant Phil Arantz of the new computer analysis division, showing that the New South Wales Police had been overstating clear-up rates for years. Friends and contacts in the force, from the Police Commissioner down, shunned Sweeney for the rest of his career.

While my own brief career in police rounds is not the central theme of this memoir, there is one more story I must tell, because it illustrates the conflict of interest that was growing as I became more closely involved with the constabulary. In our leisure hours, my friends and I had become rather too fond of LSD, spending many nights wandering around the city marvelling at the colour of park benches or street lights. There was plenty of acid available, but the quality and strength varied wildly. It must have been a particularly hot batch that led into the early morning I found myself wandering around, marvelling at the texture of everything, only to be hit by a sudden stab of reality. I was due at the Criminal Investigation Bureau for the eight am press conference.

I remember sitting in the briefing while the CIB boss, Superintendent Lendrum, read his brief report, occasionally lifting his eyes from the paperwork to look directly at me. He was clearly aware that I was heavily under the influence of a mind-altering and totally illegal substance. All I could do was stare back and wait to be arrested. In my twisted state it seemed to me that he was clearly aware ...

Convinced that my newsroom career needed all of my attention, I'd put university on hold for a year (and ultimately never got there). I had moved into a studio flat in Glebe with three other cadets (one bed, three of us on mattresses on the floor) so I could be closer to the action, but in doing so, I'd distanced myself from the surf. I was desperate to get back into the waves.

I kept thinking about our trip to Byron Bay and the Gold Coast two years earlier. It was the right time of year for the points to be firing, but I'd only been in my job a few months. I couldn't possibly ask for time off. Then I saw a brief court report in the *Herald* about a young man who had been given a good behaviour bond in Lismore Court for possession of marijuana. He told the magistrate that he had taken a year off uni for a surfing holiday, and was living in a shack in the hills behind Byron Bay. This tallied with what I'd been reading in *Surf International* about a new movement called 'country soul', and with the stories I'd heard around Sydney about people 'splitting for up north'. Some of these were lifestyle choices, some were dodging the draft. I smelled a story.

Since Brian Johns had introduced me to his friends in the pub, I'd seen the features editor, Guy Morrison, a few times in the corridors or at the lifts and nodded politely. Although he wore a standard business suit, he had longish hair and seemed like a bit of an old hippie, so I plucked up the courage to phone his secretary and request an appointment to discuss my idea for a feature. To my surprise I was given a meeting. I nervously explained my plan, which was to visit Byron Bay, pose as a drug-taking surfer, and infiltrate the cult.

Morrison nodded as I talked, and jotted down a few notes. When I'd finished he said, 'Okay, sounds like something we could use. I'll see when Brian can spare you for a week or so. Jean will organise your travel expenses. Anything else?'

As I floated out the door he added, 'Don't be too harsh on these guys. You'll probably wish you were one of them!'

CHAPTER THIRTEEN

UNDERCOVER

My flight to Coolangatta in May 1970 was the first time I had been on a plane. If I was nervous, I was also extremely pleased with myself. Not yet nineteen, I was a hotshot reporter for a major metropolitan daily, tasked with exposing a growing youth cult that threatened the very fabric of Australian society. It never occurred to me that I had also just signed up to rat on my mates.

Because I was more or less going undercover, I had toned down my normal reporter's uniform and wore a surfer's parka over my business shirt and tie. When I realised that everyone else on the flight looked like they were on holiday, I ripped the tie off and hid it in my pocket. Having retrieved my naked surfboard (this was pre-boardbags) unscathed at baggage claim, I took a taxi to Coolangatta and found a cheap hotel across the street from Greenmount Point. It was Friday afternoon and I had until the following Monday week to get my story and get back to work. There were waves on the points, so I decided to get the fun out of the way first.

Surfed out and exhausted, I hitchhiked down to Byron Bay on Sunday afternoon, checked in to the Great Northern Hotel and slept like a baby. First thing Monday morning I put my tie on and crossed the railway tracks to meet with Sergeant Ron Dobson, officer in charge of Byron Bay Police, which comprised himself and a senior constable. The sarge was an affable enough guy, but he got very serious and at times quite angry when he discussed the difficulties that he and his one deputy faced in trying to control the spread of the dope-smoking surfie/hippie cult.

'We raid their hovels from time to time,' he said, 'and often charge them with offences relating to marijuana, usually just possession, but sometimes we find a small plantation. But with only two of us, we've got no hope of controlling it.'

Sergeant Dobson lit a cigarette and rocked back in his chair. Then he looked at his watch and said, 'Come on, I can spare an hour. I'll show you.' We climbed into the cabin of the paddy wagon and headed out towards Broken Head. The sarge turned off the road and onto a steep bush fire trail. 'This is where you'll find the biggest concentration of the bastards,' he yelled over the engine noise.

He pulled up in a small clearing and we tromped on foot along a track until I could see three basic tin-roof shacks about 200 metres apart in a valley below us, with a common area and a campfire in front. It looked like none of the bastards were home, for which I was thankful. I wanted to interview them, but I didn't want to be introduced by the Boss Pig. Sergeant Dobson led me to the clearing in front of the shacks. There were hot ashes in the fire pit and the area around it was tidy, with some tools and cooking utensils stacked against a tree stump.

I followed the sergeant into the unlocked shacks, but there was nothing to see—just camp mattresses, sleeping bags and clothing. A newish surfboard stood in the corner of one shack, so I took it outside and propped it next to the water tank for my photo. That was the best I could do.

Over the next couple of days I interviewed real estate agents and found you could rent a disused shack for as little as $2 a week—it was sounding better and better. Shopkeepers told me the 'blow-ins' were good customers. Wal Clarkson, the president of the Ratepayers Association, told me, 'Without them the tourist trade here would be dead. The good surf drags them in and the council does its best to push them out.' Then the swell came up again and I spent the rest of the week surfing. One morning at Broken Head I got talking to a feral-looking guy who turned out to be a shack-dweller. I asked him if I could see where he lived. 'Nah,' he said. 'No-one knows where it is, better that way.' We smoked a joint after our surf, then he picked up his board and said goodbye.

No-one at the beach knew I was a reporter from the *Sydney Morning Herald*, either. Better that way.

Part of me was ecstatic when 'The surf is running at Shangri-la, by Phillip Jarratt' appeared on the feature page of the *Herald* later in the

The surf is

By Phillip Jarratt

IN THE HILLS behind the tiny North Coast town of Byron Bay a new breed of farmer is emerging.

Scores of disused shacks there have become the homes of young people who have gone north from Sydney to escape the smog, crowds and hassles of city life. The year-round warm weather and good surf at Byron have made it the capital of a back-to-nature movement.

Young men have settled here with their wives or girl-friends on tiny farms and have become health enthusiasts, living on a diet of home grown fruit and vegetables — and sunflower seeds.

Some make and sell handicrafts and exist on the sales of their wares. A girl produces excellent leatherwear, and an American surfer living in the hills makes fibreglass vanity wash basins.

But nobody makes much money or works very hard, Byron isn't like that. Surfers who work in the San Juan surf shop in Byron Bay's main street tell you that in Byron you don't need much money.

Former city dwellers have found that they can do without many things they need in the city. Some have traded in their cars for bicycles.

With the coming of winter the annual influx of surfers from the south is under way. Many give up their jobs in the city and for four or five months live at the Bay, taking occasional days off work at the local meatworks or butter factory. The more established and more affluent surfers, one of them a former world and Australian champion, own their farms. Some rent homes to other surfers.

The blow-ins, always short of money either take over disused farmhouses and humpies or rent shacks.

An estate agent, Stan Johnson, told me "We rent these places for as little as $2 a week. They're not much on comfort, but quite a few have electricity."

At one shack set in the bush just off the dirt road leading to Broken Head a sign on the door reads: "To pass a policeman — we have a man." Inside was a battered old bed, several candles, a tin full of tobacco, a umbrella

My first feature published, *Sydney Morning Herald*, 1970.

month, alongside my photo of the surfboard next to the water tank. But part of me was slightly embarrassed by the somewhat indignant pro-Establishment tone of the article. Byron Bay was probably evenly balanced in its views towards the New Settlers (as they would eventually become known), but that's not the way my article came across. If anyone in the police rounds room was a mouthpiece for the coppers it was me, not Basil Sweeney!

Memos of congratulations on my first published feature from the cadet counsellor, the news editor and, amazingly, from the editor himself, former war correspondent Guy Harriott, helped dull the pain, but rock writer Michael Symons suddenly stopped talking to me and one of the graduate cadets gave me a free character reading before shorthand class. I just hoped that people in the surf magazine world didn't see my article, or if they did, that they didn't see me as a Judas.

And then embarrassment followed embarrassment. The photographer and journalist John Witzig had formed a partnership with photographer Albert Falzon and a rock magazine publisher named David Elfick, and published a revolutionary newsprint format surf magazine called *Tracks*. I had submitted a couple of unsolicited articles to Witzig while I was still at school, when he was editor of *Surf International*, and had never heard back.

First *Tracks* cover.

Everything about *Tracks* was confronting and exciting, including the cover story, which tipped a bucket on the city of Newcastle, where I had just been posted.

Desperately wanting to see my work published in the new magazine, I quickly tapped out a rebuttal, pointing out that the Steel City had good waves, good surfers and 'hot chicks'. When the second issue appeared on the newsstands, I bought a copy and flipped straight to the News and Opinion pages. There was my name. But exultation turned to mortification when I realised that it was attached not to my Newcastle piece (that was buried somewhere else) but to one of the bubbly essays I had sent to Witzig back when I was an immature schoolkid. It was called 'It's hot and sticky', and with no apologies to Bob McTavish, it began in free-form:

It's hot and sticky and the flies in that classroom are as bad as the teacher and it's worse because this is November and it's results time and some one throws 37% for History in my face and the guy outside is back at the pneumatic drill and I feel bad. I'm walking home and the westerly gale's drying the sweat on my face and there's dust in my eyes and the flies are worse and now I'm home and it's hotter and the History mark doesn't jazz the oldies and they're saying things like surfbum, one-track mind, lazy, you're gonna have to sell your board next year ... Then Pat comes and says the surf has improved and I grab my pretty pink pintail and chuck it on top of his car and we're away and Joe Cocker's screaming on the tranny and already it's better.

It went on, but you get the drift. I was horrified that my childishness was there in print for all to see, but after reading it through a couple of times I realised something that horrified me even more. I flipped through the magazine until I found my defence of Newcastle, and within that I read:

The current 'we gotta get out of this place' attitude towards city life is understandable, and in some ways commendable ... (but) to succeed you've either got to have money behind you or you've got to be willing to work hard. The majority of surfers dud out in both respects—so unless you're content to lead a hobo's existence in the country, you're stuck with the city.

I hadn't been in the workforce a year yet, but I'd become one of Them. Sure, my 'hot and sticky' ramble was trite and childish, but it carried within it the mindset of a surfer. As a fledgling newspaperman I'd started to lose that. I was becoming a mouthpiece for The Establishment. This had to change.

But that wasn't going to happen in Newcastle, where I'd been sent for a three-month term as assistant to the *Herald*'s correspondent. It was spring, 1970. In those days Newcastle was an important centre of heavy industry and a busy seaport, not to mention the fact that three hours' drive north of Sydney, it was considered the gateway to the north coast and the rich Hunter Valley. It probably would have made sense to pick up stories from the Fairfax-owned *Newcastle Herald*, but this was the golden age of newspapers, when the thicker-than-a-house-brick Saturday classifieds produced 'rivers of gold', so our paper maintained an independent two-room bureau run by a local journo named Brian Cogan.

Cogan and I hit it off immediately. He was about eight or nine years older than me, balding, reasonably fit but with a bulge at his belt that said he liked a drink. He was a good writer and an even better operator, but he was a mess of contradictions. Cynical about everything we reported, he was a hopeless romantic when it came to his hometown. Newcastle was his San Francisco, and when it became clear I didn't appreciate that, he loaned me his prized copy of *Don't Call It Frisco*, a collection of schmaltzy columns by Herb Caen of the *San Francisco Chronicle*. Seemingly happily married, with a pretty wife and two small daughters, he prowled the bars and clubs until late most nights, often with me in tow.

The Newcastle posting came with accommodation of sorts, a grimy flat attached to a house in the backblocks of East Newcastle. It had one proper bedroom with another room, not much bigger than a broom closet, that might have been an office or surfboard storage, but for the fact that it was already occupied by a former *Herald* cadet who had struck a deal with the previous incumbent. He offered me eight bucks a week rent so I let him stay, well ahead of the game now.

What the company flat lacked in comfort, it made up for in convenience. It was a short walk to four surf spots between Nobby's, at the mouth of the Hunter River, and the south end of Newcastle's main beach; about the same distance to the office, the courthouse, the cop shop, the Masonic Club, and the Great Northern Grill and Café Continental, where Cogan was keen on a waitress and thus where we often ate.

The business college was also just around the corner. The Newcastle Business College was one of many quaint heritage buildings in that part of town, but it differed from the others in that its employees seemed to be part of a time warp. The pursed-lips woman who ran the school wore old-fashioned lace-up shoes, thick stockings and a dowdy suit. She never smiled and she was not to be tangled with. But the business college had one great attribute—the hundred or so sexy young things who were its students.

I was required to attend shorthand classes for three hours each Thursday morning. I was the only boy in the class, and I managed to date about half the girls I fancied within the first couple of weeks. Some afternoons I would slip away from the bureau and meet a student for a quick dalliance at the company flat before she caught her train home. It was fun, but I was soon distracted by a beautiful Chinese nurse I met at one of the late-night Greek clubs in the west end of the city. Wendy was with some girlfriends, but we danced, kissed in a dark corner of the club and exchanged phone numbers. She lived in a boarding house so I asked for her surname, for when I called.

'No,' she said. 'You'll laugh.' She was deadly serious. I promised I wouldn't. She whispered it softly in my ear. 'Hor.'

I started to crack up, I couldn't help it, and she looked at me with such sad eyes that I hated myself. But she took my call the next day, accepted my apology and we spent most nights together until I left town. We promised to stay in touch, but we didn't.

I developed an affection for Newcastle, in part because it was a place where you could live a louche inner-city lifestyle and still surf every day. I surfed wherever there were waves, but I really enjoyed the left-breaking point at the north end of the main beach. It wasn't particularly consistent, but on its day it offered fast inside sections across scattered outcrops of rock. It was here one morning that I watched in amazement as a small kid carved huge backhand turns all the way down the point, flapping his arms around and cutting deftly under soupy sections. He finished his ride with a big roundhouse cutback before plopping into the deeper water, almost on top of me.

'Hey, nice wave,' I said. He said thanks, but looked like he might cry, and paddled faster to get away from the creepy older guy. This was my first encounter with Mark Richards, a decade away from establishing himself as the greatest surfer of his generation.

CHAPTER FOURTEEN

John Witzig and Albe Falzon (background) in the Tracks office at
Whale Beach, 1970. (Photo Rusty Miller)

PLAYING POLITICS

Back in Sydney I was contacted by John Witzig, who thought it was time we met. Since starting *Tracks* he had published everything I'd sent him, so I had forgiven him for publishing my embarrassing schoolkid nonsense, and happily agreed to drive out to Whale Beach for breakfast and a surf. I had read just about everything this guy had published over the past five years or so, admired his photos and his clever-arse in-jokes. I wanted to be him, or someone like him, but more importantly, I wanted to know the people he knew. As far as I was concerned, that list covered everyone in surfing worth knowing.

He was not at all what I expected. I knocked on the door of his rented cottage overlooking the beach. There was music playing inside, but it wasn't Tamam Shud. I'd taken great care in choosing what to wear—my most Californian T-shirt, with a surfboard logo on the chest pocket and a crew neck, and a new pair of Mrs Platt's cord walk shorts—but the man who answered the door looked nothing like a surfer. He had long-ish hair, but it was neatly groomed, and I remember being struck by the clean creases of his neatly pressed and collared shirt. He turned down the volume on the classical music, ushered me into a seat at his utilitarian table, served me delicious coffee and offered fruit, yoghurt and muesli.

'Well,' he said, flexing his knuckles in front of him, 'what are you going to write for us next?' It was the start of a mentoring relationship that would drive my career in the coming years, and of a friendship that has endured close to fifty years, despite us being near opposites in so many ways. We've had our differences—many of them—but John and I have always shared a love of surfing, good conversation and good wine, and that has been the glue.

In those days, Witzig was an architecture student at Sydney University, as well as a magazine editor, and he had become part of the growing student dissent at the Vietnam War that had just exploded into the Vietnam Moratorium movement. He was also on the side of the ocean, the forests and the original inhabitants in the development debate. In short, like most young Australians, he was sick and tired of the conservative government that had ruled Australia for a generation. I was a long way short of being radicalised, but John's take on building a better world—sometimes sardonic, sometimes sarcastic—had a huge influence on me. I needed a political viewpoint and I didn't really have one, so I borrowed his.

The second year of my Fairfax cadetship seemed a blur of new journalistic experiences—town hall rounds, court rounds, airport rounds, sport (very briefly), general reporting and sub-editing—plus rushed surf trips, drunken nights, share houses, girls, drugs and protest marches. I kept up the articles for *Tracks*, mostly about environmental issues, or my fairly lame attempts at humour, but I also started to send short articles to *Nation Review*, an entertaining leftist news weekly out of Melbourne. It didn't take long for Fairfax management to issue an edict forbidding staff writers to contribute to rival publications, but by this time my ego had reached such proportions that I simply switched to signing my tomes 'Jill Pharratt'. Much of what I sent was never published, and for a while no-one of consequence noticed.

By the middle of 1971 I had become politicised enough to march in Sydney's third Vietnam Moratorium march and feel that I belonged in that passionate throng. It was a heart-stirring occasion, and while no harm came to me or my immediate circle, I was close enough to the action to see people manhandled by the police, which, in a sense, was what we were there for. But as usual I had another motive. Having turned twenty in July 1971, I had received papers requiring me to register for National Service, or to provide reasons why my consideration should be deferred. Since I had failed to pick up my deferred university entrance, the question was, would my journalism cadetship be enough to keep me out of khaki?

I didn't want to think about it. A few of the boys were heading down to the far south coast to surf the little-known Tathra to Pambula area.

I swapped some shifts around and got five straight days off so I could join them. It was the middle of winter but at last I had a decent wetsuit from a new mob called Rip Curl. This was the first time in more than a year that I had teamed up with the old home-town crew, and the first thing I noted was the truth in that old saying: you can't go home again. We were surfers, we were friends, there were plenty of memories to laugh about over the beers, but it wasn't the same. Our lives had moved on, as they do when you're still a work in progress, and I knew I would never spend time with some of these guys again.

On the other hand, I would definitely revisit the Merimbula Bar lefthander. Many years later I would liken it to Spain's Mundaka without the angst. At the time, I just knew I would come back again and again, and I did.

From the start of 1971, the political climate had continued to heat up. Two global issues dominated the student agenda (which I felt a part of, despite technically not being a student)—the war in Vietnam and the hideous apartheid doctrine in South Africa. The former was in front of us every day, despite Prime Minister John Gorton's seemingly genuine attempts to scale back involvement in what was increasingly being portrayed as an unwinnable war. The latter was suddenly front and centre in June 1971 when the all-white South African rugby team toured Australia. I wasn't one of the protestors (perhaps it clashed with the Merimbula Bar sessions) and I never reported on the apartheid demonstrations, but I remember absorbing the hateful wash-up of that tour and thinking only that no matter how much you might love rugby, you could not support this violation of human rights. I felt the same way a decade or so later, when surfing went the same way, and only the courageous few refused to go.

On the national front, dissatisfaction grew as the long-reigning conservatives replaced one idiot leader with another. That assessment is probably a little unfair on John Gorton, who was a war hero and a supporter of the arts but came unstuck when he followed his second (and lower) brain into some murky matters of infidelity. But it's not unfair at all on his successor, Billy McMahon, who in my opinion was a self-serving fuckwit with no redeeming qualities.

On the other side of politics, Labor leader Gough Whitlam could do no wrong in the eyes of media, despite their valiant attempts at even-handedness. As 1971 ended, McMahon was the laughing stock of the politically aware and Whitlam the adored saviour, promising to end conscription and our involvement in the nightmare of Vietnam, and give Australia a fresh start. An election was due by the end of 1972.

Early in the new year Brian Johns invited me for a lunchtime beer at the Australian Hotel and let me in on a secret: he had been appointed chief political correspondent for the *Herald*. It was an election year and the country was politically charged, he said. This was going to be a year like no other. Would I like to come to Canberra and be on his team?

I have to say, my first thought was, how far is Canberra from the coast? That must have been long enough for the bullfrog eyes to darken. Then, perhaps just in time, I broke into a big grin, slurped on my schooner, and put out my hand for my mentor to shake. It was a big deal in my career, but even so, I said, 'Any chance I could take a couple of weeks off first?'

We took off north in mid-January, me and a kneeboarder mate named Greg Wilson, in his Beetle rather than mine, which was dying. We had a pup tent and a few bucks, so we had fun in all the old familiar places— Forster, Crescent, Hoey Moey at Coffs, Yamba, Byron, Kirra—whether there was surf or not, but as the clock wound down on my time off, we noticed something happening on the Gold Coast.

The sea seemed to click into a different rhythm. Suddenly you were paddling more than you were riding waves at Burleigh. The next morning, however, Burleigh was wild and crazy—pretty much unmanageable—and someone suggested Noosa, three hours north. We arrived at about three in the afternoon on the last day of January 1972, and as we drove out to the park entrance, we saw perfect lines breaking across three points. Our jaws dropped.

We surfed until after dark, slept in an on-site van on Hastings Street, got up and surfed again. By the third day the swell was still pumping, but I had to go. Greg 'Grotty' Wilson farted at me from his sleeping bag. 'Tell 'em to get fucked.'

'No-one tells Brian Johns to get fucked and lives.'

Canberra was different. I'd been there once before, on a school excursion in fifth form, when a schoolfriend named Kerry and I had shared a half bottle of Gilbey's Gin and a few moments of passion, but I have to confess that Walter Burley Griffin's greater vision for the town and the gravitas of the affairs of state that surrounded it hadn't really registered.

Contrary to expectation, I loved the place from the start, when the late summer nights were still warm and the night workers from Parliament

House, Charlie's Bar and the other haunts around the CBD would gather at a sandy bank of Lake Burley Griffin in the early hours and drink, smoke dope and skinny dip.

As the summer waned, the realities of life as a political journalist kicked in. There was a lot to learn. I was told that when the first Parliamentary session of the year began in a week, I would be seconded to the Australian Associated Press (AAP) as a Parliamentary reporter, meaning that I would sit in the press gallery above one chamber or the other and take shorthand notes on anything that was remotely newsworthy. That last bit was important. There were people paid by the government to report everything for a record called Hansard, but media access to Hansard took time. AAP provided an almost immediate verbatim record of news from the House of Representatives and the Senate—or at least it did until I was seconded.

The boss of AAP was a hard taskmaster called David Barnett, who went on to become an apologist for failing right-wing prime ministers, but it's fair to say that his assessment and subsequent dealing with me was nothing less than fair. I just couldn't stand to hear the truth from such a man.

'You've come to me highly recommended,' he said after my first major fuck-up, fiddling with his Coke-bottle glasses, 'and I really don't understand why.'

On one of my last days in the gallery for AAP, I sensed someone standing behind me, reading my notes. Fearful that it was David Barnett, I ignored them for a while, but curiosity got the better of me and I turned to see a man in early middle age flashing me what seemed like a laboured smile, coming out of a forest of creases across his forehead. He was tapping a rolled-up newspaper against his leg, *tap*, *tap*, *tap*. I smiled, nodded and turned back to my work. Later, when he showed up in the Non-Members Bar, it was explained to me that this was Rupert Murdoch, who had just bought the *Telegraph* newspapers from the Packer family.

For a while I made surf runs to the coast (about two and a half hours away) whenever I had a couple of days off in succession. Once or twice I met up with my Wollongong mates at Ulladulla, but mainly I travelled alone and slept in the Beetle (a new one, a 1964 model) with the seats pushed back. I'd never been a seeker of solitude before, but I quite enjoyed the adventure of finding waves at places like Bawley Point and Dalmeny. I rarely surfed alone, but when I did I found that enjoyable, too. I began to study weather maps in the daily papers and take note of low pressure systems and the sections of coast they might influence. This sounds like a no-brainer today, but I thought it was cutting edge back then.

Canberra was getting cold, freaking cold, when suddenly after a long Parliamentary session I found I had five days off for time in lieu. It was late in the season for a Coral Sea low, this much I knew, but the national weather map in *The Australian* clearly showed one moving west from a position north of Fiji. Its trajectory indicated that southern Queensland would feel its impact in about three days. When the Houses of Parliament got up for the winter recess very late the following night, I headed not for the Non-Members Bar, but for my Beetle. I climbed onto the front and pissed the frost off the windscreen, picked up my surfboard, sleeping bag, wetsuit, and a box of food from my flat in Campbell, and hit the road.

Somewhere out on the freezing plains of the Newell or Olympic Highway I pulled off the road and slept for a couple of hours, then drove hard all of the next day, pulling into the car park at Noosa National Park about an hour before dark. Nothing. Nada. Flat as. There were a few car-loads of surfers sitting around, drinking beers and moping. I walked along the track until I could see dots off Tea Tree Bay where a few hopefuls sat in wait in the bleak, grey afternoon. This was my first impulsive surf trip, driven purely by my own forecast, and there was nothing. I was monu-mentally depressed, but too tired to turn around and drive the twenty-two hours back. Instead I drove up Noosa Hill to the pub, where I sat by a red brick wall and drank schooners of Castlemaine beer while I read my book, Germaine Greer's *The Female Eunuch*, a gift (perhaps tongue-in-cheek) from a Canberra girlfriend. It did nothing to lighten my mood.

I was woken from an uneasy sleep in my car when the large pebbles on the shoreline below started to rumble. I climbed out and saw in the moonless dark lines of whitewater rolling to shore where there'd been none ten hours before. I could sense more power in the ocean. The swell was coming. I got back in the car and pulled the sleeping bag over me, but I didn't sleep. At the first sign of pre-dawn I waxed my board and made my way along the track to the top of the point. I launched myself off the flat rock between sets and paddled into a scrum of surfers already waiting. We nodded and smiled in anticipation.

It was another hit and run on Noosa's points—more than two days on the highway for a mere day and a half of actual surfing—but it was worth every pothole and kangaroo dodge. On my way out of town I picked up

Surfers camped at Noosa National Park. (Photo Bob Weeks)

a surfer hitchhiking at Cooroy. We babbled so much about the quality of the waves that I drove him out of my way to the Gold Coast. Then I babbled to myself until I was west of the Divide and drawing a straight line back to the cold heart of the capital.

There was one wave I couldn't get out of my mind afterwards. I'd taken off just inside what we now call the Boiling Pot. (If it was called that in 1972, no-one had told me.) I turned hard to make the first section, but the wave grew as it curved into the bay, and the fast-breaking section just kept coming at me, the power of the breaking wave threatening to fling me from my board, but letting me just squeak through, again and again. As I drove along the plains, I found myself leaning into the gentle bends of the empty night highway, still riding the wave, still beating the sections.

CHAPTER FIFTEEN

OUR MAN IN CANBERRA

In stark contrast to the weather in the frosty lakeside city, Canberra's political climate was heating up. An election was due by the end of the year and there was a growing belief within the parliamentary press gallery that Gough Whitlam's Labor Party would finally end the twenty-three-year conservative stranglehold on the country.

There hadn't been a federal Labor government in my lifetime, so the prospect of change was enough to make me partisan, but even more compelling was Whitlam's promise to end military conscription and bring the last of our troops home from Vietnam. My National Service deferment was up for review at the same time as the election, so I needed Labor to win to get that monkey off my back. I put my name down as a campaign volunteer for Kep Enderby, the member for Canberra, who was also a civil rights lawyer, a scratch golfer and a good bloke.

By this time I'd become friendly not just with my *Herald* colleagues but with many of the legendary press gallery members and the never-ending stream of politicians who did the rounds of the offices at old Parliament House. Within our own office, Brian Johns was the ultimate boss, but it was not an undisputed position. Ian Fitchett, a Colonel Blimp of a man who had been the paper's chief political correspondent through-out the '60s, still held the position of defence correspondent but, now well into his sixties, was clearly being phased out.

'Fitch' didn't like Johns and he didn't hold back. 'You're a cunt, Johns, and you've always been a cunt,' he thundered once, while we shuffled papers and looked downward. Fitch was fat and slow, but he'd been known to throw a punch to settle an argument in the Non-Members. And he was well connected. I was often given the Saturday shift for the *Sun-Herald*, because in politics nothing much happened on Saturdays. Fitch would already be at his desk when I arrived for my shift, the racing forms scattered about him as he worked the phone. Andrew Peacock, the new shining light of the Liberal Party, was usually on the other end of the line, comparing notes from the Melbourne stables.

My favourite crazy in the office was John Stubbs, a laconic rural Queenslander and a passionate Labor man who, convinced he'd been gazumped for the top job, was not a Brian Johns fan either. Stubbs loved drinking and telling outrageous stories about politicians in his broad Cunnamulla drawl, but his political instincts were highly developed, and he was such an entertaining character that he had many friends on both sides of the House. Through Stubbs I met many of the leading politicians of the day, not to mention press gallery characters like Laurie Oakes of the Melbourne *Sun-Pictorial* and Mungo MacCallum of the *Nation Review*, while regular visitors to our office included the veteran Labor man Tom Uren (a former boxer who would always throw me a feint as he danced into the room), the Queensland Liberal maverick Jim Killen, Labor Party secretary Mick Young, the suave New South Wales senator 'Diamond' Jim McClelland and, whenever he was in town, the potty-mouthed ACTU boss Bob Hawke.

Among the politicians, I really only made one close contact of my own, and that proved to be about as useless as it was bizarre. I was alone in the *Herald* office one day (probably a Saturday, after Fitch had placed his bets) when the phone rang. A croaky old voice asked me to find a two-week-old paper in our files and bring it to his office. I had no idea who I was talking to, so I had to ask. He mumbled something I couldn't pick up, so I asked again. 'Calwell!' he spat down the phone. 'What's yours?' I told him. 'Phil Jones, you say? I know your father, good man. Now hurry down here.'

I looked up Calwell in the parliamentary directory. There was only one. I jotted down his office number, found the edition he had asked for and set off. I knocked on the door. 'Come in.' The old man's voice sounded like he was talking through a mouthful of unchewed food with a peg over his nostrils. He was a lumbering old wreck of a fellow, hunched over an untidy desk. This was Arthur Augustus Calwell, the former Labor opposition leader who had lost three elections to Menzies. He was a champion of White Australia who had once famously said in Parliament, 'two Wongs don't make a White'.

Calwell took the paper and motioned for me to sit opposite him. 'And how is your father?' he asked. 'Good man.' I could never disabuse Calwell of the notion that I was the son of the chairman of the *Herald and Weekly Times* newspaper empire, Sir Philip Jones, and over the next couple of months, as I ran errands for the old man and was frequently called to his presence, I gave up trying. In a few months he would be out of the Parliament, and in a year he would be dead.

Arthur Calwell stood for everything I found repugnant about old Labor—a bitter racist demagogue, I thought, from my scant research in the clippings files—but I grew to like the old bugger. I was pleased to discover, after his death, that Calwell had opposed the war in Vietnam from the beginning, and that he had visited his would-be assassin, Peter Kocan, in the prison psychiatric ward to forgive him, and corresponded with the young man right up until his death.

If I learned anything from this strange, brief friendship it was that it is too easy to apply political labels, and that people are rarely one hundred per cent anything—good or bad, right or wrong. That was pretty much the way I felt about another new friend, John Newfong.

I had been sent to report on the Aboriginal Tent Embassy, which had appeared overnight on the parkland directly in front of Parliament House. The tents had been erected in protest after the land claims of the

John Newfong (centre) at the Aboriginal Tent Embassy, 1972.
(Photo Sovereign Union)

Northern Territory's Yirrkala people had fallen on the large but apparently deaf ears of Prime Minister Billy McMahon. To this point I'd had virtually no contact with Indigenous Australians, although I remembered as a child being intrigued by the prominent activist Charles Perkins, who my father brought home for dinner once, when he was to speak at a Rotary meeting. Now I was sympathetic to their cause, but I didn't really know how to relate to them. I was welcomed with friendliness, and willing answers to my dumb questions. I took to visiting the embassy every couple of days. My main point of contact was John Newfong, a large man in his late twenties who had also been a cadet journalist with the *Herald*.

As spokesman for the illegal encampment, Newfong was on the television news almost every night. I could see that he was dealing with petty jealousies within his own ranks, but he was always ready to sit down and talk to me. While he didn't exactly exude warmth, he was an intriguing character and I grew to like him. Our conversations sparked an interest in Aboriginal culture and history that has stayed with me.

In the weeks leading up to the election, Gough Whitlam strode across the national consciousness like an unstoppable colossus. Our televisions were still tiny black-and-white boxes, but Gough beamed out of them, too big to be contained as he spread his gospel of a new and fairer Australia.

Whitlam talks to Aboriginal Embassy protestors while Kep Enderby looks on, 1972.

No previous Australian election had been so clearly fought on issues of personality. Now that his minders had thrown away the Brylcreem and fluffed his hair up, and surrounded him with youthful celebrities (Little Pattie holding her surf flag high), Whitlam was clearly today's man, while creepy little Billy Big Ears was clearly not. Mungo MacCallum had turned dissing McMahon into an art form. Even his own staffers could be seen pissing themselves with laughter in the Non-Members Bar when the *Nation Review* appeared. Respect for the hapless prime minister and his party had evaporated. It really was time.

On election day, I gave out how to vote cards for Kep Enderby, then went to work at the National Tally Room at Belconnen High School in one of the new housing estates that had been built to cater to Canberra's huge public sector growth. I can't recall what my exact role was, but I know I was on the phone a lot, trying to get reaction quotes from candidates and sitting members as the progress scores were posted for each marginal electorate.

'Are you looking at the latest numbers, sir? It looks pretty much like you're gone.'

'I think it might be a little too early to call. Goodbye.' Bang.

Within the one-eyed confines of the press gallery, we had predicted a Whitlam landslide. It wasn't a landslide, but it was still comprehensive enough to file last copy and get to the after-party while it still had legs. (It wasn't long before I didn't.) There was much to celebrate. Australia was a brave new world, I wasn't going to be donning khaki, and I would soon be a fully qualified, graded journalist.

CHAPTER SIXTEEN

Newquay in the fog, 1970.

THE OLD COUNTRY

Brian Johns had been right when he promised an exciting election year, but it looked like Whitlam's first months in government were going to be just as exciting. I would have been happy to remain in Canberra for another year, consolidating my political credentials, but there was a hitch.

I had received a letter from Fairfax management confirming that I had completed the third year of my cadetship to their satisfaction, but stating that the company would not hire me as a D-grade journalist until I had attained the required speed in shorthand and typing. For me this was a lost cause. I'd gotten this far with two-finger typing and marginal shorthand, and I wasn't going back to business college—although I was considering going back to Newcastle.

Brian Cogan, my old boss at the Newcastle bureau of the *SMH*, was now the lead writer at the *Newcastle Herald*. Although the paper was also owned by Fairfax, Cogan's inquiries revealed that their management would look favourably on a job application from me. I sent a mailbag of press clippings and a gushing letter about my love of Newcastle, and was offered the position of feature writer on a C-grade salary, starting as soon as I had served my notice.

Within days of returning to Newcastle, I had moved into a share flat at Cooks Hill with Neil Jameson, a cadet journalist on the paper who shared my love of surfing, a cold beer and a good laugh. Tony Dixon, who worked in the front office, was also a keen surfer, and since we all worked mostly in the afternoons, we started making pre-dawn runs up the coast to Treachery Head when conditions were right. That summer and into the autumn we enjoyed many days of beautiful waves with few, if any surfers in the water. Treachery was at least a ninety-minute run each way, but Tony was a kick-arse driver, and Jamo and I would sometimes sleep all the way home, showing up for work refreshed, although often dripping saltwater from deep in our nasal cavities.

My job application apparently had plenty of support from the top, but it seemed none of it had come from Jim Hooker, the staid, dour news editor. After a year of wearing suits in Canberra, I was relishing the much more casual dress code in Newcastle, but apparently showing up in board-shorts and thongs after our morning runs up the coast was going too far. Jim read me the riot act for not taking the job seriously. He didn't know the half of it.

Although I'd had access to some drugs during my time in Canberra, alcohol had become my go-to panacea for the long hours, the tension and the stress. We drank at the Non-Members Bar every afternoon and then filled the office fridge with Fosters Lager to get us through the evening. I had put on a lot of weight. In Newcastle I was back surfing every day, and marijuana and LSD had joined beer as my drugs of choice. It all seemed more or less harmless, but Jim Hooker was right: I wasn't taking my job seriously enough.

But sometimes it was hard to. Instead of the rowdy political arguments in the Non-Members Bar, now I drank with police rounds journalists and detectives at the bar of the Masonic Club. One of the clean-cut young detectives used to get a few on board and borrow the motto of a popular paperback cop, shouting melodramatically, 'I hate crime!' He didn't know I was a stoner, and I didn't know that he was already taking bribes and building the foundations for a spectacularly messy exit from the Force.

Jamo and I spent a lot of time together, often stoned, and cooked up wild schemes to travel the world. He was the sweetest guy, salt of the earth, but with an analytical edge and a wicked sense of humour. We had very different outlooks on the world, but we seemed to bond on the important things—leftist politics, booze, dope, music, chicks and surf—and figured if we could share a small flat, we'd probably be good travel mates. There was no argument about where we would go—London, of course. The movie version of Barry Humphries' outrageous *The Adventures of Barry McKenzie* had just been a big hit, depicting the naive hero chundering his way around the fleshpots of still-swingin' London. This alone probably wasn't enough incentive to jump on a plane, but we had also seen good waves in Europe in Paul Witzig's surf film *Evolution*.

Our plan was to get ourselves to London, find work as journalists on Fleet Street and make enough money to surf our way around Europe.

But first we had to get there. I was on a decent wage at last and I had a car to sell, but Jamo had only a cadet's paltry income and a motorbike. Still, he managed to eat less and save more of his pittance, and we made a pact to buy our airline tickets in July and leave in August.

And then I met the girl.

On surfless Saturday afternoons we used to drink in the back bar of the Star Hotel, where Bob Hudson's Electric Jug Band kept us amused by taking the piss out of drunken local yobbos. It was there that we learned that Hudson and the band would be headlining the May Day Ball at the town hall. We bought tickets and rocked up in our best op shop clobber.

In those days Newcastle was still very much a working man's town, a stronghold of old-school Labor. But it was also a university town with a vibrant and volatile student body. This combination was very much in evidence in the lobby of the Newcastle Town Hall, steelworkers and union officials in ill-fitting suits at one end, long-haired stoners at the other. Somewhere in the middle I spotted a student body I was particularly interested in, a beautiful girl in a long blue dress, her dark hair held back by a bandana and flowing down below her shoulders. She shook her hair as she laughed, perhaps a little nervously, and I caught her eye and held it until she walked away towards the bar. Before becoming lost in the crowd, she turned back and smiled.

Her name was Valerie. She was Scottish, but she had that olive skin you sometimes find in Scots and the Irish, a nod to Iberian invaders back in history, perhaps. She came home with me that night, but after we'd made love she couldn't sleep for Jamo's foghorn snoring in the next room, so I drove her home. We sat in my car outside her student digs and talked until the sun came up. She was smart and funny and deeply sexy. I had to see her again.

Valerie was an arts student who had already exhausted Newcastle's small stock of interesting galleries, so we took to spending winter weekends in Sydney, doing the art rounds, catching a band or a movie, then sleeping in a tiny hotel we found in Kings Cross, attached to a cheap and cheerful Italian restaurant. By the time the deadline for buying airline tickets came around, I was head over heels in love. I had to keep reminding myself that I was twenty-two years old and I hadn't seen the world yet. I had to keep telling myself to get a grip.

Although he thought our trip was youthful folly, my dad found the cheapest one-way London ticket available—via Manila, Karachi, Damascus and Amsterdam on Pakistan International Airways. I forget how much the tickets cost but it cleaned Jamo out. He had a month to make his spending money.

There were tears when I told Valerie I was leaving, but then we concocted a plan. At the end of the university year she would fly over to join me. We would have a white Christmas in Paris, or somewhere equally exotic, and maybe she would defer her studies and stay. I don't know how committed she was to this, but it made us both feel better. I had a farewell drink with Brian Cogan. 'Don't worry about the girl,' he said. 'I'll look after her.' He winked lasciviously.

The flight was interminable. We got drunk and sobered up twice, and felt like crap as we took the long train ride from Heathrow. My cousin Lynnie, one of the fun-loving twins I'd first lived with in Sydney, was sharing a basement flat in Upper Addison Gardens, Holland Park, so once we'd mastered the complex multi-coloured Tube map, we made a beeline for her place. There were no spare beds, but we were welcome to floor space, which we gratefully accepted. The basement flat was home to an ever-changing cast of young people on working holidays, many of them attractive young girls. The rule was, if you paid real money you got a real bed; if you were freeloading, you got the floor, but there was a lot of nocturnal movement, and you could never be sure where you might wake up, or who you might meet in the hall. (One night I was woken by the American actor Ty Hardin, a boyhood hero of mine from his role in *Bronco*, wanting to know where to find the toilet.)

We loved London, but I had about a hundred quid to live on until I got a job, Jamo had less than half that, and we were chewing through it in the city, even without paying rent. Everyone said we should put off working until after the summer, so we decided to cycle to Cornwall and get bar work for what remained of the season. We bought two ancient fixed-wheel bikes at an op shop on the Kensington High Street for a couple of quid each and took them back to Holland Park to prepare them. Someone's boyfriend said, 'You'll never get there. In England we have hills.' He offered to buy them for a quid each to use as garden decorations, and we went to a sporting goods shop in Shepherd's Bush and bought bikes with gears instead.

It seemed to take forever to find our way out of London, but eventually we made progress down the A3 until we decided to stop for a ploughman's lunch and a pint or two. After a long nap, the afternoon ride seemed twice as difficult, but we rode until almost dark, then slept the sleep of the dead in a park behind a pub in Winchester. We'd gone out too hard and spent the next day admiring the cathedral before pressing on with aching butts. On the third afternoon we walked our bikes into Exeter and caught the train to Newquay, the surfing capital of the south west.

You may have already detected that a pattern was emerging for my adventures: spontaneous action, zero preparation. Who knew that the south west of England was one long hill?

As we walked our bikes through the quaint streets of Newquay we passed a surf shop and heard the unmistakeable strains of a broad Australian accent. 'Look mate, I can basically surf anything. Take this door off its fuckin' hinges and I'll give it a go, you know what I mean?' I recognised the voice. It belonged to Stuart 'Twizzle' Entwistle, a good surfer from Manly whom I'd come up against in a couple of schoolboy heats, to my cost.

Newquay.

The Old Country

We parked our bikes and walked in. I don't think Twizzle remembered thrashing me but he made a good show of the reunion. I walked out with a very good deal on a six foot four inch Bilbo swallowtail, and directions to where we could rent a cheap cabin for the night.

Jamo and I found live-in jobs at opposite ends of the town. Mine was at a Fawlty Towers-like establishment at the top of the hill on the way to the wonderfully named Lusty Glaze Beach. The Basil who ran the shabby little private hotel seemed greatly impressed by my claim to be a journalist. 'I have a typewriter you can use!' he shouted over his shoulder as he guided me down the back stairs to a tiny room stuck in between the kitchen pipes. The walls were greasy with cooking fat and the smell of bacon and kippers pervaded everything, but there was a neat little single bed with a bedside table that could serve as a desk. Basil disappeared and then came back with a battered portable typewriter.

'In perfectly good nick,' he said. 'What are you going to write?'

'A novel,' I lied.

There was barely time to surf, let alone write anything substantial from my desk in Bacon Fat Alley. I'd been hired as a handyman, but it soon became obvious that there wasn't much I was handy at, so I became a kind of bellboy instead, even donning a jacket and cap when large groups arrived. I was responsible for keeping the front of the house meticulous at all times, which involved rising at dawn to pick up rubbish and empties left on the front lawn by the lager louts who paraded noisily past after the pub closed. Then I would clip the edges and sweep the path, before polishing the brass doorknobs to within an inch of their lives. Then I might be able to sneak an egg and sausage from the kitchen before helping the first departures with their luggage. From about ten to midday, or a little after, was my window to surf, unless the lady of the house had other ideas.

Basil's wife—surely her name was not Sybil!—ran the front office, but if she had errands to run, or perhaps lunch with the girls, I had to put my bellboy jacket on and deputise behind the reception desk for an hour or two. The wife was much younger and more attractive than Basil, and the similarities stacked up so perfectly that in later years I wondered if they had modelled the hotel on John Cleese's hilarious television series. But in fact my summer season on the hill above Lusty Glaze predated Fawlty Towers by a couple of years. I guess there were a thousand such joints in Devon and Cornwall, just waiting to have the piss taken out of them.

The closest beaches to the hotel were Great Western and Tolcarne, divided by a clump of rocks, and neither had a great reputation for attracting swell or quality surf. But beggars couldn't be choosers. The best waves on the town beaches were generally to be found at Fistral, on the other side of the port, but I could never make it there and back on my break. The water temperature was too cold for my one and only Rip Curl wetsuit (a long-sleeved spring suit) but I soon got used to the level of discomfort, and I loved the feel of my new board. I discovered that tide made all the difference at Great Western and Tolcarne: if it was too low, it closed out; if it was too high, it didn't break. But if it was no good for the morning session, I knew there would be something there for the after-work session, although these were sometimes cut short so I could get to the pub.

Jamo worked different hours to me so we only met up in the evenings, invariably over a beer. There were many pubs in Newquay, but for surfers there was only one that mattered, the Sailor's Arms. Its small spaces were always packed to the rafters with the crowd flowing out onto the footpath and narrow Fore Street. Here you could buy a board or a bag of dope, get a surf report for the morning or a ride to London. We would normally drink a few beers with the locals or the other summer workers before heading out on the cobblestones for a cheap curry or fish and chips, but one coolish night towards the end of the season we lingered in conversation with an Australian surfer who had just shown up in town with a rather prim-looking girlfriend, a Bedford van set up for camping and a plan to get down to France and Spain before winter kicked in.

The Sailor's Arms.

His name was Graeme, his girlfriend was Isabel, and although he was from the western suburbs of Sydney, he was a Coffs Harbour tragic, driving up the coast to surf there as often as he could. I said, 'We've probably had a beer or two at the Hoey Moey.'

'More than likely,' Graeme said, ordering another round. By the time the Arms heavies swept the last of the rabble out onto Fore Street, we had agreed to join them on their grand adventure. Or perhaps they'd agreed to let us.

CHAPTER SEVENTEEN

Guéthary coast.

SURF AND SARDINES

We were tromping around the magical ring of Stonehenge one grey afternoon when Jamo and I decided that Graeme and Isabel were just a tad loopy. They wore matching parkas, for Christ's sake. It was our second day on the road and, despite Graeme's professed hurry to get to the warm water of the Bay of Biscay, he couldn't drive past a cathedral or a monument without stopping. I liked the fact that he was a history buff—so was I!—but Jamo and I had less than a hundred quid between us now, and we wanted to get to the bottom of Iberia before the money ran out.

At a roadhouse on the A3 I phoned Lynnie and asked if I could bring some friends home, just for a night or two. She wasn't exactly enthusiastic, but she had come around by the time we parked the Bedford in Upper Addison Gardens. Over drinks in the basement flat that night, she took me aside and asked, 'Are you sure you want to travel through Europe with these people?' I told her we didn't have a plan B. Besides, Graeme and Isabel were growing on us. They had their funny ways but they were generous to a fault, and most importantly, they had wheels.

On the ferry to Calais I remember sitting in the upstairs bar with Graeme, watching the white cliffs of Dover recede into the glare of the sunset, when he started to talk about William the Conqueror, his march on Westminster Abbey in 1066 and all that. The campaign had been staged from Hastings and historic Dover Castle, on the coast we were looking at. He knew his stuff, and he spoke with great passion about the events that had formed modern England.

'Why didn't we visit Dover Castle?' I asked.

He responded, 'There isn't time. We have to surf.' Damn straight we do, I wanted to say, but he'd already gone to the bar.

We had one more historic excursion before we made for the Atlantic surf coast of France, and that was to the fabulous Gothic Roman Catholic cathedral in Rouen, once the tallest building in the world, immortalised by the oil paintings of Monet. Graeme was ecstatic, and even Isabel showed some emotion. I was glad we had stopped, and I started to feel more optimistic about the rest of the journey.

Jamo and I had bought the cheapest nylon pup tent we could find. It kept out stray animals but not the rain, or even a heavy dew. So if conditions looked inclement, we used the tent as a groundsheet and slid under the cover of the Bedford in our sleeping bags. There wasn't much clearance but we could make do, so long as Graeme didn't get too excited while exercising his conjugal rights.

Both Newquay and Biarritz, situated on surf-rich stretches of the Atlantic coast, were considered to be the surfing capitals of their respective countries, but that was where the similarities ended. While Newquay was a rough old fishing port with a veneer of Blackpool bad taste tacked on, Biarritz was an elegant, even regal little city that spread from the Hôtel du Palais, once Napoleon's gift to his Empress Eugenie, along a craggy coast of hidden coves and pirate bars. We camped on the beaches south of the city and found waves everywhere, although we avoided the crowded main city beach, La Grande Plage, after lifeguards confiscated my board for the day for surfing too close to the swimmers. After Cornwall, the water seemed warm, and in the mornings before the wind got up it was wonderful to paddle around the clear water at the edges of the Bay of Biscay, sharing waves with just a few friendly locals.

Like Newquay, Biarritz had but one meeting point for the transient surfing crew—a noisy bar and restaurant called The Steakhouse, situated conveniently at the top of the stairs that led from the surf beach known as La Côte des Basques. Like the Sailor's Arms, The Steakhouse was a clearing house for everything a travelling surfer might need, and many of the leading surfers of the day passed through and left their signatures on the wall.

The Steakhouse was a lot more stylish than its name or its clientele would lead you to believe. In fact, everything along the Pays Basque strip was stylish, at least to my unsophisticated eyes and palate. I loved the cheap red wine, the crusty baguette dipped in olive oil, the small plates of sardines or squid, and the pimientos grown around quaint villages in the foothills of the Pyrenees.

Armed with every phrase and conjunction I'd memorised to impress Glenda, my French teacher, I thought myself French. I bought a beret and a red neckerchief and wandered around the village squares of Bidart and Guéthary like I owned them. And then Graeme pulled up stumps and we headed south as the days started to close in.

Although the grandness of San Sebastián and the grime of Bilbao, and the mountainous and wave-rich coast between them would become familiar to me later, I recall nothing of them from this first trip. It's possible that we drove straight from the Pays Basque to Santander, because that is where I remember first experiencing Spanish tapas, of the raw and unhomogenised type that you found on bare wood bars in rural towns in Franco's Spain. The mysterious little concoctions and pastries were oily and often bland, but my god, they cost nothing!

On the wall of one of Santander's numerous tapas bars, we found a small poster advertising the fiesta of a village called Ampuero, in the mountains not far away, with an extended weekend of bullfights and a running of the bulls each morning. This was a godsend. Jamo and I were huge fans of Hemingway, we'd read Michener's *Iberia* and its silly sibling *The Drifters*. We'd wanted to experience the fiesta of Pamplona but we'd left our run too late in the season. Ampuero would have to suffice.

Guéthary town square.

Running of the bulls, Ampuero.

About an hour inland from Santander, Ampuero was little more than a cobbled street leading up a hill with a town square in the middle, a church at one end and a bull ring at the other. But it was full of bars and people and laughter, and it was framed by dark, moody mountains. As we lingered over a beer in the square, a throng of young Basques paraded by, singing and chanting about El Lute, a criminal who was number one on Spain's most wanted list, and believed to be hiding out in the hills. El Lute had become a Robin Hood figure in Franco's poor and divided Spain, a symbol of resistance to the feared Guardia Civil.

We fell in with a bunch of American students and finished the night sprawled in a paddock above the town, swigging from goatskins of cheap wine to combat the cold. And in the morning we ran with the bulls.

Later in life, when my wife and I became regulars at the Festival of San Fermín in Pamplona, I always felt grateful that I'd got running with the bulls out of my system when I was young and dumb and in the relative calm of Ampuero, which at that time had a population of less than a thousand, though this doubled during its fiesta. Pamplona, on the other hand, becomes sheer bedlam as fifty thousand drunks strive for death or glory. That day, so long ago in the hills of Cantabria, was my only bull run, and I would have to describe it as running from the bulls, rather than running with them. But it had its scary moments, and I remember Jamo and I being so elated that we got drunk all over again.

We were heading for Portugal but couldn't make the border before dark, so Graeme found a roadside cutting to park the van and we pitched the pup tent in a nearby field. Some time later I woke with a start. I first registered bright lights outside our tent, then I saw the silhouette of a man holding a submachine gun. I shook Jamo awake so he could die like a man, and we both quaked in fear as a hand undid the drawstrings and opened the tent flaps.

I recognised the intruder by his Nazi-like uniform as a Guardia Civil, who in northern Spain at that time were always on the lookout for movements of Eta, the violent Basque separatist movement. He flicked at our sleeping bags with the barrel of his gun, said something that made his colleagues outside laugh, perhaps drunkenly. I was trying to process whether their good humour was a good thing or a bad thing, when he leaned forward and said directly to me, 'This golfing. Golfing!' He motioned to us to get out of the tent, where our bedraggled appearance caused another round of laughter among the Guardia.

Sure enough, under the strong beams of the Guardia Civil searchlights, it was quite clear we had camped on the manicured lawn of the ninth hole at a fancy country club. I didn't know the word for sorry in Spanish, so I just kept mumbling, *Je suis vraiment désolé* as we packed up the pup tent at gunpoint and departed the way we had entered.

Portugal was at war on two fronts that year, trying stupidly to hold onto its African colonial outposts of Mozambique and Angola, so there were very few young men in the village of Peniche when we arrived in October and set up home in a dusty free camp at the edge of town. This became evident when we attended home games at the town's soccer ground just behind the camp, Jamo being a soccer tragic, and saw that the average age of both sides was a paunchy forty. But if we thought this shortage of young men would work to our benefit with the local young ladies, we were soon disabused of this notion. They wore black shawls and smiled rarely. The older women were even less friendly, sneering and even spitting when we passed by in the market.

Our camp was near the end of a sandy track that finished at a rock seawall, which formed the southern boundary of the fishing port. Seeking to afford Graeme and Isabel (or Donald and Daisy, as we had rather cruelly christened them) a little privacy, we had set up the pup tent behind some scrub at the edge of the rocks, which turned out to be populated by large and aggressive rats that would scratch around the walls of the tent all night and occasionally fight their way inside. We found that the best way to handle a rat invasion was to lie very, very still, and pretend it wasn't happening.

Most of the time we shared the free camp with about a dozen other vans, but few stayed long enough to form a community, whereas we fell into a pattern of life in Peniche that seemed to suit all of us, so we stayed. A couple of articles had been written about the surf potential of the area, but it certainly wasn't yet the magnet it would become. Most days we surfed a lazy righthander just off the rock wall with a few others, or if the wind came onshore, we would drive to a reef break across town that offered a fast left. If the swell dropped away, we would trudge way up the beach to an A-frame peak that formed at the run-off from a large sardine processing plant. The waves here were fast, hollow and fun (in years to come this break would become known as 'Supertubos') but the water was often pink with blood, and when the wind was offshore the stench from the sardine plant was almost unbearable.

When we weren't surfing we would sit in the sun outside Madame Sirly's café and drink good coffee as thick as mud, or play mini-soccer on the table inside, then order a huge plate of Madame's excellent chips and wash them down with cheap wine from a plastic bottle. When the fishing boats came in we would wander over to the old port and haggle with the fishermen over the price of sardines. Often they would just laugh and throw us a plastic bag full of the fresh catch. Sardines were the currency of Peniche, and these rough, friendly men were millionaires. Night after night, we swigged wine and grilled sardines over a fire at our camp, and threw the heads into the rocks for the rats.

One of the fishermen, José, became a regular at our campfire and he never came empty-handed, bringing vast quantities of sardines and occasionally other fish. It transpired that he had suffered a severe head wound in Angola and had returned with what we now know as post-traumatic stress disorder. We never got the full story, but perhaps domestic violence had been a factor, for now he was an outcast among his own. So, José would trade sardines for a broken English conversation about the weather, about the rats, about a woman he saw at the market and fancied. When I wrote an article for the *National Times* about our

Portugal feature article, *National Times*, 1973.

time in Peniche, an editor pulled out a quote for the title—'"No money, no wife, no friends—only sardines": a taste of life in Portugal'. It was a quote from José, but it could just as easily have applied to us.

But man cannot live on sardines alone. Madame Sirly would not take conversation for wine, for example, and our pile of escudos was dwindling rapidly, despite the fact that, as Jamo (who kept records of such things) has reminded me, we were paying the equivalent of sixteen cents for a litre of wine and eight to ten cents for a beer.

One of the vans that rolled into our camp and stayed belonged to a laid-back, long-haired Kiwi hairdresser named Russell, his beautiful blonde Dutch wife Marija, and their sweet little girl, Mia. Russell had surfed in his youth, but establishing successful salons had taken his eye off the ball. Still, he enjoyed fooling around on my board on the small waves by the wall, and pushing Mia into foamies. Jamo and I liked Russell a lot, but we were both desperately in love with Marija. She was smart and sassy and wore her long hair up and her perfect breasts bare beneath a ragged T-shirt.

Marija keeps an eye on our surfing preparations, Portugal, 1973.
(Photo Russell Smith)

Russell could see our infatuation from the start—I'm sure he saw it everywhere they camped—and generally found it quietly amusing, but one night in the old port, sharing a rare proper restaurant meal, Marija fed the jukebox, we danced and I went too far.

'I know you've had a few,' Russell whispered in my ear as we returned to the table, 'but you'd better ease off.'

I did, and the group dynamic was never quite the same, but eventually it was another lesson learned. Marija had been indulging in flirtatious play and I simply wasn't mature enough to recognise the boundaries of the playground. I found that a problem in those years.

Money was an issue for most of us in the free camp, and one day over coffee at Madame Sirly's, a Cornish surfer named Rob Job came up with a possible short-term solution. 'The government's paying good money for blood in Lisbon,' he declared. 'They're desperate for it down in Mozambique. All you need is a passport and your blood type.' We all drove down to the capital together and presented ourselves at the blood bank where, surprise, surprise, the queue of young travellers stretched around the block. We waited for hours and some of us were eventually rewarded, but neither Jamo nor I had the desired blood type.

The moral ambiguity of selling my blood for US$20 a litre had never really occurred to me as I waited to be tested, and I thought about it even less as we celebrated the windfall of the others over a steak and red wine lunch. In those days in rural Portugal, twenty bucks went a long way. It'd probably have bought another week in Peniche.

But we hadn't. Graeme and Isabel were heading for Morocco but we realised that our money could stretch no further. We stayed with them down through the Algarve and back into Spain, but somewhere around Cádiz we said goodbye and hitchhiked north. We lucked out with a couple of long rides and were soon back in Biarritz, where I sat on the terrace at La Grande Plage with a 'for sale' sign on my board until it was swooped on by a local for a fraction of its value. But we could eat again, and after shouting ourselves a farewell dinner at The Steakhouse, we sat by the Route Nationale with our thumbs out until someone picked us up.

As it turned out, it was the best ride I ever got in my hitching career, all the way to West London on the smell of an oily rag. They were a rather stitched-up Kiwi couple in early middle age, doing Europe in a Kombi. The nights were cold now, but they liked to roast chestnuts over a campfire and drink a glass of wine. Apparently chestnuts can cause flatulence, and he was in the habit of walking around to the other side of the vehicle to fart, thinking the noise wouldn't carry. It did, but she didn't laugh, so we didn't either.

We were in luck at Upper Addison Gardens. Some tenants had moved on with the summer and there were spare beds. Jamo and I immediately went off in search of work. Within a couple of days Jamo was happily stacking boxes at Bejam; it took me a bit longer to score some casual shifts on Fleet Street. Working on the Street was the dream of every young Australian journo, but my reality was less than romantic, doing graveyard shifts sub-editing (about which I knew nothing) on the tits-and-arse tabloids. But I discovered that some of my Canberra mates, including the venerable John Stubbs, were now at the Fairfax London bureau, so not only did I have drinking pals, I also had an outlet for my travel writing at the weekly *National Times*, where my Portugal feature ran over two pages.

Soon I found a full-time job just across the Blackfriars Bridge as a feature writer on a magazine romantically titled *Truck and Bus*. The prat of an editor immediately christened me 'Kanga' (or sometimes 'Roo') and sent me off on ridiculous assignments. The most contentious issue in the world of heavy transport at the time was a device known as 'the spy in the cabin', which recorded the number of continuous hours of driving. I was sent to somewhere outside of Glasgow to cover a huge protest meeting about this imposition. I had a list of people to interview but I couldn't understand what anyone was saying. I scribbled notes to be polite, but on the train back to London I realised I had no story. Fortunately, at *Truck and Bus* this was not a deal-breaker.

At last I was making more money than I was spending—just. The nightlife was fun. A Kiwi band I'd loved in Sydney called Max Merritt and the Meteors had a residency at the Windsor Castle on Harrow Road at Maida Vale, and we became their cheer squad, drinking pints with them in the breaks and grooving on their soul and rhythm and blues sets.

I'd reconnected with my former French teacher, Glenda, but it was a brief fling. I think we both found that there was something lacking without the danger of being found out. My favourite movies at the time were the sexy subtitled Italian rom-coms that always seemed to star Marcello Mastroianni as the lover and cad. One scene in *Casanova 70* that resonated with me had Marcello, with a beautiful woman waiting in his bed, slipping into an adjoining room so he could edge along a frightening precipice to get back to his conquest. That was pretty much Glenda and me in London in 1973.

Max Merritt and the Meteors, London, 1973.

As winter kicked in I was beginning to get a little concerned about my long-distance relationship with Valerie. Admittedly, since we had professed undying love as we kissed goodbye at Sydney Airport just a matter of months ago, I hadn't exactly been faithful, except when there had been no alternative, as in Peniche, but I'd written many heartfelt aerograms, and suddenly the heartfelt responses had stopped coming. She was meant to be flying over to join the party very soon—I needed communication!

A roommate called Angie (the one who Ty Hardin had been visiting) had a brilliant scheme for defrauding British Telecom, so we had unlimited free calls home. I started phoning Valerie at her parents' Canberra home, but she was never there. Then one evening her father, Andy, phoned me back. 'She's not coming, son. It's a difficult situation. You might want to think about coming home.' I'd only met Andy on a couple of occasions, but we'd hit it off. He even offered to help me with the fare back.

I had no right to, but I felt gutted by this betrayal. There'd been another guy before me, and I knew he was back. I knew I had to go home and put up a fight.

It took me a while to extricate myself from London. For starters, I was seeing another girl, and I'd also made deals with the magazine that I had to complete. But the prospect of losing Valerie cast a black pall over my London. We were in the middle of a fuel crisis and half the country was on a three-day working week. England was in the middle of its bleakest winter since the Blitz, and suddenly, so was I.

CHAPTER EIGHTEEN

Kim Baily at the Wedge, early 1970s. (Photo Simon Chipper)

DOWN AND OUT IN WHALE BEACH

Soon after take-off from Heathrow, late on a black and blustery night, my plane suddenly hit an air pocket and dropped like a stone, before shuddering sideways and regaining its upward momentum. People were screaming, and the guy next to me, who'd just been bragging that he'd won a contract to play football for Prague Sydney FC, puked into his sick bag. This frightening start to my trip home seemed like an omen, and it left me with a fear of flying that would take years to overcome.

I flew straight to Canberra from Sydney and had my showdown with Valerie in the full flush of jet lag. She looked beautiful, standing in the little terminal in a simple summer dress. Because I couldn't fit it in my bag, I was wearing my London work suit, a heavy, shapeless brown thing, and a shirt that had been soaked with sweat and dried at least four times since I'd put it on. My hair was long and matted and I stank. She recoiled a little as I kissed and hugged her.

On the way to the family home, she pulled her dad's car into a leafy park in Campbell and switched the motor off. It was time for the talk. It was the Other Guy, of course. She hadn't meant to let it happen, but it had, and now she didn't know how she felt, and why did I have to go away and leave her anyway? There were some tears.

I said, 'Do you want me to go away now?'

'No. My dad's expecting you to stay. For tonight. Tomorrow you'll have to go.'

When we got to the house I stood in the shower for half an hour and pondered my future. Nothing much came to mind. I opened my travel bag, pulled out all the Carnaby Street dresses and tops I'd spent my last quids on at the Oxford Street sales, stuffed the stinking suit in their place and took the clothing to her room. She seemed genuinely pleased (either with the clothes or the fact that I'd showered), and this time when we kissed, some of the old passion had returned.

The next afternoon I hitchhiked to Corrimal and walked into my family's travel agency. Now that the kids were out of her hair, Mum had gone to work in the business. She looked up from the counter and nearly had a heart attack. Things had been moving so fast I guess I'd neglected to mention I was coming home. And I wasn't coming home. There was nothing for me on the coast. In the morning I caught the train to Sydney and started looking for a job.

I slept on the couch at Greg 'Grotty' Wilson's flat in Freshwater until I got a job, which proved surprisingly easy. I landed a C-grade salary at the *Sunday Telegraph* and joined the small staff of newsroom reporters. Since I'd been a copy boy at the *Daily Telegraph*, the Packer family had sold it and its Sunday stablemate to Rupert Murdoch, who'd taken both papers even further downmarket. But I didn't mind the job, and our newsroom pack had plenty of places to eat and drink near the News Limited headquarters in Surry Hills, which was becoming trendy.

I found a small flat in the city and within a few weeks Valerie, who was finishing her arts course in Sydney, had moved into a shared apartment not far from my office. We were back together, but it was a rocky road. Just when things seemed to be coming together, they would start to fall apart. I was spending a couple of nights a week at her place, but one night I came home from work earlier than expected and found her in bed with the Other Guy. There were some angry words, then I poured a glass of wine and sat out in the postage stamp of a back garden and waited for them to get dressed and leave. (Since I had another place to go to and she didn't, I'm not sure why it went this way, but it did.)

When I heard the front door click shut, I took a pair of scissors from the kitchen drawer, removed all the Carnaby Street clothes from her wardrobe and cut them into tiny pieces, which I scattered over her bed. Then I picked up the few belongings I had there and left. I never saw her again.

I was heartbroken, but the drugs helped. There had been a little weed along the way in Europe, but in Sydney I was reasonably connected and soon found myself spending strange evenings tripping on LSD. To be honest, a lot of the fun had gone out of acid that hideous morning when I fronted the CIB press conference off my tits, but there were extenuating circumstances now, so until I found another girl, I embraced my psychedelic other. And I wasn't exactly Robinson Crusoe among the drugged-out journalistic misfits who gathered in the evenings at the News Limited local, the Evening Star (known as the Evil Star, with good reason).

Knowing I was a surfer (although I didn't even have a board at this point), the chief of staff sent me out to the northern beaches to cover the biggest thing that had happened in Sydney surfing since the surf boom of the early '60s—the world's richest professional surfing event, Surfabout, sponsored jointly by Coca Cola and the rock music radio station 2SM. I had continued to contribute to *Tracks* while I travelled, but I hadn't kept up with what was happening in the culture or the contests, which was a lot. The previous year Rip Curl, the company whose wetsuit I had proudly worn around Europe, had funded the first professional surfing contest in Australia, the Rip Curl Bells Beach Pro, following a trend that was already well established in California and Hawaii and was now beginning to gain traction in Australia, with Coke and 2SM determined to blow the Victorian upstarts out of the water.

The prospect of making real money out of surfing had lured the sport's first world champion, Midget Farrelly, out of his Brookvale surfboard factory, and several devotees of the 'country soul' movement, led by former world champion Nat Young, out of their north coast lairs. It had also enticed many of the leading surfers from America. And it all seemed to have happened so quickly.

I stumbled around the rocks at Fairy Bower feeling like an alien in my brown London suit. I'd been a surfer all my young life, but I knew no-one here, and I was so not one of this cool crew. Fortunately I found Graham 'Sid' Cassidy, a journo I knew from the Fairfax days who was moonlighting as the contest director, and he introduced me to a few of the stars. While I was interviewing Hawaiian surfer Barry Kanaiaupuni (who mostly grunted his responses, shades of the Glasgow truckers from my *Truck and Bus* experience) a nearby cameraman heard my name mentioned and came over to introduce himself. It was Albert Falzon, the publisher of *Tracks*.

He pumped my hand and said, 'I've been meaning to get in touch with you. Give me a number I can call you on.'

Sid Cassidy got me invited to the Surfabout presentation party at a bar in Woolloomooloo and introduced me to Michael Peterson, the young Queensland surfer who'd just won the biggest payday in surfing, and another trophy to put on an already crowded mantelpiece. If Barry Kanaiaupuni had been uncommunicative, Peterson raised the bar several notches. He was twitchy and weird and seemed desperate to get away from me, which he did as soon as Sid moved on.

Nat Young was much friendlier. He had come third, and when he went up to receive his $600 cheque, he stunned the sponsors by donating it to the Australian Labor Party. Gough Whitlam's government had run into a bit of strife since that euphoric December election night in Canberra, and was now facing a critical new election. I sniffed a story in Nat's patronage of Labor, and went along with a photographer when he handed the money over to the secretary of the party, a slippery customer named David Combe, who later lost his Labor credibility over allegations that he was a Russian spy. In hindsight, it seems rather funny. Nat had no idea that Combe was a wheeler-dealer who would flirt with espionage, and Combe probably didn't know much about Nat's position on soft drugs, which would soon see him facing serious charges. Politics makes strange bedfellows. They just smiled and posed for the photo, which ended up on page three. A few weeks later Nat Young sat beside Gough Whitlam at Labor's campaign launch at the Sydney Opera House. Nothing is for nothing in politics.

Albe Falzon and I met for lunch at a bistro the News Limited crowd frequented on Elizabeth Street called L'ognion. Over a bottle of red he explained that John Witzig had moved on and that *Tracks* had been staggering along with part-time editors. He felt it was time to put a full-time pro in the chair. He put his glass down and looked across the table at me. 'Well? Are you interested?'

By the end of the following week, I had handed in my resignation, slithered out of the lease on my city flat, junked my London suit, bought a $200 FJ Holden at a car yard on Parramatta Road and a second-hand six-four rounded pintail from Chris Henri at Curl Curl, and rented a house overlooking Whale Beach for $35 a week. (Greg Wilson, who was now working in radio, moved in to help with the rent.)

On the first morning of my new life I walked down the hill with my new board and surfed the Whale Beach Wedge with just a few locals. I saw John Witzig paddle out off the rocks and pick up a couple of beautiful waves further out. I liked the effortless glide of his surfing, although it made me realise how rusty I was. He invited me for a coffee at the small cottage he was now renting at the northern end of the beach, and as we sat on his patch of lawn in the autumn sun he congratulated me on my new job, and said he hoped I'd throw him the odd bone. (He'd gone back to university to finish architecture.) I left my board on the grass and walked along the beach towards the *Tracks* office to report for work. Even though it was almost winter, there were girls sunbathing topless in a sunny corner out of the breeze. Big Afghan hounds and red setters roamed free on the sand. Ahh, life was becoming good again.

I walked up the narrow pathway at 182 Whale Beach Road and entered a large, sun-filled room with a long workbench built along two walls. In the far corner Albe Falzon was sitting having morning tea with an attractive young woman he introduced as his secretary, Mary Camarda. She greeted me warmly, but then scurried away to another office. Albe leaned back in his cane chair and put his hands behind his head. He said, 'Ah, we have a bit of a problem.'

We did. I'd just quit my job and moved to Whale Beach to work at *Tracks* and now he was telling me that someone he'd promised the editor's job to long before me was winging his way to Australia to take him up on the offer. I'd gone from hero to zero in less than a minute. I was gutted. To be fair, Albe felt terrible about it all, so much so that he promised to give me enough freelance work to keep the wolf from the door, but the money was only part of it. I'd told everyone that I was the new editor of *Tracks*, and now I wasn't.

I expected to hate the new editor, a freelancer from San Francisco called John Grissim, but in fact we hit it off from the start. Grissim was a tall, good-looking guy in his early thirties, with a big moustache and a quick wit. He also had a limp, the result of a pinched nerve in his right leg. He confided in me that as soon as he'd made enough money at *Tracks*, he was going to the Philippines to see a faith healer. I asked how long he thought that might take, but he was noncommittal.

Although Albe had met him at the 1972 world surfing championships in San Diego, Grissim was not a surfer. But he was eager to learn, so I took him on as a project, limp and all. We went on surfari down the south coast in my blue FJ. Albe had loaned him one of his boards, a beautiful gun shaped by Mitchell Rae, a young shaper who had been working out of Gonsalves Boatshed at Palm Beach. It wasn't exactly a learner board, but Grissim could stand up and turn a little by the time we got back to Whale Beach. He was a highly opinionated fellow, but fun to travel with.

I was amazed when we walked into a country pub and he sat down at an old piano and belted out honky-tonk for half an hour.

Despite having very little money, I started to enjoy the Whale Beach lifestyle. I dated a couple of local girls and hung out with the *Tracks* crew of photographer Frank Pithers and advertising salesman Stephen Cooney, who Albe was teaching to design the magazine, which in those days meant gluing columns of text onto art boards and making headlines out of Letraset. Frank was a thickset, macho kind of guy with curly hair and a disconcerting habit of stroking the fairly prominent bulge in his tight jeans as he spoke to you. But he had a wicked, earthy sense of humour. Stephen was the prodigy surfer who had starred in the Bali sequences of Albe's movie *Morning of the Earth*, filmed in 1971 when he was just fourteen. He was a beautiful surfer to watch, and had turned into a street-smart operator, mature beyond his tender years. We soon became good friends.

I also developed a friendship with Tony Edwards, whose cartoon creation Captain Goodvibes was fast becoming the most popular feature of the magazine. Tony had grown up on the northern beaches but he had never surfed, and had city sensibilities. Despite this, he and wife Sally had moved to Palm Beach, where they rented a magnificent but crumbling sandstone cottage overlooking Lion Island at the mouth of Pittwater. 'Windyridge' was a salon for our crew, a place where much wine and dope was consumed while the master of the house entertained with a hilariously depraved wit.

Albe shooting 'Morning Of The Earth', 1971.

Tracks crew at Windy ridge, 1974.

I was hanging gloomily around the *Tracks* office one day when a loud, jovial, chain-smoking fellow walked through the door. He was introduced to me only as 'The Mexican'. David 'Mexican' Sumpter turned out to be a fan of my work in *Tracks*—he particularly liked 'As Tall as a Grafton Jacaranda', a satirical piece I'd written about Nat Young's political donation. He told me he had just made a surf movie called *On Any Morning* and asked if I would go on the road with him to promote it. He said, 'You can write a funny story, and my whole life is one big funny story, so it shouldn't be too difficult.'

David 'Mexican' Sumpter, 1973.
(Photo Dick Hoole)

The Mexican was delighted when I used my contacts at the *Sunday Telegraph* to get them to run a feature article titled, 'Surfie filmmaker lives on dog food and yoghurt to finance new movie'. We hit the road up and down the coast, with him gluing posters all over towns while I chatted up the local papers and radio stations. His personal hygiene was highly questionable, but he was a funny man with a good heart and we did good business.

After the Melbourne premiere he handed me $250 in cash and advised me to give it all to a photographer named Rennie Ellis, who was a partner in Bali Easyrider Travel Service. 'You need to go to Bali,' The Mexican said. 'It'll fix your broken heart and you'll get some perfect waves all to yourself.'

I visited Rennie Ellis at his Prahran office, thus beginning a friendship for life, and he said he could squeeze me onto a Rip Curl trip leaving in a few days. With the return airline ticket, three weeks' bed and breakfast and a motorbike thrown in, it cost $49 more than The Mexican had paid me, but I was in.

CHAPTER NINETEEN

ISLAND OF THE GODS

I knew a little—very little—about Bali.

When I hooked up with an old schoolfriend, Kerry Goonan in London, she told me she had started her overland trail in Bali, and got all misty-eyed as she related wonderful stories about the huts in the jungle next to the perfect waves, the gorgeous, friendly people and the fragrant aroma of frangipanis, satay sauce and clove cigarettes. Albe Falzon and Stephen Cooney had also told me stories about the mystical aura of the place and the incredible waves they had found on the lonely Bukit Peninsula. The Mexican had filmed around Kuta Beach with Nat Young and Wayne Lynch, and he, too, had colourful tales.

In time Bali became such an important part of my life that eventually I had to write a book about it, so I won't dwell on too many elements of that story here, but I need to share how that first visit changed my life.

I still vividly recall the excitement as the plane broke through the clouds on descent and we saw glistening waves breaking along the coastal cliffs to the south and either side of the runway. I remember smelling that intoxicating mix I'd heard about as soon as we disembarked, followed by the craziness of the tiny terminal, and waiting forever for our surfboards to appear, and the pandemonium outside as the porters and drivers hustled for our buck. I loved it immediately.

We sat in the back of a three-wheeled *bemo* (local taxi-bus), facing each other on benches on either side, our boards and bags stacked down the middle. I peered through the small barred window at the driver in the cabin, surrounded by garish ornaments hung from the rear-vision mirror and roof. He jabbered away to his offsider in the passenger seat, one eye occasionally on the narrow sealed section of road, his hand never far from the horn.

Our unofficial tour leader was Brian Singer, the co-founder of Rip Curl at Torquay in Victoria. Brian had been to Bali for the first time the previous year, so he knew the ropes, and this year he'd brought along some of his employees and some of Torquay's better young surfers. When we arrived at Kodja Inn, a humble *losmen* not far from the beach on Jalan Pantai, the first thing the Torquay surfers did was unpack their boards and start waxing the decks. They fastened cords to fibreglass loops

The crew at Kodja Inn. Mexican, Peter Troy and Jack McCoy front row.
(Photo Dick Hoole)

on the tail, which they would then attach to their leg by means of an adhesive strip. By contrast, no unpacking of my single board was necessary. It had travelled naked, a solitary 'FRAGILE' sticker pasted to its bottom. The previous year I had surfed all over France, Spain, Portugal and Cornwall, and since returning to Australia I had surfed up and down the coast from Sydney, but I had never seen a board bag or a leg-rope.

After a warm-up surf in the friendly beach-break waves at the end of the sand track, Brian took me aside and suggested that, since the swell appeared to be rising and we might surf the new reef-break discovery, Uluwatu, in the morning, it would be advisable for me to use a leash so I wouldn't damage my only board on the reef.

'But I haven't got one of those thingies,' I protested.

'A rovings loop,' he supplied. 'After dinner I'll take you over the way to meet a guy who should be able to fix that for you.'

Having settled his young family for the night, Brian came across the garden to the bungalow I was sharing with Bob Pearson, a schoolteacher from Santa Cruz, California. 'Grab your board,' he said. 'We'll go see Boyum.'

On the other side of the track, perhaps 30 metres closer to the beach, we turned in to a dark laneway and then right into a candle-lit courtyard, from which point we could gaze into a house where a mixed group of Western and Balinese men were sitting around a table. A muscular blonde fellow with a slightly protruding jaw got up and shone a flashlight in our direction. He smiled and said, 'Sing Ding! *Apa kabar?*'

Brian introduced me to Mike Boyum and explained my predicament. In an instant Boyum had issued some instructions in Indonesian or Balinese—I had no idea which—and two young men grabbed my board and took it away to be modified. 'Take about half an hour,' Boyum said to Brian. 'We're just having some soup. Join us?'

I was rather pointedly excluded from the conversation, which was mainly about the great Hawaiian surfer Gerry Lopez, who was either about to arrive or had just left, I can't remember which. I was handed a small, chipped bowl of murky mushroom soup that I neither needed nor wanted after our seafood binge at dinner. Noting Brian's enthusiastic slurping, I joined in and put away perhaps half before pushing it aside.

I can remember laughing madly about nothing as we danced back to our *losmen* in the dark, me carrying my surfboard fitted with its sexy

Author at Windro compound, Uluwatu, 1975. (Photo Dick Hoole)

new leggie loop, Brian Singer loping along in front, saying, 'Jesus, what a first night!'

I slept fitfully and uneasily, and at one point, fearful of waking Bob in the next bunk, I sat outside on the porch and smelled the night air, alternately counting my blessings and imagining large animals in the garden.

I wasn't right for days thanks to the mushroom soup, but we surfed Uluwatu the next morning. My new leash kept my board from danger, I caught a few waves that tested me, and between sessions I had time to ponder what this adventure would mean to my life. Like so many people in those days, I had experienced a psychedelic mushroom trip upon arrival, but I had few negatives to report, other than that I would have preferred to know what I was getting myself into. Although I had messed around with LSD quite a bit, tripping on psilocybin was not to become part of my long-term Bali experience.

On the other hand, sharing my first night in Bali with Brian Singer (who would become a multi-millionaire surf industry mogul, and remain a friend) and Mike Boyum (who would get weirder and weirder and die young in mysterious circumstances) profoundly influenced my perceptions about the freedoms and opportunities this island seemed to offer. I had just turned twenty-three and this was such a cool new world. I couldn't believe how so many things—getting ditched by my girl, meeting Albe, getting the editor's job, not getting the editor's job, meeting The Mexican, meeting Rennie—had fallen into place and allowed me to be here at this point in time.

On the third day of my first trip to Bali, someone advised me to cycle across the cow paddock behind our *losmen* to a place called Arena Bungalows to see a man named Dick Hoole. Apparently he could organise a fake student pass for me so I could buy airline tickets at a discount. When I arrived at his door, Dick distractedly called for me to come in. I was somewhat shocked to find him stretched out on the floor of his room stuffing Thai marijuana sticks into the hollowed-out balsawood stringer of his surfboard. 'Won't be a sec,' he said. 'There's a thermos of tea on the porch, help yourself.'

At the time, Dick was a struggling surf photographer who needed to subsidise his lifestyle in whatever ways he could. He wasn't the only one. Practically every long-termer or regular visitor I met in Bali that year had some kind of scam going on; some comprehensively illegal, others just a little bit dodgy. Cheap clothing made from colourful local fabrics seemed to be low-hanging fruit, so Brian Singer and I and a couple of other Torquay likely lads travelled overland to Yogyakarta, Java—a horrendous bus and train journey in those days—to buy batik print shirts to smuggle back into Australia. I had no idea, and barely made my money back on the hideous shirts I bought, but if it was good enough for the boss of Rip Curl, it was good enough for me.

When I returned from Bali, John Grissim told me he had contacted a faith healer in the Philippines and booked his plane ticket. I would be taking over as editor of *Tracks* for the first issue of 1975. I was so grateful that I used the money I'd so far made from the batik shirts to buy him a slap-up dinner at The Scullery in Avalon Beach. We drank far too much and I backed the FJ into a lamp post on the way home.

Grissim and I had one last hurrah before he left. David Elfick, one of the founders of *Tracks* and Albe's film production partner, had bought an old farmhouse in the hills behind Byron Bay and invited all the magazine crew to camp on the property over Christmas. Only Grissim and I took him up on the offer. We travelled north separately, because I was helping a girl called Elizabeth desert her husband. She was a strange little hippy

David Elfick with John Witzig. (Photo Albe Falzon)

thing, but we were well into a fling before I realised that this was her Summer of Love, seven years after everyone else's. How could she remain married when everywhere she looked was sexual opportunity?

To avoid becoming a punching bag in a marital dust-up, I waited for her in the FJ at a Central Coast railway station, and we drove up the Pacific Highway together, stopping to skinny dip whenever she saw a body of water, preferably in full view of passing cars. By the time we arrived at Elfick's farm, the party was in full swing. David seemed to know everyone in the countercultural world, including several people I was in awe of. Everyone was given a job, regardless of fame, so that first afternoon I found myself digging a latrine with the outspoken *Oz* editor Richard Neville and experimental filmmaker Albie Thoms. It was the beginning of a long friendship with both.

That night Elizabeth and I were about to bed down in the tent I had pitched when she pulled me aside on the verandah and explained that another guest had asked her to sleep with him, and she kind of liked him, and it would only be the one night. Hadn't seen that one coming. I wasn't so uncool as to ask any questions, but I wondered if it was Grissim who was mowing my grass. If not that night, then maybe the next, or the next— after which I threw the tent in the boot of the FJ and slipped away before dawn without Elizabeth, and without saying goodbye to John Grissim, so I never found out.

The next time I saw him, a couple of years later in California, still limping, I forgot to ask.

CHAPTER TWENTY

MAKING *TRACKS*

If I had any kind of plan for my editorship of *Tracks* it was probably to loosen it up a bit. Although I'd been a fan since the first issue, I often felt its tone was just a little too cool for school. It could be a bit superior, a bit up itself.

Of course, if you'd done a vox pop survey of the morning coffee crowd at the Whale Beach Store, or at Bommie Beacham's surf shop next door, you would have found many intelligent, articulate, well-educated Peninsula surfers who loved the magazine for those very reasons. But the *Tracks* circulation had been in a growth spurt for the better part of a year, and the new readership represented a very different demographic. This had become apparent in the middle of 1974, when one of the jobs I'd been given to 'keep the wolf from the door' while I waited for the editorship was to pore over the responses to the first ever *Tracks* questionnaire and develop a statistical profile of the readership. The big news was that the overwhelming majority of them were bog ordinary—schoolkids from the outer suburbs who only got to the beach once a week, surf-mad tradies who lived for weekend trips up or down the coast, teenage surf chicks who wanted an introduction to Mark Warren. There was also a disproportionate number of readers in jail, almost all of them for drug offences.

The most popular features in the magazine were surfing pictures, funny articles, the Captain Goodvibes comic strip and, of course, the cheerfully obscene letters page, which probably told you more about the readers than a survey ever could. A frequent theme on the letters page was parental outrage, but this could cut both ways. Just before he vacated the editor's chair, John Grissim published a letter from one T. Slocum, from leafy Killara in Sydney's north. 'So many young, impressionistic, lost and directionless minds read *Tracks*. Give them a direction, both good and positive,' pleaded Slocum.

Grissim's response was, 'Aw, get fucked!—Ed.' He left the country and I got the blame.

In the beginning the *Tracks* founders liked to think they were writing the revolution, but the questionnaire results didn't sound too radical. In fact, they described the recipe for surf magazines that Californian John Severson had developed when he created *Surfer* in 1960. While we didn't go back to the future entirely, I realised from the start that on the *Tracks* staff we had exactly the right people to give the readers what they seemed to want. Frank Pithers was a good surf photographer, and Steve Cooney also had a good eye. There was a memorable and usually disgusting gag line about to happen every time Frank or Tony Edwards opened their mouths, and, despite my abysmal shorthand, I was good at jotting it all down. We would make the readers laugh so hard they'd cry. And we would be even more outrageous! That was my plan.

Tracks office at Whale Beach, early 1970s. (Photo courtesy John Ogden)

When I first started reading *Surfer* magazine in the mid-'60s, my favourite features were always the road trips undertaken by cartoonist Rick Griffin and photographer Ron Stoner, related as a series of increasingly desperate telegrams between the travellers and their long-suffering boss back at the office, editor Patrick McNulty. I could see the same dynamic developing between Pithers, Cooney and myself, except that I had no intention of staying in the office and missing all the fun. Realising that the blue FJ didn't have many miles left in it, Albe Falzon had allowed me to spend $1000 on a company car. I'd bought a near-new, ex-Fire Brigade shiny red Holden station wagon. The first road trip for the *Tracks* fire truck was the 1975 Rip Curl Bells Beach Pro.

We took off for Bells in the afternoon and drove through the night, one sleeping in the back, one driving and one opening the beers and lighting the ciggies and joints. We listened to the new ABC rock radio station, 2JJ, at full volume, which killed any hope of conversation, so I didn't share the news that Tony Edwards and I had just signed on to present the new station's morning surf report, me playing straight man to Tony's Captain Goodvibes persona. Frank already thought I was a wanker; this news would only have confirmed his view.

Steve Cooney and I had already become friends, but when Frank was around, Cooney became a 'Mini Me', laughing at Frank's jokes (which were usually pretty funny) and taking his side against mine. When we arrived at our Torquay rental house, Frank took the best bedroom and spread his shit liberally around the place, camera bags and tripods in doorways. His rationale for claiming alpha male status was that he'd been at the magazine the longest. My rationale for equal billing was that I was the fucking editor! There were going to be tears.

The waves were good at Bells that year, and although I was outclassed by almost everyone in the water, I paddled out with Cooney and enjoyed some good sessions at Winki Pop, the fast, steep right-hander down the line from the Bells bowl. Frank never surfed with us. Although he would paddle out on a canvas surf mat to take photos in any conditions, he seemed to think normal surfing was beneath him.

We were clearly heading for a dust-up. If I asked him to take a portrait shot of a particular surfer or a mood shot for something I was writing, he would snarl at me as though this was a calculated insult. One morning on the Bells cliff-top I retaliated with an angry, 'I'm not asking you, I'm telling you!'

He nodded a couple of times, placed his camera gear on the ground slowly and deliberately, then turned around and took a swing at me. At school an older but smaller guy called Roy Norris had taken a set against me, and used to lie in wait outside Darrell Eastlake's surf shop. He was angry and he was quick, but he never laid a fist on me because I was quicker. And so it was a decade later at Bells Beach. I ducked and weaved and avoided contact. The fight was over before it really began because another photographer, laden with bags and lenses and sporting a ponytail and an extravagant moustache, got between us. 'Cool it, you guys.'

I recognised him immediately, from a meeting at the Bali Easyrider Travel Service nine months earlier, but it was Frank who said, as the peacemaker walked off, 'Fuck, that was Rennie Ellis!'

In addition to being a Bali travel pioneer and the best known photo-journalist in the country, Rennie was a name in the world of surfing for a series of articles he wrote for *Surfing World* magazine in the mid-'60s called 'Odyssey of a Surfer', which detailed his adventures looking for surf and love in all the wrong places, often in the company of another legendary surf adventurer named Peter Troy. I sought him out at the contest later in the day and we had a few drinks that evening at Jack McCoy's Summer House restaurant, where an eating contest was taking place featuring some of the leading surfers, who were renowned for their gluttony. This was just the sort of loony stuff I wanted to include in our Bells coverage, and Rennie was on hand to shoot every gruesome angle as Wayne 'Rabbit' Bartholomew from Queensland (chicken salad) fought out the final against local hero Maurice Cole (enchiladas).

Fortunately my new friend Ellis left before the drinking contests began, and I was spared the ignominy of him seeing me standing on a table pouring flaming shots of Southern Comfort down my throat next to top surfer Peter Townend, who managed to singe off his blond goatee. I had to be helped down from the table, but that didn't stop me driving the *Tracks* fire engine the three or four blocks to our rental, where I misjudged the driveway and ploughed into the red brick wall.

Technically, it was my car, but that didn't stop Frank from exploding when he saw the damage the next morning. We were in for a wild ride, I knew that. Conversely, Rennie Ellis and I hit it off from the start and worked well together. Both men were brilliant photographers in their own way, but it would take years and many more screaming matches before I could call Frank a friend.

Rennie Ellis, 1975. (Photo Bob Bourne)

My lease on the Whale Beach house had run out so Stephen Cooney and I decided to rent together. We found a sprawling bungalow in Rayner Road at the southern end of the beach, on a couple of levels, with magnificent views across the beach to the Wedge, and beyond to Lion Island and the Central Coast off in the distance. It was definitely a party house, with a vast living area and deck on the top level and a games room with a ping pong table below. It was the perfect pad for a budding media star, which I imagined myself to be.

Tony Edwards and I had started doing the morning surf reports on 2JJ, up against surfboard builder Shane Stedman on 2SM. Shane had a lovely, bubbling personality and a great sense of fun, but he took his surf reports very seriously, combing the coast every morning in a sponsored Mini Moke. Since it had burst onto the airwaves earlier in the year with the banned Skyhooks song 'You Just Like Me Cos I'm Good in Bed', JJ had modelled itself as the bad bastard child of Sydney radio, flouting all conventions. Our brief was to be outrageous, play it for laughs. So, patched through to the one line from our separate home phones, Captain Goodvibes and I would engage in banter that was as obscene as broadcasting standards would allow, and then some.

'You don't know what the surf's like, Jarratt, you piece of turd, oink, oink,' the Pig of Steel would scream, using the hoarse porcine voice that was doing untold damage to his vocal chords. 'You're probably still in bed with some piece of fluff you picked up at the Rissole [RSL]. Oink!' Sometimes we worked out a little script beforehand, but our go-to routine was that I was either too drunk or too hungover to have actually seen the surf (sometimes this was true), so listener beware.

David Elfick and Albie Thoms were producing an interesting and mysteriously named short program on youth culture for the ABC, and decided that JJ's debauched surf report duo was good fodder for the show, *GTK*. (Years later I found out that the name stood for 'getting to know', which was so lame I can understand why they kept it a secret.) They decided to pursue the conceit that I phoned in the surf report from bed, and I was so blinded by my louche self-image that I agreed. When they arrived just before sunrise to shoot the piece, they found me in bed with the nanny from across the street. I asked for a moment's privacy so she could dress and take her leave, but Elfick said, 'No, this is perfect!' My embarrassed bedmate shrunk beneath the bedding while the cameras rolled.

When my *GTK* episode went to air a couple of weeks later, the woman who would one day become my wife was cooking dinner when her then-husband called her to watch something on TV. 'Would you take a look at this asshole,' he said, shaking his head. I imagine there were similar reactions across Australia.

But I couldn't stop. A law student at Sydney University named Craig Leggat had started doing a bit of work with us at the magazine, and when the university's own magazine, *Honi Soit*, decided to run a surfing supplement, Craig was invited to edit it. He interviewed me at home on a beery Saturday afternoon and ran the unedited transcript over a full page with a photo of me holding a beer in one hand and giving him the finger with the other. The piece was a disaster. I managed to insult just about everyone I worked with and appear racist, sexist, homophobic, boorish and stupid all at the same time. The photo caption was a direct quote: 'I'm interested in surfing and fucking women'.

The *Honi Soit* coverage didn't win me any friends, and I wasn't very happy with Craig Leggat, who showed his complete lack of judgement by putting a photo of himself doing an off-the-lip on the cover. He continued to work for *Tracks*, however, writing a column called 'Browneye'.

Mr Obnoxious, 1975.

Despite this dodgy start to his professional life, he eventually matured and became an esteemed barrister. I did neither of those things.

Steve Cooney and I were beginning to have some interesting house guests. Rabbit Bartholomew was a friend of Steve's and had a standing invitation to crash at our place whenever he was passing through Sydney. He and his young Burleigh friend Guy Ormerod had been slowly making their way up the coast from Bells with Keith Paull when they checked in to Rayner Road for one night that became three or four. 'Keith's been acting weird,' Rabbit whispered. 'He's starting to scare us.'

Rabbit on the Keith Paull trip, 1975. (Photo Stephen Cooney)

Within twenty-four hours he was scaring all of us. Keith had been one of the real stylists of the '60s, a surfer whose flowing forehand turns and cutbacks were a joy to watch. An Australian champion in 1968, he made the transition to shorter boards with ease and it seemed he'd be a force to be reckoned with for years to come. But Keith had started to act rather strangely in recent times. In 1974 he had turned up for the Pa Bendall Memorial contest on Queensland's Sunshine Coast wearing silver knee-high boots and blue Superman briefs, with concentric blue circles painted on his shaved head. After the conclusion of the event he drove his van up the steps of the pub where the presentations were being held, before being taken away by the police for questioning. People shrugged and said he used too much acid.

Keith looked and smelled like he'd been wearing the same clothes for a couple of weeks. I tactfully suggested he might like to take a shower and freshen up after the long drive, and went off to make up beds for the guests. When I came back half an hour later I found Keith slumped on the floor of the shower recess, fully clothed, drenched and steaming, surrounded by empty bottles of Brem rice wine that I'd kept on a shelf as souvenirs of Bali. When I asked what he was doing he stared blankly into the steam.

Within a year or two Keith Paull had disappeared from surfing, another victim of undiagnosed schizophrenia who would die alone in a hotel room, too young, a lost soul.

Michael Peterson was another visitor who was showing signs of increasing weirdness, even as he cemented his position as the world's leading professional surfer. I hadn't been able to talk to him when we first met a year earlier, but for some reason Michael and I had begun to get along quite well, and during the 1975 Surfabout, we spent time together while I did an extensive interview. He didn't stay with us during the contest, but he popped in frequently, thrashing all comers on the downstairs ping pong table.

One night I was awoken by voices in the house, followed by what sounded like nails being hammered into a wall. I looked at my watch— it was just after three in the morning. I heard laughter. Since it seemed unlikely that armed intruders would be cracking wise while on the job, I got out of bed to investigate. I pushed open the door of the games room and found Michael Peterson stripped to the waist and dishing out another flogging to someone at the other end of the ping pong table while six or seven others stood around drinking our beer and cheering him on. Peterson didn't even look around as I came in and surveyed the scene. He just threw the ball to the other end and called for service, as if it was the most normal thing in the world to come into someone's home in the middle of the night and commandeer the games room.

The budding friendship survived the ping pong night, but it didn't fare so well when we painted a monogrammed attaché case into his hand for the cover of the magazine that featured my interview with him. Most people who saw it thought we were taking the mickey out of Mick, so to speak, but Michael was furious because it was true. He did carry an attaché case around with him, but would never be photographed with it. (He also wore a suit on plane rides, long after that era had passed.)

On a contest lay day I surfed the Whale Beach Wedge with Michael and a few others. Watching him surf at close quarters, even in those scrappy, wind-affected peaks, it dawned on me that truly gifted surfers

Michael Peterson winning Bells, 1975. (Photo Frank Pithers)

are not like us. I had caught glimpses of this growing up around Kevin Parkinson and Bobby Brown, and over the years I was to see it again and again, this other-worldly ability to become one with the wave, to sense its subtle movements and match them, to freakishly predict what the ocean is going to do and harmonise with it. You can see it from the beach sometimes, or even on a television screen on rare occasions, but you only really understand it when you are there, in the moment, with the greats, or at least close by, in the channel or paddling out of the way, watching in awe. And while it is not only the champions and the recognised names who have these gifts, they are usually the ones who can perform minor miracles on a regular basis.

In my own long but inglorious surfing life, I have been blessed to share such insights at close quarters—let's call it the view from the channel—with the very best, from Michael Peterson at Kirra and Paul Neilsen at Burleigh, to Tom Carroll at G-Land and Gary Elkerton at Staithes in Yorkshire, of all places, and Shane Dorian and the incomparable Kelly Slater at Cloudbreak. We used to say of reading *Tracks*, it's the next best thing to being inside. Well, this was being pretty damn close, and it was better than the next best thing.

CHAPTER TWENTY-ONE

Highway One poster art by Tony Edwards, 1977.

ROAD WARRIOR

***Tracks* was going** gangbusters, its circulation growing by a thousand a month and advertising revenue up ten per cent every issue. It seemed like people were lining up to throw money at Albe Falzon, who was now the sole owner of the magazine.

One of the more interesting benefactors was the American Express corporation, who wanted us to partner in a travel venture to be known as the Tracks Travel Company. Bali surfing packages were starting to mushroom, largely due to the groundbreaking work of Jack deLissa and Rennie Ellis at Bali Easyrider Travel. AmEx had its eye on that, but its initial interest was in the fiftieth of the United States: Hawaii. The general idea was to create a Bali-style surfer holiday in Hawaii and give it some cred by putting the *Tracks* name on it. In my view it was never going to work—in those days the vast majority who went to Hawaii for the deeply challenging waves of the North Shore were elite surfers and self-starters. But how quickly I fell into line when Albe asked me to fly to Hawaii and put together a magazine supplement to promote the new partnership!

As an afterthought Albe said, 'They're giving us two tickets so Frank will go with you and take the photos.' Great. It was a nine-hour flight. I wondered how we'd survive that much proximity, but we did. Maybe our relationship was making progress.

Our mission was to sample what the AmEx tour intended to offer and present a glowing report that would be the centrepiece of the introductory editorial and advertising campaign. The problem was that it was a winter season package and we were there at the height of summer, which meant that the North Shore of Oahu, the home of the biggest waves in the known world, would be like a lake. And that was only one of the problems. Another was that the North Shore accommodation for the tour was not on the North Shore but a half-hour drive away at Laie, and yet another was that the motel was attached to the Mormon-owned Polynesian Cultural Center, and was alcohol-free.

Frank and I bonded over our desire to spend as little time as possible in the AmEx Mormon prison. In fact, we didn't last a night, driving our cheap rental car back to Waikiki and checking in to a motel in the middle of the Ala Moana sin strip. This was the first experience of Hawaii for both of us, and we badly needed direction, but none of our pro-surfer mates were in town to give it. In the morning, however, Frank, I had to admit, had a very good idea.

Queensland surfer Paul Neilsen, the 1972 Australian champion, had been one of the first Australians to establish solid social connections in Hawaii, a fact demonstrated by his closeness to the legendary Aikau family, and underlined when he flew his glamorous Waikiki squeeze, Faye Parker, out to Australia for the 1975 contest season. We had both met Faye at Bells and in Sydney and instantly liked her brash charm and naughty aunty persona. Mysteriously, Frank had her number.

'So glad you called,' Faye gushed. We were invited to lunch at the Outrigger Canoe Club and a luau dinner at her home in the hills above Diamond Head. Faye had been married to the actor Doug McClure and the star footballer Don Parker, among other prominent men. She was well connected with the local entertainment crowd, as well as the surfing fraternity and the point where those two groups collided, which was the hit TV show *Hawaii Five-O*. At the Outrigger she introduced us to the former world surfing champion and boss of the emerging pro movement, Fred Hemmings, but her real coup for the day came when we arrived at her place for the hilltop luau to be greeted by James 'Jimmy' MacArthur, 'Danno' in *Hawaii Five-O*.

Ironically, given that Faye, Paul Neilsen and his older brother Ricky were all staunchly anti-drugs—Ricky had famously flushed another surfer's stash down the toilet at the 1972 San Diego world titles—that evening at the luau was my first encounter with cocaine. I walked into a bathroom and discovered several of the guests chopping up the powder on the marble top. No-one said a word, just handed me a cut-down straw and watched as I nervously hoovered up a long line. I discovered that Frank was already in on the action, and suddenly we were the life of the party, laughing uproariously at our own jokes and sharing tales of derring-do. It was a long night, probably much longer for those who hadn't taken the magic elixir that removed self-doubt.

After a couple more days surfing and soaking up the atmosphere of the South Shore, we headed for the airport, less than confident that we had covered the job—but Frank would have to be the one to explain that to Albe. He was going home, I was going to California. For some reason, when we picked up our complimentary tickets from Pan American Airways they were round trips to Rio, via Honolulu, Los Angeles and Guatemala City. I had work obligations in Sydney, but seriously considered blowing them off and doing the whole trip. Given our failure to produce the goods in Hawaii, this may have been too much, even for as easygoing a boss as Albe, so I compromised with a stolen week in California.

California was another first for me, and I have to admit I was horrified as we dropped through the intense grey marine layer that I took for smog on descent into Los Angeles International. I rescued my naked Brothers Neilsen swallowtail (I still had no board bag) from the baggage carousel, rented a Ford Pinto and headed for the freeway. It was six on a gloomy Friday afternoon and I had no idea where I was going. I turned right onto the 405 and edged south, listening to a new band called The Eagles on the radio.

The stop-start traffic was too much to bear so I took the first beach exit south of the airport and found myself at Redondo Beach. A few blocks back from the beach a neon sign caught my eye: EL RANCHO MOTEL— COLOR TV NO POOL—WE JUST LOOK EXPENSIVE—VACANCY. I pulled into the drive and paid fifteen bucks for a room on the first floor.

That night I drank at a sleazy Tiki bar on the Redondo Pier and listened to a country rock outfit butcher the Eagles songs I'd heard on the radio earlier. It could have been depressing, but I found myself in the first throes of a love–hate relationship with southern California style (or lack thereof) that endures to this day.

I skipped Hollywood and the theme parks and drove north on the 101, casting an eye over the famous but ridiculously crowded Rincon Point and coming to rest somewhere on the Montecito coast just south of Santa Barbara, where I could see waves breaking beyond the beachfront estates. I parked down a side street, grabbed my board, jumped a few fences and paddled out to a glassy head-high right with only a handful of surfers on it. As I reached the zone I nodded and smiled, as you do when you're new to a break. No-one smiled back, but one guy paddled directly over to me and asked where I was from. I told him.

'Australia! No shit! That probably explains it. See, this is Hammond's Reef, it's private.'

'I'm sorry, I had no idea.' (All those signs, all those fences, who knew?) 'I'll catch a wave straight in.'

'Hell no, you're here now, let's surf.'

My new friend was a long-haired, moustachioed Aussie-ophile named Tom Sims. When he found out I worked for *Tracks* and Albe Falzon he almost lost it. 'No shit! Hey fellers, this guy writes for *Tracks* and he knows all the *Morning of the Earth* dudes!' I was no longer an intruder, I was an honoured guest.

After our surf, Tom guided me up into the Montecito hills to his mud-brick cabin, set between Spanish-style stucco mansions. I was staying with him, no excuses accepted. We'd skate the hills all afternoon, party all night and surf again in the morning. I suddenly realised there were skateboards everywhere I looked, but most of them were unlike any I'd seen in Australia. They were around a metre long with beautiful polished wood decks that gave a very different kind of spring as you leaned into turns. These were the big guns of the skate world, and after he'd whipped up an avocado salad (was avocados being another thing that were plenti-ful) for our lunch, and we'd smoked a fat joint, Tom took me out to show me how to ride them.

I've never forgotten that session, speed-warping down smooth, paved hills in the blue-grey of evening, occasionally catching glimpses of the ocean below us. Tom was fluid and fast, no tricks, just speed-lines all the way. Following behind him, I was scared shitless, but I made the runs unscathed, and when we settled back at the house and drank some beers, I felt a wave of contentment come over me that skating has never induced since. I invested $50 in two of his guns to take home, but they were rarely used.

Before a fire that night, a little twisted to be sure, Tom Sims told me about his bold plan to make the sliding game his own. 'I'm going to take skateboards to the snow,' he said. One of his financial backers nodded sagely from an armchair opposite us, sucking a joint through his teeth. 'I'm gonna make a fucking fortune!' He cackled maniacally and got more drinks.

Tom Sims styling his gun skateboard at Montecito, 1975. (Photo SimsSnow)

Before the end of the '70s Tom Sims had won a world skateboard title and patented a snowboard design. By the mid-'80s he'd added a world snowboard title to his collection and the name Sims was synonymous with the best skateboards and snowboards in the world. He made his fortune, and then some. We'd just gotten back in touch through social media when he died of a heart attack in 2012.

I had only been back at work for a month or so when it was time to go to Bali again. A big influx of leading surfers was underway and I convinced Albe that, since he'd virtually invented it, we needed to keep covering the island of the gods. I'd been dating a girl who worked at The Scullery in Avalon, so I invited her to come with me.

In those early days of surfer settlement, everyone tried to be 'Bali-er than thou'. Considering I'd only been there once before, my own contribution to the argument over whether we were indeed destroying the

Bali we came to enjoy was as naive as it was trite. However, it speaks of the times.

The Kutarese, the hippies will tell you, are prime examples of what the tourists are doing to Bali—these people who live close to the sea and the devils within, far from the gods who guide the mountain people. It's hard to tell just what the Kuta locals think of us. They realise that tourism has brought them wealth that much of the population will never know, but they cling to their family traditions, make their offerings to the gods, respect authority at every level and generally shun the freedoms of western life. 'They're funny little people,' my girl said, watching them take breakfast of tea and toast to a statue in the garden. But no doubt they think we're funny big people, giving them enough money for a week's rice in exchange for clothes we'll never wear and paintings we'll never hang.

That season I worked with Jack McCoy and Dick Hoole, good photographers who had formed a business partnership called Propeller, and together we documented the return of Gerry Lopez, fast becoming the surf god of Bali, and the performances of the young Australians Tony 'Doris' Eltherington, Larry Blair, Peter 'Grub' McCabe and Terry Richardson.

Mr Obnoxious, 1975. (Photo John Witzig)

Jack and Dick, 1973. (Photo courtesy Dick Hoole)

Surfers were arriving from all over. You never knew who you might find paddling out. One morning Jack McCoy screeched his bike to a halt in front of my room at Sunset Beach Bungalows. 'Grab a tape recorder and jump on,' he said. 'Dora's in town and he's agreed to an interview.'

Miklos Chapin Dora, better known as Miki, was the black knight of Malibu, a legendary figure in Californian surfing, probably the best to ever ride the fabled waves of First Point, Surfrider Beach. It was said that Miki had never worked a day in his life, that he was a conman and a fraudster who was on the run from the FBI. And now he was waiting for us in his room at the Legian Beach Hotel. Dora was gruff when we knocked on his door. It looked like we might have woken him. As he let us in he said, 'No interview, no photos.'

But we spent two hours with him in that darkened room. Then in his early forties, Miki was deeply tanned, unshaven and wild-eyed. He spoke in staccato bursts about all kinds of weird shit. I was fascinated by his unusual delivery, by his dark-eyed outlaw aura. The rant, not so much, but I listened intently, then got McCoy to drop me at the cane juice bar in Kuta, where I sat in the corner and scribbled down every bit of the conversation I could remember. We published this 'unofficial interview' in *Tracks*. It took Miki more than twenty years to forgive me.

CHAPTER TWENTY-TWO

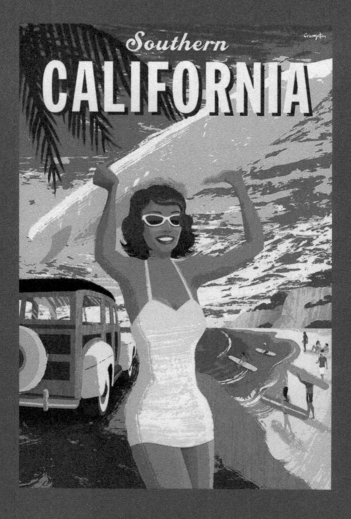

CALIFORNIA DREAMING

Tracks **continued to** assault the senses and grow ever more popular. Effectively, this meant that, editorially speaking, we could pretty much do whatever we wanted.

At the same time, the magazine's content was becoming more diverse. We looked for ways to marry diversity with outrage, and found them constantly. When an earnest hippie named Jan Whiting (who was to become a colleague and a dear friend) contributed an article about saving trees by using water rather than paper in your ablutions, we titled it, 'How to wipe your bum'. When an excellent rock journalist named Annie Burton wrote a considered piece about misogyny and sexism in surfing, Frank Pithers talked our beautiful secretary, Mary, into posing naked on the sand with a paper bag over her head to illustrate the point, which unwittingly I'm sure it did.

Mary, our secretary, 1975. (Photo Frank Pithers)

We seemed to have no filters, but nor did anyone else in the youth culture of the time. After hearing the hit Melbourne band Skyhooks belt out a moving rendition of their party anthem, 'Why Don't You All Get Fucked', on a paddock near Bells Beach, I had become friends with lead singer Graeme 'Shirley' Strachan. A tradie and a surfer from Phillip Island, Shirl seemed diametrically opposed to the Carlton arty-farty sensibilities of his band mates Red Symons and Greg Macainsh, and whenever the Hooks were in Sydney, he would bail out on the band and make a beeline for Whale Beach to surf and hang out.

On one of these visits, after a session at the Wedge and quite a few beers, I persuaded the rock star of the year to drop his dacks and pose sitting on our backyard dunny, reading the latest issue of *Tracks*. We ran Shirl on the bog as a full page. Only fervent pleading from his manager, Michael Gudinski, stopped us from putting it on the cover.

Shirl on the dunny, 1976. (Photo Martin Tullemans)

I seemed to be surfing less and enjoying it more. Or at least enjoying the fact that I could hang out with the surf stars without having to pretend to be one. One of the reasons the act of surfing had taken a step back in my life was that I had fallen in love with another girl who worked at The Scullery. It might seem like I was working my way through the female staff, but this one was special, and, of course, she had history. She was the former wife of one of Australia's greatest rock stars—then battling heroin addiction—with whom she had a young son.

I took on the baggage gleefully, with no thought of consequences, and proposed to her when we stayed at Brian Singer's house for the Bells Rip Curl Easter Pro. I even bought her a dog! We planned to marry, soonish. It was always going to end in tears, and I should have known that from the very early days, when I was hustled out of bed and out of her house on Christmas morning because the rock star was coming to see his son. But love is blind, and I hung in until the bitter end.

Heartbroken again, I moved into a rental house just a few doors down from the *Tracks* office, sharing with some new friends from Cornwall, surfboard shaper Paul Holmes and his partner, Simonne Renvoize. Paul was a talented writer who had also done some editing, so he soon became associate editor while shaping part-time. We also had a job for Simonne when our secretary, Mary, unexpectedly landed an extra's role on the feature film *Mad Dog Morgan* and, on completion, ran off with its star, Dennis Hopper, to Texas. Simonne took over as my secretary.

I threw myself into work, as many surf trips as I could fit in, and an increasing flirtation with cocaine, which suddenly seemed to be everywhere on the Peninsula. Then I met another girl. Her name was Jackie and she lived right across the street. She had just split up with her American musician husband and was sharing an old beach house with another American musician. I knew she had a young son, Sol, because he used to find his way up to the *Tracks* office from time to time to play with Frank Pithers' young son, Zahn. I didn't find out about her one-year-old daughter, Sophie, until Jackie appeared at the door one day with a little cutie on her hip.

Jackie Sadler had arrived from England with her parents and sister as 'ten pound Poms' on the liner *Oriana* in 1963. A dozen years later there was no trace of an accent. She was a slinky, sexy thing who spent a lot of the summer on the beach topless, her tan complete but for a tiny white bikini stripe. But she also had a sharp mind, a wicked tongue and

Jackie with Sophie and Sol, 1976. (Photo John Witzig)

And with grandkids Beau, Hunter and Jackson, 2010. (Photo Jason Mccallum)

we laughed about the same things. She'd seen me on TV, doing the surf report from a lumpy bed. Her friends had warned her off me as a shallow, self-obsessed womaniser, but it still began to happen. And it happened very fast, and once again I found myself taking on the mantle of stepdad with no thought for the consequences, nor any comprehension of the years of bitterness and rancour that lay ahead before time would heal the wounds, and the children's father and I would form a friendship based on, among other things, our mutual love of surfing.

And once again, just as a relationship was developing into something serious, perhaps even lasting, I was committed to a long trip away. I kissed Jackie and the kids and took off for California and Hawaii for two months.

My second trip to California was on another weird cheap ticket, this one requiring me to enter via Vancouver, Canada. No-one knew that there was good surf a ferry ride away on Victoria Island, so I didn't plan to linger there, but I found I couldn't rent a car to take over the border, so I took a cheap room near the bus terminal and grabbed a Greyhound to Seattle in the morning. Again I had trouble negotiating a one-way rental to Los Angeles, but for an arm and a leg National kitted me out with a white 1976 Buick Century coupe with layback seats, one for me and one for my board.

I filled the centre console with ice, jammed a few Coors beers in there and drove south through the redwood forests of the Pacific North West, Waylon Jennings thumping out of a country music station and keeping me awake. In the early hours I pulled into a parking lot behind a roadhouse, pushed back my seat and slept like a baby. In the morning it was a short drive across the border into California, where I found inviting waves at Crescent City. Over the years I've surfed up and down the west coast, and had plenty of good sessions and plenty of shockers. I've surfed lonely coves in Big Sur and been chased out of the water by a psychopath at Huntington Pier. Much of it has become a blur, but I can remember every detail of those first surfs, with Tom Sims at Hammond's Reef in 1975, and with a couple of throwback locals in ducktail wetsuits at Crescent Beach in 1976. My diary notes tell me that the water was a chilly 49 degrees Fahrenheit and that the large pebbles on the shore made minced meat of my feet, but they don't mention the head-high sets bobbing up in the murky water or how I had to learn to dodge the logs in the line-up. All of that is etched in the memory bank.

In the afternoon I drove the beautiful coast road through tall stands of redwoods to a town called Fort Bragg, where I rolled into an old-style saloon and drank a beer while I consulted a tourist map. Mendocino was just down the road. I'd heard of Mendocino, courtesy of a '60s hit for a band called the Sir Douglas Quintet.

'What goes on in Mendocino?' I asked the bartender.

'Ain't nothin' there but hippies an' drugs,' he said. I left a couple of bucks on the bar, ran to the Buick and pointed her south.

Just outside of town I picked up a hitchhiker in a fringed buckskin jacket who squeezed under my surfboard and directed me to the Caspar Inn, where the joint was jumpin' to a very good three-piece band. The clientele ranged from ageing flower people in robes to hip cowboys and bikers in leather. I made some friends, and as night turned into morning we progressed to the Seagull Inn, where a shambling drunk of a man joined our group and began dunking cigarettes into a vial of hash oil and passing them around. I was introduced to Gene Clark, founding member of The Byrds, who had moved to Mendocino to overcome his drug and alcohol problems. That didn't seem to be going well.

Nursing a hangover, in the morning I drove to Marin County, north of San Francisco, and found my way to John Grissim's converted wine barrel home at Stinson Beach, where the former editor of *Tracks* limped out to greet me. (Clearly the Filipino faith healers had let him down.) Grissim had a supersized can of Foster's beer in one hand and a fat joint in the other.

'Jeez, mate,' he called in mock-Aussie, 'how ya bloody been, ya bastard?' I had never heard Grissim talk like this. I guessed he was excited to see me.

Grissim said that between Stinson and nearby Bolinas there was plenty of surf, though I noticed that his board, which stood decoratively between the fridge and a framed *Rolling Stone* cover, was not waxed. But we tried, and were rewarded with a few small sessions at a break out in front of the Bolinas Lagoon and at Stinson's main beach.

I liked the pace of life in West Marin, full of hippies and dreamers, and Grissim did a good job of introducing me around. In the main street of Bolinas there was a saloon on one side of the road called Scowly's and on the other, Smiley's. Behind the bar at Smiley's we found Jim Anderson, the least known of the London *Oz* obscenity defendants but a better known gay rights activist. Down on the beach I met the famous Mitchell brothers, Jim and Artie, who were then making a fortune out of porn films like *Behind the Green Door*. We went back to their beachside compound for drinks and the ubiquitous lines of coke. They seemed like fun guys—or so I thought at the time. Jim would later shoot his brother dead.

Grissim also spent a lot of time on the phone lining up interviews for me in San Francisco. The prize among these was a marathon three-hour session with the enigmatic Grace Slick of Jefferson Airplane. I walked into that one a little bit in awe, and walked out a little bit in love.

On my final weekend in the Bay Area, Grissim got me invited to the party of the year, at the crumbling North Beach mansion of the avant garde German-born artist Wilfried Sätty, famous for his psychedelic poster art and his illustration of the works of Edgar Allan Poe. There seemed to be bars set up in dark alcoves on every floor of the rambling house, and around each of them the star power was dazzling. In one corner Jack Nicholson juggled several drinks as he moved to a table; in another, Grace Slick was deep in earnest conversation with Paul Kantner; over there was the singer Dan Hicks and *Rolling Stone* publisher Jann Wenner. It was Disneyland for starstruck drooling dickheads. I tried to stay cool but just couldn't.

When most of the guests had drifted off, I found myself with Grissim and Sätty and a few others in a vast drawing room, full of overstuffed furniture and with dark art on the walls. When I enquired about his art, Sätty signed a collection called *Time Zone* for me. I still have it, with its scrawled pencil inscription, 'to Fil', and its Gothic panoramas, so many years after he, too, died young. Two men at the drawing room table, who turned out to be half of a San Francisco band called The Tubes, were pouring powder onto the glass top and arranging it in thick lines. I asked Sätty what it was, fearing it might be heroin. 'It's called green,' he said. 'It will take you to places you never dreamed existed.'

A Tube pushed a straw under my nose. I inhaled deeply and the night developed a mind of its own. I still had my copy of Sätty's book as I made my way through the grey dawn streets to my hotel, but that is all I can tell you.

I was running out of time. I ditched the Buick and flew to LA, hoping to renew my acquaintance with surfing. Two things were different about Southern California this time. One, the weather and the surf were a lot better in November than in the gloom of June. Two, the longboard was back. Less than a decade since the nine-foot plus malibu disappeared off the face of the earth, expunged by the shortboard design revolution led by Bob McTavish in Australia and Dick Brewer in Hawaii—a shift that sent many big manufacturers to the wall—the damned thing was back.

'Herbie Fletcher is making and surfing eight foot nose riders,' I wrote in the December 1976 issue of *Tracks*. 'Art Brewer at *Surfer* has a brand new double-ended Stretch ... and up at Pacific Palisades, yesterday's hero Lance Carson is back in business with nine foot hot doggers.'

Although it would take nearly another decade to reach Australia, California's longboard renaissance was laid out for me in all its glory when Denny Aaberg took me for a surf at Malibu on a very late-season south swell. Denny, who with brother Kemp was Malibu aristocracy, had been to Australia and we had many mutual friends. He was a writer too, and had written a hilarious and well-received article for *Tracks* called 'No-Pants Mance'. As we cruised around the First Point line-up, sneaking waves off shortboarders with our superior paddling speed, Denny commented, 'I think eventually there will be two accepted styles of surfing, shortboard and longboard side by side. The guys who were hot ten years ago will be stars all over again.'

If you'd said this at 54th Street in Newport Beach or at Narrabeen or Kirra in 1976, you would have had to wash your mouth out with soap (as my mum was wont to say), but Denny was proven right.

Denny had developed 'No-Pants Mance' into a screenplay that glorified surfing's golden years and lamented their passing, and the Hollywood producer and director John Milius—himself a one-time Malibu surfer—had purchased the rights. *Big Wednesday* was now in pre-production, and Denny arranged for me to interview Milius at Burbank Studios. I wrote in *Tracks*:

> I found Milius in a plush director's office going through the final draft of the script with Denny Aaberg. The walls of the air-conditioned suite were lined with a curious blend of culture symbols: stuffed bears and hunting trophies and faded photographs of great days at Malibu in the 1960s. Milius himself looked a little like Sean Connery in *The Wind and the Lion* (a recent Milius film) ... he played menacingly with a paper knife while we talked.

Milius was a big man with a penchant for a grand gesture and grandiose turns of phrase. Waving his stogie around, his feet on the desk,

Milius (centre with beard) with cast and extras during Big Wednesday shoot, 1977. (Photo courtesy Peter Townend, who is on Milius's left)

the afternoon sun filtering through the window and catching the smoke in blue shafts, he said, 'This is probably the most personal film I will ever make. This is surfing's *How Green Was My Valley*—the loss of an aristocracy, the end of an era.'

John Milius may have been overcooking the egg, particularly in light of *Big Wednesday*'s mediocre box office when it was released in 1978, but it did speak to my generation of surfers, and to all those who have followed. It's still surfing's leading cult classic today.

Mary Camarda's romance with Dennis Hopper was over and she was living in West Los Angeles at La Cienega. I stayed for a few days and was amazed at her connections. She was another John Grissim! I found myself sitting four tables from the stage at the Troubador Club on Waylon Jennings' opening night, courtesy of *Billboard Magazine*. The back of my ticket read 'Unlimited free drinks'.

While staying with Mary I received a phone call from Simonne Renvoize in the *Tracks* office, relaying bad news. The pioneer surf film-maker and publisher Bob Evans had died suddenly of a brain haemorrhage in Florida while roadshowing his movie, *Drouyn and Friends*. He was forty-seven. When Stephen Cooney and I rented together in Whale Beach, 'Evo' was our neighbour, and I dated his kids' nanny. We became friends, frequently sharing an evening scotch on his verandah. I was at the media preview of *Drouyn*, which Evo believed was his best work, and celebrated with him and Peter Drouyn, the temperamental but hugely entertaining subject of the film, into the wee hours. I was devastated.

As an afterthought, Simonne said, 'Oh, and Albe has sold *Tracks*.'

'He's fucking what?'

But he had, to an English publisher named Philip Mason, a stuttering dandy of a man who in those days bore a passing resemblance to the singer Bryan Ferry, and dressed the part. Philip published *Rock Australia Magazine (RAM)*—where my Grace Slick interview was published—and was looking to create a stable of youth publications. I had no right to, but I felt slighted that Albe hadn't consulted me before the deal was done. I felt like he'd thrown us to the wolves. Overnight we'd gone from a boss who was a laid-back surfer to one who was an ambitious businessman with one eye forever on the budget. I wondered if *Tracks* would survive.

CHAPTER TWENTY-THREE

NORTH SHORE

I flew out for Hawaii on election day, Jimmy Carter against the incumbent Gerald Ford, who had taken over mid-term when Nixon was impeached. It seemed a terrible choice, between a plodding Republican vice-president who was clearly out of his depth in the Oval Office, and a homespun Southern Baptist Democrat, but compared with what was to come in American politics, this was a win/win situation.

I'm sure there were television screens all over airports by the mid-'70s, but I have a distinct memory from that day of seeing men—I only remember men—hurrying across the terminal at LAX with transistor radios to their ears, getting exit polls or early results from back east. Election fever was much less evident in Honolulu, particularly when I arrived in the early evening at the Kuilima Resort Hotel on the North Shore and found a group of worried Australian surfers huddled around a bank of phones in a corner of the lobby, trying to deal with their own political crisis.

Paul Neilsen was on the phone with Eddie Aikau, the shining star of Oahu's leading surf dynasty, trying to organise a 'peace' meeting to stop further threats of violence against the Australians. I knew that there had been a lot of ill feeling among the Hawaiians over what they regarded as the 'disrespectful' behaviour in the surf of some of the top Australian professionals, particularly Rabbit Bartholomew and the big West Australian Ian Cairns, both of whom had added insult to injury by being less than diplomatic about their superior surfing skills in the surf media. Just before coming to Hawaii, Cairns had formed, with Peter Townend and Mark Warren, a promotional troupe called the Bronzed Aussies, which was also seen by the Hawaiians as confrontational.

While we waited for Neilsen to get off the phone, Cairns and Rabbit filled me in on the recent backstory. Rabbit had been the first to arrive, in mid-October, and was viciously attacked in the water on his first session at Sunset Beach. The attacker, a prominent member of the Hawaiian Hui Nalu, or Black Shorts club, finished the job on the beach, leaving Bartholomew bruised, battered and in fear for his life. He lived in hiding in bushland near the beach for a few nights, before seeking refuge in the secure enclave of the Kuilima condominiums. Another Australian surfer received thirteen stitches in the face after an attack at a North Shore restaurant, and Cairns had been subjected to verbal threats of violence since arriving.

Perhaps sensing the air of unreality that I was feeling, Rabbit looked me in the eye and said, 'Kanga (Cairns) and I are sleeping with baseball bats under the bed. It's that fucking serious!'

Paul Neilsen hung the receiver in its cradle and said, 'Crisis meeting here tomorrow night at seven, Eddie's going to chair it. Let's get a drink.'

Over dinner that night I learned that Eddie Aikau had taken it upon himself to visit the Australians the previous day at their condo hideaway to warn them that the situation had gotten out of hand, that the threats were now being issued by underworld elements who had little to do with surfing but liked kicking *haole* (white man) butt. The threats are real, was Eddie's message.

The crisis meeting at the Kuilima was held in a small and crowded meeting room on the hotel's seaward wing. Eddie Aikau and his younger brother Clyde took the top table, with Mark Richards sitting like a deer in the headlights between them, bookended by Aikaus. The young Newcastle surfer, who was becoming a big enough surf star now to be known by his initials, MR, stared resolutely at a spot on the back wall of the meeting room while the Aikau brothers pointed at all of us—bad Aussies (Rabbit wasn't there, still in hiding)—and then to MR—good Aussie. None of us had any respect, Eddie said. 'Rabbits and Ians in particular, got no respeck, but dis guy Mark Richard, he got respeck.'

The Aikaus meant well—they really did want to prevent further violence—but it all seemed so petty and stupid to me, like a bad B-grade movie. Respect (or 'respeck') was, and still is, code for localism—nothing more or less—but it was underwritten by a century of no respeck that began when the *haole* planters and offspring of missionaries uprooted the Hawaiian royals and installed military rule and ultimately a government led by one of their own. In the eyes of many old-school Hawaiians, their culture had been in decline ever since, and a bunch of foul-mouthed young *haoles* colonising the sport of the Hawaiian kings was further evidence of this.

The only thing wrong with this interpretation of history was that the people making it were themselves among the greatest enemies of Hawaiian culture, being the conduits of bad drugs, cheap guns and racist ideas to impressionable young minds in the poorest parts of town (Honolulu) and Oahu's Westside. The surfing dynasties like the Aikaus and the Keaulanas knew only too well that the lunatics were suddenly running the asylum, and when I look back on it now, having studied Hawaiian history and become friends with both Eddie (until his tragic death at sea in 1978) and Clyde, and the Keaulanas of Makaha, I see that strange and spooky meeting as a measure of their genuine concern.

There was no further violence that winter, although there were some tense moments at Sunset a few days later when it looked like Australian rookie Bruce Raymond was going to beat Hawaiian veteran (he was thirty-one) Barry Kanaiaupuni in the final of the season-opening Pro Class Trials. The Hawaiians in the gallery on organiser Bernie Baker's back lawn went silent for a while, but when BK prevailed, they started happily chanting, 'He's Hawaiian, he's Hawaiian!' We were so relieved we joined in.

Aussie camp at Bernie Baker's house, Sunset Beach, 1976. (Photo Jeff Divine)

North Shore

There was also a new policy from Lightning Bolt, then the world's biggest surfboard brand, on supplying the top Australian pros with 'comped' boards. It had been considered good business for a couple of seasons to supply the best surfers with boards to guarantee that the Bolt logo appeared in every movie and every magazine cover. Suddenly the Australians were being told they had to pay $200 a board like mere mortals. Peter Townend and I drove into town to confront Lightning Bolt boss Jack Shipley about this. Shipley, a big and normally affable man, looked embarrassed. He said, 'I don't like to treat you guys this way, but, you know, I gotta live here, so that's the way it is.'

PT and I pulled up at Sunset Beach on a smaller day. He started to get boards out and prepare to surf. I wasn't very keen at all. It might have been smaller than previous days but there was still a big fat peak moving around unpredictably out there in the ocean—and what if some local knew who I was and didn't like something I'd written!

'Jarratt, you need to get out there and experience what it's like in the line-up. If something happens, I've got your back.' This wasn't terribly reassuring. PT had proven himself in huge waves in recent years, but not in huge brawls. He was smaller than me! But we paddled out together and after a couple of shoulder hops my confidence began to build and

Peter Townend, Rocky Point, 1976. (Photo Dan Merkel)

I moved onto the peak, snuck a few and enjoyed the session. Nobody welcomed me to Sunset or waved me into a ride, but no-one gave me the stink-eye either.

That Peter Townend would take the time to tutor me at Sunset was indicative of the relationship that had formed between us, even as the magazine I edited was taking pot shots at his dream team, the Bronzed Aussies. Of the three original Bronzed Aussies—the one who found them the gold jumpsuits and insisted they wear them, for god's sake— PT was the only one who believed that all publicity was good publicity. He was also slyly amused by my numerous (and often cruel) piss-takes.

A few years ago a friend from Los Angeles, filmmaker, longboarder and bon vivant Takuji Masuda flew me to Hawaii so he could film me wandering around the grounds of what used to be the Kuilima (now the Turtle Bay Resort) trying to look pensive and nostalgic (perhaps) for the good old days. Later, we spent hours at musician Jack Johnson's home studio near Log Cabins while I read parts of my January 1977 profile of a man named Bunker Spreckels into a microphone.

All this was for a feature documentary called *Bunker 77*. For me it was pretty weird shit. I hadn't really thought much about my brief interface with Bunker for decades, but I was intrigued by Tak's near-obsessive interest in a man who accomplished very little in his life and was dead not long after my friend Tak was born. But Takuji Masuda was by no means the only surf culture vulture to have become besotted with the short and murky life of Clark Gable's stepson and heir to the vast Spreckels sugar fortune.

I wasn't a member of the Bunker fan club that season on the North Shore, but I had certainly heard about him, courtesy of *Surfer* magazine's coverage of his adventures in Africa with Art Brewer and Rory Russell, and some late-night storytelling by Rory himself, the fun-loving heir apparent to 'Mr Pipeline', Gerry Lopez. The word was that Bunker, this trust fund kid who at twenty-seven was just a couple of years older than me, was seriously bent, but likeable. Within his intimate circle he was known as 'The Player'.

'He's your kind of guy,' Rory told me when I said I wanted an introduction. Like everyone else in the North Shore surf scene, I was intrigued by a man who often described himself as the 'master of divine decadence', and who was actually an able and innovative surfer, despite all the late nights.

If he was my kind of guy, he was better at it than I was, I thought as I watched Bunker sitting on the roof of his Mercedes Sports, fondling a gorgeous, long-legged woman in a brown one-piece. The girl stroked his moustache ends while he blew cigarette smoke in her face and ashed on the hood of the Merc. True love.

I took a deep breath, sidled up and introduced myself, telling him I was a friend of Rory Russell. He was a bit aloof and monosyllabic at first, but he eventually slid down to ground level, offered a limp handshake and invited me to visit him at his luxurious cabana at the Kuilima the following afternoon.

When I showed up the next day, the gorgeous girlfriend was sprawled on a daybed, smoking a cigarette in a dainty holder, which she pointed in

Bunker Spreckels article, *Tracks*, 1977. (Photo Gary Terrell)

the direction of the stairs. As I started upstairs, the pro skater Tony 'Mad Dog' Alva came bounding down, pumped my hand and told me *Tracks* was his favourite surf magazine. He was talking fast and sweating profusely despite the air conditioning. I had a fair idea what that meant. I followed him up the stairs to Bunker's chamber of horrors.

Bunker sat in the middle of the man cave fondling a dildo. He wore a silk headscarf, a Thai silk bathrobe and a pair of martial arts pants with the string drawn tight over a soft little gut. All around him were surfboards, workout weights and sex toys. 'The whole male thing,' he explained.

Over the next few hours, and into the next few days I was drawn into the spider web world of the self-styled 'master of divine decadence'. The experience had its pleasurable moments but it was all too weird for a kid from Wollongong. I helped play out The Player's slightly sicko fantasies in print, while trying to distance myself from where he was going with it. It was only ever going to end badly.

The last time I saw Bunker was at the bar of the Kuilima in early December, just before I flew home. We drank a few Cuba Libres, but our session was terminated by The Player getting verbally assaulted by a drunken surfer. Apparently this was a frequent occurrence, although I hadn't seen it. Bunker didn't hit the guy, he excused himself politely, leaving the drunk lurching and muttering behind my shoulder. He returned a minute or two later with the security manager of the hotel, who removed the offender quickly and quietly. As the guy was strong-armed out, Bunker leaned in to him and whispered menacingly, 'Next time I'll have to hurt you.'

Less than a month later Bunker Spreckels was found dead in his cabana. I was saddened by the news. He was an intriguing fellow, but Rory had been wrong—he wasn't my kind of guy.

CHAPTER TWENTY-FOUR

THE WAVE GAME

Jackie and I were in love, in that first wonderful bloom of romance when you just can't get enough of each other. Technically, I was still living across the street with Paul and Simonne, but I spent most nights at Jackie's comfortable old renter, baby Sophie and Sol close by, behind thin curtains.

I gave Alan McGirvan, the breakfast announcer on 2JJ, a new number to call in the unlikely event that I failed to phone in my surf report on time. This had unforeseen consequences almost immediately. While I was sleeping off a big one, Jackie answered the phone.

Romancing Jackie in a quiet corner at a Whale Beach party, 1977.

'Ah, that must be the new Mrs Jarratt,' gushed the always smarmy McGirvan.

'Well, not exactly,' she replied. 'The boys were laying out the last pages of the magazine until late, and then I guess they celebrated with a few hundred drinks. I can't wake him up.'

'I see,' said McGirvan. 'So how's the surf looking?'

She peered out the window across the length of Whale Beach. 'Well, it looks okay to me, but I don't surf.'

And so it went. As soon as she'd hung up from McGirvan, the phone started to ring off the hook, with friends telling her she'd just made her radio debut. McGirvan had gone live to air with the whole conversation. It didn't look good for me, but my whole radio act was starting to come apart anyway. Tony Edwards had been told by a doctor that his pig voice was destroying his larynx, so it was decided that Captain Goodvibes would only speak once a week, on the new Friday night surf show, to be hosted by Holger Brockman with me playing straight man to The Pig of Steel again.

At the time the station had a promotional slogan (used in its *Tracks* advertising), 'Go to bed with Holger Brockman and wake up with Alan McGirvan', which was a frightening thought for 2JJ's many groupies. Although they both came from commercial radio, Holger (or Bill Drake, as he'd been Anglicised at 2SM) was everything Alan was not. He was a bearded longhair with sleepy eyes and a laid-back patter that suggested he was stoned most of the time, though this turned out to be not quite the case.

For the first live surf show, I organised an all-star cast that included pro surfer and surfboard designer Terry Fitzgerald and the legendary Nat Young. As we went over the loose script in the green room, Nat pulled out a huge number and lit up. By showtime we were off our faces.

Inside the studio as we counted down to the start of the two-hour program, Nat lit another bunger and handed it to Holger, who took it, stared at it while he read the introduction, then went to a record and took an almighty toke. The script was out the window almost immediately. I have no recollection of what we talked about, but I remember we all thought it was both hilarious and hilariously entertaining for the listeners. Listening from home, station manager Marius Webb apparently didn't share this view. There was a muted phone on the corner of the console inside the studio, which was flashing green in Holger's face, but he didn't see it. He was too busy trying to stay conscious. Finally, a message was conveyed via the night duty manager: get this rabble off air and play out the time slot with music.

The Friday night surf show had lasted about forty-five minutes. It was out the door, and my radio career went with it.

My new boss at *Tracks*, Philip Mason, turned out to be not such a bad guy. We didn't have a lot in common, but we bonded over a mutual love of magazines and cricket. He was the antithesis of a surfer, but in a way that was a good thing. Apart from controlling the purse strings (which suddenly got very tight) he left us to our own devices at Whale Beach, although I did have to report our progress about once a week at the Glebe office of his company, Soundtracts.

The only real editorial interference was a new policy of integrating his staff across different publications. Suddenly I was contributing to *RAM* magazine, and *RAM* was supplying *Tracks* with music articles. When Philip and his business partner, Barry Stewart, started a third publication, *Ragtimes*, I found myself occasionally writing about fashion too, which never sat well.

I made Philip promise that he would never move *Tracks* into the city. 'My staff would all quit and the magazine would lose its unique character,' I said in a prepared speech. He humoured me for the moment, although I suspected there were a couple of staff members he would like to see leave. There was certainly no love lost between Philip and Frank Pithers, each regarding the other as being preposterously arrogant, but Frank had pre-empted a sacking by moving on from *Tracks* during the awkward courtship dance between Philip and Albe.

Professionally, Frank was far more interested in shooting high fashion (his girlfriend, Louise De Teliga, was a leading model) than he was in shooting waves, and his personal life had moved into rather dangerous territory. It was customary for all of us to get good and drunk on the final night of magazine production as we laid out the pages on cardboard art sheets and spread them around the floor of the cottage, so that we could literally 'walk' through the magazine from cover to cover. So when Frank threw up all over pages nine through thirteen, necessitating a late night redesign, I put it down to excessive drinking. But I soon discovered that this was a by-product of his increasing drug use. Frank was heading into a period that would distance him from his friends and yet eventually turn him around. Curiously, as he distanced himself from the magazine, and thus there was less chance of direct conflict between us, I found myself appreciating his natural intelligence and his dry wit. We were still a decade away from becoming friends, but the shift had begun.

In the final months of 1976, Paul Holmes and I had started to blood new photographers to take over from Frank, including Queensland-based Martin Tullemans, while locally we started using more of a talented young photographer called Richard Bailey, and a crazed kneeboarder turned photographer named Peter Crawford. Marty came with his own set of problems, and I didn't think he had Frank's clever eye, but he was the most enthusiastic photographer I'd ever worked with—nothing was too much trouble—and eventually he took over as staff photographer.

During the troubled Hawaiian pro season Peter Drouyn had announced the introduction of a new professional event for Queensland, to be sponsored by the Stubbies clothing brand, famous for its indestructible work shorts but now bringing out a range of truly horrible surf shorts. As contest director, Drouyn had adapted a controversial new two-man heat format pioneered by George Downing in Hawaii. Under Drouyn's rules the 'man-on-man' concept was more like gladiatorial combat than surfing. A month or so before the Stubbies Pro was scheduled, I flew to

With Peter Drouyn, Sunset Beach, 1976. (Photo Jeff Divine)

the Gold Coast to interview Drouyn about it. By now we'd socialised on several occasions, but we were not friends. I found him difficult and abrasive, but I always remembered Bob Evans' assessment of him, when I'd had the temerity to suggest that Peter was a little bit too old and paunchy to be the star of his movie. He'd said, 'Never underestimate Drouyn. He's sensitive, he's colourful, he's slightly crazy and he's guts-up. I see in him everything I love about surfing.'

We met for lunch at the old Surfers Paradise Beer Garden and after about three beers and thirty questions, Drouyn became very animated. 'There's got to be a blow thrown. If surfing is going to progress, there must be physical contact.'

I responded, 'You're not seriously suggesting that surfing should be a contact sport?'

Drouyn had spent a year at the National Institute of Dramatic Art. He ran his fingers through his long hair, took a swig of beer and clenched his fists. Then he spoke with real passion. 'Phil, it *can* be. It's the only way forward.'

Paul Holmes and I had decided to turn the Australian pro contest season into a surfing road trip. Surprisingly, Philip Mason agreed to fund our travels, but only with the provision that as well as producing a special issue of *Tracks*, we use the opportunity to create a 'one-shot' magazine about the birth of professional surfing. In the years since, *The Wave Game* has come to be regarded as the first 'book' about the pro sport, but at ninety-six pages and riddled with typos and ridiculous captions (Cooney and I on the midnight drunken layout shift), it is very much a magazine, never meant to stand the test of time. Still, back then I was happy enough to see it on the newsstands with my name on the cover and call it a book. Apart from co-authoring a collection of short stories called *The Adventures of Nemo and El Gato* in 1975, it was my first.

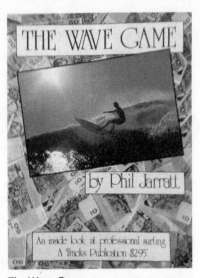

The Wave Game.

My coverage of the 1977 pro tour is mostly a disjointed ramble of bar stops and manic, alcohol-fuelled all-night drives, owing a considerable debt to Dr Hunter S. Thompson, but written with inferior drugs. Within it, however, are a few nuggets, like surfing Burleigh Cove in august company two days before the historic Stubbies contest began:

As I paddle around to the Cove, let me describe the first wave I see. Midget Farrelly and Terry Fitzgerald take off together and share the first section. Michael Ho drops in on his five-four, works it for a while and flicks off. Shaun Tomson takes the inside section and disappears inside, leaving the rest to Reno Abellira and Col Smith. That was just one wave!

It was a roll call of some of the most dynamic surfers of the day—and that was barely scratching the surface. Not only had Peter Drouyn invited an eclectic field of international surfers (as many chosen for their legendary free surfing as for their contest records), but the Stubbies Pro had also attracted a huge attendance of great surfers who hadn't made the cut, leading surfboard designers and shapers, industry figures, groupie girls in string bikinis, media hacks and, of course, drug dealers. Everyone wanted to share a piece of history, and maybe, just maybe, see a touch of gladiatorial combat on the waves. While this was Drouyn's dream, it was more like a nightmare for the Australian professional and amateur surfing associations, and they were determined to see it didn't happen.

The contest crew worked through the weekend erecting a giant hessian wall around Burleigh's beach park so they could charge admission (another first for the event). The top surfers began moving into apartments overlooking the surf. Paul Neilsen moved his entourage into the penthouse suite at Goodwin Towers. The O'Neill team of Shaun Tomson and Reno Abellira plus wives and girlfriends moved into even more salubrious digs further down the hill. Out on the park and in the water the excitement was palpable, far more so than at any surf event I had attended previously. A lot of it could be attributed to the Drouyn effect—a sense that if he was involved, anything could happen.

Although we shared the excitement on the park for most of the daylight hours, the *Tracks* budget didn't run to dress-circle digs. We were holed up in a backstreet rental at North Burleigh, splitting the rent with surfer/shaper Simon Anderson and his Narrabeen buddy, Dave West.

The Narrabeen boys seemed to spend most of their time on a rotating shift between couch and kitchen, either watching daytime television or cooking sausages and replenishing beer supplies. Anderson was a big, beefy fellow who played up his bogan image for the amusement of himself and his friends, but also hid behind it a sharp intellect, a wry and self-deprecating wit, and a fierce determination to win. Sitting in front of *Days of Our Lives*, bloating out on bangers and beer, Simon was, in his own way, preparing himself for the events ahead. I had never seen him look more determined.

The favourite for the Stubbies was, of course, Michael Peterson, at unbackable odds on his home turf. But unbeatable as he had been from 1973 through to the end of 1975, there were chinks in his armour now. Peterson watchers like myself were beginning to detect signs that Michael's fragile temperament and perpetual drug use were exacting a toll on his performance. While he'd won an event in New Zealand at the start of 1976, he'd failed at Bells (won for the first time by a foreign surfer, Jeff Hakman of Hawaii) and at the Coke Surfabout, which was taken out by Mark Richards. Richards was just one of the young surfers barking at his heels. Others included South Africa's Shaun Tomson, Simon Anderson, and the other 'Coolie Kids', reigning world champion Peter Townend and Rabbit Bartholomew, a style-master at Burleigh.

But then there was the new man-on-man format. If anyone could psyche out a single competitor, it was Michael Peterson. The disappearances moments before the heat, the weird looks, the manic paddling up and down the point, the shrill whistle from up the line: 'Comin' through, chine.' As drug-fucked as he seemed, sitting by the brick wall of the amenities block with Hawaiian Owl Chapman, Peterson could not be written off.

The mayor of the Gold Coast, Sir Bruce Small, a shrivelled little man in Bermuda shorts and socks who had made a fortune selling Malvern Star bicycles and canal estates, threw a reception for the surfers. Paul and Rick Neilsen wore dress slacks, Hawaiian shirts and puka shell necklaces. Eddie and Clyde Aikau wore faded beach boy singlets and thongs. Michael Peterson didn't show. Later, when we arrived at the Southport Yacht Club on the invitation of Stubbies boss Brian Calvert, the sponsor had to have a quiet word with committee members to get a temporary suspension of dress code for the Hawaiians. The reward was a sunset singalong of all the old beach boy favourites, Clyde taking the lead with his powerful, true voice and amazing range. Having traded violent threats just a few months earlier, the Hawaiians and Australians were now bonded in the spirit of aloha and a haze of XXXX beer.

On the last stinking hot day of a memorable week, Burleigh was close to the best I've ever seen it. Long lines of stand-up barrels pitched endlessly over the sharp rocks. The standard of surfing matched the quality of the waves, which peaked during the semi-finals. Peterson versus Rabbit, the Coolie duel from hell, was extraordinary, two surfers who knew the wave so well, positioning perfectly, even arrogantly, and emerging from tube after tube. Richards versus Tomson was more one-sided, with Mark swooping enough to join Peterson in the final.

None of us knew it, but this would be Michael Peterson's last world-rated final. Within a year he would be off the tour, within two off the radar, within three off the planet. So I'm glad I was there to see this performance. The barrels gone with the rising onshore wind, Michael had to bludgeon his way through sections, his hand jive getting more frantic with each wave. When they called him to the presentation podium, there was no response. I was standing next to his mum, Joan, who suggested that he might have gone home, exhausted, and that she was happy to accept the cheque. The officials were having none of it.

Lord Blears announces MP the winner, Stubbies 1977. (Photo Dan Merkel)

Then there he was, shuffling through the crowd in aviator sunglasses, a brown striped T-shirt with two small holes under the left armpit, a tattered pair of jeans and bare feet. He looked slightly embarrassed by the presence of two bikini girls wearing sashes. The former heavyweight wrestling champion, Lord Tally Ho Blears, introduced him as 'Mr Cool in the water but Mr Nervous on the land'. Michael squirmed, muttered something monosyllabic, accepted an empty envelope and shuffled towards the car park.

That was how he played it, and how he ended it. Well, almost. There was one last shining moment in international competition for Michael, but unfortunately it took place on a cold, bleak afternoon at a break called Express Point in front of about thirty people.

The Alan Oke Memorial had made its debut on Victoria's Phillip Island the previous year as a tribute to a local surfer. In 1977 it was picked up as a spoiler for the Rip Curl Bells Pro by the rival wetsuit company O'Neill, and held the week before Bells. The Rip Curl founders were furious.

Holmes and I drove the *Tracks* fire engine at breakneck speed all night across backroads Australia, with our passenger, Bob Pearson from Santa Cruz, screaming at us from the back seat to stop speeding, stop drinking, stop smoking! After a flat tyre at Narrandera and a fender bender in outer Melbourne, we missed the Oke opening party by an hour and twenty minutes.

Pearson was furious. 'You guys drove like maniacs halfway across the country for a free drink!' Pearson had been my roommate in Bali a couple of years earlier, and even decades later, after his Pearson Arrow Surfboards had become one of America's most respected brands, he was still telling two stories against me—something about a sea snake and a bottle of beer in Bali, and that beer-soaked dash to Phillip Island.

The contest was an on-again, off-again affair in gnarly weather—even another Skyhooks gig in a paddock couldn't lift the vibe—but it finally got to quarter finals, called on late in the afternoon when the rain stopped and Express Point suddenly lit up with groomed grey double-overhead grinders across a slab of rock.

Our slightly decadent and totally stupid dash south paled into insignificance when compared with that of Michael Peterson and his co-conspirator Owl Chapman, who arrived three days late and somewhat wasted after spending at least one night in a country lock-up. (No-one could get the full story out of their gibberish.) Now I found myself lying in the long grass overlooking the break, trying to stay out of the wind, with Owl, MP and Rabbit Bartholomew. Joints were passed around. MP and Owl giggled about nothing. Every time a big set rolled over the slab, Michael would murmur, 'Heavy shit, man,' and then giggle again.

Suddenly Rabbit was standing in the long grass, shaking Michael by the shoulders. 'They're calling your heat, Mick! Your heat! You're on, man, you gotta get your singlet.' MP passed the scoob to Owl. 'Huh, what?' Exasperated, Rabbit said, 'Listen. They're calling your name. That's you. You're in a heat. Now. Walk, don't run, along the cliff and get your shirt.' Now Michael stood up. Seeing him emerge from the grass, the commentator called him again. 'Michael Peterson, your heat starts in two minutes. Please pick up the white singlet.'

Michael was smiling now. 'Hey, that's me, that's my name. Cool!' He sauntered along the cliff towards the marshals.

MP gave the others at least a five-minute start. Even when he was in the line-up he let a couple of sets go by. Then a mother of a set started marching towards the slab. He let the first one go and swung on the second. Air drop, still there. The water sucked up the face ready to spit. MP threw an arm into the face and applied the brakes, disappearing inside a mutant double-up. Over and over, he set it up and let it eat him. He only made two waves but it was enough to win.

I can't remember what happened in the semis, but Michael didn't make the final. Probably a no-show. Pressing engagement with a man in a back alley.

At Bells I broke. A month on the road already and I was missing my true love. I flew her down to join me, and waited at Tullamarine to pick her up on a wild and wet night. In a bar I watched Rory Russell do a guest spot on the *Don Lane Show*. He explained how you could die riding Pipeline, and then Don and Bert Newton demonstrated how you could die on TV simulating surfing. We were supposed to be joining Rory at a city nightclub after the show, but the flights were hideously delayed, so I called the club.

'Hello, I'm meant to be meeting a world champion surfer there tonight. He's from Hawaii and his name is Rory Russell. I'm delayed at the airport and I'm not going to make it. Is there any way you could get that message to Mr Russell?'

'I doubt we can do that sir, unless we can eyeball him. Would he be wearing a team uniform by any chance?'

'He was just on the *Don Lane Show*, for chrissakes! Can't you page him?'

I hung up. Jackie's plane had landed. I grabbed her and drove as fast as I could to our renter at Anglesea.

Simon Anderson had to surf through the qualifying trials to the main event at Bells, but once there he whipped the field, in good surf and bad.

Back in Sydney, the Coke Surfabout was plagued with lack of surf, but Simon, despite his size, was still in the hunt when the event went into hiatus waiting for waves. On one such morning at Narrabeen, I chatted with 'Snow' McAlister, an Australian surfboard champion of the '20s who still rode waves on a surf ski. I asked him who he favoured to win the Surfabout.

'Oh, Simon Anderson's got as good a chance as any, don't you reckon? He knows these waves and he rides his own surfboards beautifully.'

Snow was prescient. Simon took two on the trot and was also named Australian Professional Surfing Champion for 1977. I liked Simon a lot and was thrilled for him. At the presentation I whispered that *Tracks* might throw a sausage sizzle in his honour. He said with a straight bat, 'I'm trying to give them up, Phil.'

We had finished our book, *The Wave Game*, but we needed a cover. My mad mate Peter Crawford said we needed a picture of Simon Anderson, who had pocketed almost ten grand from the Australian season, backed by stacks of money. Peter already had a nice, backlit picture of Simon at Dee Why Point, so I phoned the manager at the Avalon branch of the Commonwealth Bank and asked if we could throw a bunch of money around in a locked room and photograph it. To my great surprise he said yes.

Crawford and I were given $50,000 and locked in a room. While I threw the notes in the air, he photographed them landing. And that was the cover. It occurred to both of us that if there was a back exit we should load up and take it. It also occurred to both of us that we were playing with far more money than any professional surfer would see that year, or for years to come. But it was a start.

CHAPTER TWENTY-FIVE

Empty Uluwatu, 1975. (Photo Dick Hoole)

GRANDSTAND

I took Jackie to Bali that year, just as soon as *The Wave Game* had gone to the printer. It was her first time, and if she had misgivings when I asked her to throw a leg over and straddle the nose of my board for the motorbike ride out to Uluwatu, they were nothing compared with her immediate reaction to the chant that went up as we passed by the Windro family compound on the long walk in to the Suliban surf break. 'Pilip's got new darling,' the village kids chanted, 'Pilip's got new darling!' I was embarrassed, but also rather pleased that I meant enough in their lives for them to have remembered my name. Jackie, to her eternal credit, came to see it as hilarious.

I loved those kids and their long memories, and stayed close to them through the years as they began to graduate from board carriers to board riders, and we loaned them our boards to ride foamies in front of the cave at mid-tide. We watched them grow up, only losing contact when it all grew so big, so soon. My friend Dick Hoole likes to say, 'If we discover paradise again in the next life, we will *not* teach the locals to surf!' But I cherish those years, despite the consequences.

When my filmer friend Shaun Cairns and I were making a short film to promote my book, *Bali Heaven and Hell*, almost forty years later, we tracked down the Windro family compound amidst the high-end villa cluster-fuck that is Uluwatu today, and the wife of my regular board carrier, Wayan Windro. Wayan was away working somewhere. I showed her early photos taken at the compound by Dick Hoole and she caressed the screen of my Mac at every recognition of family or friends. Despite the external changes to the Bukit Peninsula, and the enormous wealth that some have reaped, life is essentially unchanged for these villagers, hidden beyond the villa walls.

Travelling overland to Yogyakarta had been a highlight of my first Bali trip in 1974, and I wanted Jackie to experience that. I also now had media mates working out of Jakarta, so we extended our trip to the capital. The night bus to Yogya was scarier than I remembered, with overladen trucks constantly forcing us to the edge of the narrow roads. But Yogya was still a charming hippy village where we spent a leisurely couple of days poking around the antique shops.

Before we left Bali I had asked our neighbours at Arena Bungalows if anyone knew a good, cheapish hotel in Jakarta. 'Hotel Menteng,' said Meatballs, a surfing friend from Torquay. 'Cheap but charming.' He shot me a wink, the significance of which would only become apparent later. We took a taxi from the railway station and checked in at the tiny reception desk, beyond which a dissolute bunch of 'old Asia hands' were nursing their noonday beers. I noticed a sign above the door—'Hot Men Bar'. Then I noticed that along the far wall of the Hot Men Bar, hot Javanese women in tight skirts and ridiculous high heels sat in individual booths, each bearing a star sign.

Meatballs had tipped me into a brothel, but if he was laughing himself hoarse back in Bali, I was not, particularly after we were shown to our

The Windro compound board carriers, 1975. (Photo Dick Hoole)

windowless room, which was clearly meant to be used for an hour rather than a night. I looked at Jackie and shrugged. We were already late for a party at the ABC offices, with the best top-shelf booze in Indonesia supplied by the Australian Embassy. We would fix everything tomorrow. The hookers from the Hot Men Bar were on the prowl, grabbing my shirt as we came down the stairs. 'You hot man, mister?' We jumped into a waiting taxi.

The best top-shelf booze in Indonesia didn't seem to agree with me that night, and Jackie felt the same. My throat was dry and I felt dizzy and vaguely nauseous, so we excused ourselves relatively early. By the time we'd run the hooker gauntlet and thrown ourselves down on the creaky little bed, my head was pounding. By morning we were both in bad shape. We managed to keep down a slice of toast and a Coke and headed for the airport.

In those days, when electricity and refrigeration were very new in South Bali, no-one would dream of visiting a local doctor, and options for finding a Western medico were limited and expensive. We chartered a *bemo* to take us to the biggest hotel on the island, the grotesque Bali Beach Hotel at Sanur, for an appointment with the renowned Dutch doctor in residence. He checked us out, sent us out for blood tests and then declared, 'You both have either dengue fever or typhoid. If it is the former, you can recuperate here. If it is the latter, you will be flown to Australia immediately and placed in quarantine for three months. It is both dangerous and contagious. Come back in four days when I will have the results.'

This was the first time Jackie had left her children in the care of a friend while she travelled. The five weeks we had planned to be away was a stretch, but three months in quarantine! The days passed slowly and painfully as we awaited our verdict. Neither of us could bear to be outside a darkened room, so we lay on a bed, sweating, shivering, cold towels on our aching heads, eating a Vegemite jaffle a day and drinking a can of Coke.

'You have dengue fever,' said the Dutch doctor. 'You can relax and recover.' Easier said than done. When I finally felt strong enough to eat properly and move around, we rode out to the Bukit Peninsula and trekked along the cliff to surf the new spot called Padang Padang. I caught three or four waves and came in shivering in the heat of the day. I have lost a snapshot of two stick figures on the beach that day, but trust me when I say we looked like survivors of the Burma Railway.

Jackie recovering from dengue fever, Kuta, 1977.

I was starting to feel it was time to move on from *Tracks*. My tenure was coming up to four years. Paul Holmes was ready for a term in the chair and I knew Philip Mason would approve. I had a lot to be thankful for. During my time at the magazine I had learned much about my trade, and maybe even (eventually) a little humility, and I had made friends I would keep for life. My surfing friends were drawn from the best of our era, but I had also formed lasting relationships with many of the leading lights of the surf media and the fast-growing surf industry.

I felt connected, and I was confident I would be able to move back and forth as surfing grew. Steve Pezman and his new editor at *Surfer* in California, Jim Kempton, had already offered me a gig that would keep me at least partially in the surfing loop. Starting from the 1978 season, *Surfer* would fly me to Hawaii for a month and provide accommodation on the North Shore while I prepared the magazine's coverage of the IPS events and wrote enough profiles of leading surfers to see them through to the next season. This arrangement freed me up enough to pursue another dream, to publish my own magazine.

As my interest in *Tracks* had begun to wane, Philip Mason had involved me in other projects within his growing publishing empire, including editing a *Tracks*-style youth travel tabloid called *Detours*, under contract to Qantas. I felt I knew my way around a publishing operation well enough to start one, but I needed backers. I discussed with Mason my idea for a monthly all-sports tabloid based loosely on America's *Sports Illustrated* and he shocked me by suggesting we look at doing a joint venture. My concept was to marry intelligent coverage of traditional sports with the rapidly emerging action sports sector, which included surfing and its newer spin-offs skateboarding, snowboarding and windsurfing.

Philip and I shook hands on a development deal, I went off to make a 'dummy' issue we could sell to advertisers, and he went off to do his due diligence, which included a microscopic examination of the sales and advertising potential of multi-sports publications. As soon as I walked into his office a few weeks later, I knew it was bad news. He poured us both a scotch.

'M'boy,' he started. 'You have a wonderful vision for this publication but I'm afraid I can't share it. I don't think it can be financially viable.'

This from a guy who came to Australia as an executive of IPC Magazines, built his own publishing house on their dime, eventually sold it for megabucks, and then in retirement found a huge IPC superannuation entitlement while cleaning up his garage! Luck and business chops. Can't be beat. Why the fuck didn't I listen to him?

Dad, pretty chuffed that I'd come very close to actually working for Qantas at last, chucked $5000 at it. John Witzig, who had just come into an inheritance, matched it. I found the rest somewhere, and *Grandstand* hit the newsstands in March 1978 with a Peter Crawford underwater shot of a swimmer on the cover. The first edition was brilliant. We were broke by the third.

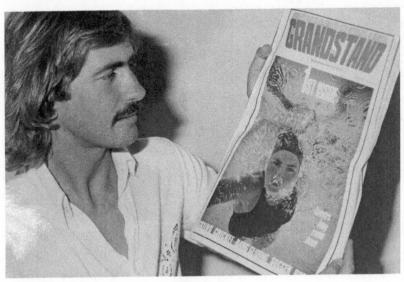

Me with the debut edition of *Grandstand*, 1978.

These were testing times. I remember flying to Melbourne to try to convince General Motors Holden to take the back page. When I was told no, I spat the dummy at the advertising agency and was escorted out. At this low point, I noticed a muscular pain spreading from my groin, accompanied by an angry rash. I had shingles, brought on by acute tension and only cured, after months of agony, by Peter Crawford's clever Chinese medicine man and acupuncturist Dean Rainer.

Dark clouds were gathering around my professional life but there was one shaft of bright sunlight getting through. Jackie was expecting our first child, due in July. I was thrilled at the prospect, horrified by the financial realities. Our publishing project couldn't pay me a wage, so when Mark Day, a friend from my News Limited days, asked me to profile surfing's current world champion, Shaun Tomson, for the new Australian edition of *Playboy*, I grabbed it with both hands. Shaun and I hadn't always seen eye to eye, particularly over the increasing spectre of apartheid hanging over sporting relations with South Africa—'People who don't live in South Africa are not in a position to tell us what is right and what is wrong,' he snarled when I interviewed him in 1975—but he had mellowed since then and I enjoyed the opportunity to hang out with him during the 1978 Coke Surfabout, being directed, for the first time, by my friend Holmes.

Sol and Sophie at Surfabout '78. Note the judges' panel for the world's richest surf contest in the background. (Photo Simonne Renvoize)

The Surfabout was also being filmed for a television series for the first time, under the direction of the Nine Network's young sports wizard David Hill, who had just revolutionised the coverage of cricket for his boss, Kerry Packer. 'Hilly' and I had never met before but we formed an instant bond (one that remains firm today). When he heard I was writing about Shaun for *Playboy*, he confided, 'Packer is throwing an absolute fortune at this thing. It's like he's just discovered tits. Don't just write an article, get a highly paid job!'

I don't know if it was coincidence or whether my name was mentioned in Kerry Packer's corridors of power, but just as the printer was pulling the pin on the next issue of *Grandstand* because I couldn't pay for the last, Mark Day phoned and offered me a staff writer position at *Australian Playboy*. The timing couldn't have been better. I got my first pay packet the day before our daughter, Samantha, was born.

Family shot with Soph and baby Sam, Whale Beach, 1979.

I was smitten from the start. She was such a cute, cheeky little thing, and she seemed to have real spirit very early on. She was my firstborn and, I admit, she owned a special piece of my heart. But Sophie, who was just turning three, had been part of my life since she was eleven months old. We were relieved to see that she welcomed the new arrival.

To be honest, I'd never been much of a *Playboy* or *Penthouse* kind of guy. I had no problem admiring photos of beautiful naked women, but since my patrol leader Max taught me how to masturbate on a Boy Scout outing, I don't think I ever sought help in that regard. If I ever bought a copy of the imported editions, I can attest it was for the articles. No-one ever believed that, of course. I was entering the wink, wink, nudge, nudge phase of my life, which would last far longer than I could ever have imagined. But I liked working for Mark Day, even though he was the quintessential tits-and-arse connoisseur—an editor who would greet you on return from an assignment not with, 'Is it a good story?' but with, 'Did you get a root?' And I liked the crew I worked with at *Playboy*, and sharing a few after-work beers with Mark and the Australian Consolidated Press lawyer, Malcolm Turnbull—the first of several future prime ministers and premiers I would rub shoulders with at Packer headquarters.

Playboy contents page photo.

Not that I was in the office much. Mark kept the assignments coming, mainly in the area of sport, drugs and youth culture. I flew to Melbourne and Canberra to report on the emergence of the Pot Party, then Mark thought it would be a good idea to travel the east coast of Australia and find out what had happened to all the Age of Aquarius hippies who had deserted mainstream society after the Nimbin festival in 1973. Mark was hoping we would find beautiful hairy-pitted women frolicking naked in every rainforest and wooded glen, and we didn't let him down entirely.

'We' was me and my now frequent partner in crime, Peter Crawford, the mad stoner kneeboarder turned photographer. Peter was an excellent surfer, a very good photographer and a hell of a joint roller. Unfortunately I crushed his fingers in the sliding door of the VW campervan we'd rented for the trip on the first afternoon.

'Whatever happened to the hippies?' was to be a two-parter (to justify our huge expenses) so we needed about ten thousand words and fifty good pictures, and we had three or four weeks to get them. Piece of piss. Our surfboards sat above the camera gear, ready for action. We studied the weather maps and what little swell information there was in those days, and planned our trip accordingly.

We scored the beginnings of a late winter easterly swell at Byron, between runs out to Nimbin and The Channon (where I found my old Sydney girlfriend Carole, now with flowers in her hair and kids at her waist), then caught its peak at Burleigh, and again at Noosa. When it kicked again, we headed north to a right point break that Peter had heard about. We reached the few fishing shacks and general store that made up Agnes Water in the late afternoon and rented a two-bunk shack on the grass above the beach. We surfed the point alone for a couple of hours. As the sun set, peacocks strode majestically around the camp.

I'd only been working for him for a few months, but Mark Day generously agreed to allow me a month off so I could cover the Hawaiian season for *Surfer*, on condition that I come home with a story for *Playboy* too. But my first North Shore season for *Surfer* wasn't exactly how we'd planned it. In the midst of preparation for the trip, Jackie had woken before dawn for no apparent reason, and gone to check on three-month-old Sammi. Her face was blue and she was emitting a weak little gurgle. Jackie woke our doctor, who told us to get to the hospital immediately. They called it arrested cot death. At the time the terminology didn't mean much to me, but I knew we had nearly lost our little girl that night.

CHAPTER TWENTY-SIX

ADVENTURES IN THE SKIN TRADE

'Oh my god! Is that a baby in that basket?' A slice of Middle Americana in a voluminous muu muu was hovering over our restaurant table in Waikiki. 'Oh, it is! Look, Marv, a baby in a basket! Isn't that just darling?'

This scene was repeated all over Oahu as I tracked down my interview subjects with lady, baby and bassinet in tow. I'd had my doubts, but it was fun, our first family holiday, and in a season of cocaine snowstorms in Hawaii, it kept me out of trouble. I interviewed a broad mix of Hawaiians, Californians and Australians, old school (like Gerry Lopez) and new (like Buzzy Kerbox, Bobby Owens, Buttons Kaluhiokalani), but one I didn't get to on that occasion was standing on the lawn of the *Surfer* house at Rocky Point at dawn when I got up to check the surf. He was taking photos of the beautiful early light, using a lens that looked bigger than him. I knew this muscular little guy, but not well.

'What's up, Tommy?'

I'd disturbed his reverie. He seemed embarrassed to have been caught taking photos when he should be surfing. 'Not much. Just checking where I'm going to surf.'

'Well, it's a beautiful day for it.'

Tom Carroll, aged eighteen, was putting his camera away in a bag. He looked up past me to the heavens and sighed, 'Every day here is a beautiful day.' Later that day he told Jackie he was going to be the world champion. Neither of us has had reason to doubt him since.

Soon after I arrived home from Hawaii I was putting in some desk time at the *Playboy* office when I got a phone call from a gruff-sounding

American. 'Huh, this is Murray. You Jarratt? Want to catch a beer?' It was mid-morning. Had the pubs even opened yet?

'I'm sorry, who is this?'

'Murray, Bill Murray. Got your number through Hunter Thompson. I'm in town two days. Let's go have a drink.'

Strangely enough, while I'd never met Hunter S. Thompson, the guru of gonzo, I knew who Bill Murray was—but only just. This was pre-*Ghostbusters* and Murray was chiefly famous for being the big, goofy guy on *Saturday Night Live*. How had Thompson had my number to pass on to Murray? I sensed John Grissim in the middle of this. I agreed to meet Bill Murray at the top floor lounge bar of the Boulevard Hotel, where he was staying, at eleven. When I arrived the bar was empty but for Murray, who was hunched over a bar stool dressed for a Sydney summer in a trucker cap and mismatched plaid shorts and aloha shirt. I noticed that he was onto his second bloody mary and had ripped a section of vinyl off the bar rest while he waited. There were no formalities, just a cock of the head, a slap on the shoulder, and he ordered two more bloody marys.

'Cheers,' he said. 'Don't normally drink in the morning, but hell, I'm on vacation and I'm still in character. That'll do for excuses.'

It transpired that Murray had just finished filming *Where the Buffalo Roam*, in which he played Hunter Thompson in a screenplay very loosely based on the gonzo classic *Fear and Loathing in Las Vegas*. He was now on his way to Bali to recuperate from six weeks of deranged method acting. *Buffalo* was savaged by critics on release and only later became a stoner cult classic. It would take a silly screenplay about ghosts to make Murray a household name. For now, he could move around Sydney unrecognised, which is what we had to do immediately, since the barman had noticed the damaged bar rest and asked us to leave. Bill gave the poor man an almighty spray before prancing out onto William Street as cars swerved and screeched to a halt to miss him while he hailed a cab, New York style.

It being Friday, the *Playboy* staff was lunching at the old Malaya restaurant on George Street, so we set off to join them, via a beer stop at a corner pub. Murray wanted coke, so I pulled half a gram out of my pocket and slipped it into his hand. When he came back from the bathroom there was very little left. He gulped his beer. 'That stuff's not very good. Can you get more?'

The Malaya was packed as usual, but the staff fussed around us and made space for two more chairs at Mark Day's long table. Food kept appearing in huge bowls and platters, wine sloshed from bottle to glass and conversation was a manic din, above which only Bill Murray could be heard. In the immortal words of Brother Buffett, some of it was magic, some of it tragic. Mark Day was not well pleased to be upstaged at his own table. When enough was too much, he summoned me to his end and said, 'Who is this yank prick again?' I told him. 'Well, I don't give a fuck who he is. He's a rude cunt and please get rid of him.'

In four hours we'd been asked to leave two establishments. Bill Murray's character comedown was going well. We adjourned to another pub where I made a few calls and got him hooked up for a couple of grams of coke. The dealer was a fan—he'd deliver anywhere if it meant meeting Bill Murray. I had a succession plan. When I got back to the bar Murray was picking a fight with a guy who looked like a sumo wrestler. It was ugly and getting worse. The minutes dragged by until the dealer arrived. Bill was in the bathroom with his goodies before I had a chance to say goodbye.

Mark Day was jumping ship. A Sydney printing company had won the license to publish an Australian edition of the rival *Penthouse* magazine and as founding editor he was putting together an editorial team, which he asked me to join at a vastly increased salary. At 54 Park Street there was hell to pay. *Playboy* was selling upwards of a quarter of a million copies a month. You didn't poach the top guy and escape the wrath of Kerry Packer. Day was allowed to say farewell to his staff (half of whom had already signed up to join him) before being escorted from the building. Then Packer's lieutenant, Trevor Kennedy, told us that the magazine was bigger than the man and that Mark had pretty much been a worthless piece of shit anyway.

Although *Penthouse* trailed *Playboy* by about a hundred thousand in the American market, it was catching up fast, its competitive advantage being its graphic photo spreads featuring close-ups of labia minora, or 'Gene Autry's saddle bags,' as Mark Day delicately referred to them. Mark had plenty of ideas about talking local celebrities into exposing themselves gynaecologically (including his first-issue scoop of Lillian Gasinskaya, 'the girl in the red bikini', who had made headlines by stowing away on a Russian ship and swimming ashore in Sydney Harbour to gain asylum), but the explicit nature of the photos put us on a collision course with the most conservative state censorship boards, those of Victoria and Queensland.

In the middle of my move from the gutter to the sewer of magazine journalism, so to speak, Jackie and I got married in the garden of the lovely old sandstone house we were renting at Palm Beach. Paul Holmes was the master of ceremonies (affecting a Cornish lighthouse keeper's accent, for no apparent reason), and Rennie Ellis and Peter Crawford were the official photographers. My *Playboy* colleague Carol Ashdown did the food, while her husband Doug, the folk singer, refused to sing a song. That great Australian sailor and bon vivant Sir James Hardy (who I had recently interviewed) supplied an enormous quantity of industrial-sized casks of wine, and my TV mate David Hill organised for Channel Nine's race caller, Johnny Tapp, to pause before the feature race at Rosehill to wish us all the best. As we all raced inside to watch this, Sol, now eight, guzzled up all the beer and wine leftovers he could find, becoming violently ill and thereby learning early that in alcohol, quality trumps quantity.

So it was the wedding that had everything, except that the groom left the next day for a honeymoon on his own. It was to set the pattern for much of our married life. The job always came first, and if the job sounded like fun, that was so much harder to take. In this case, I was going undercover as a barman/host on a game fishing mother ship off

Our garden wedding, Palm Beach, 1979.

Apres tennis on our honeymoon, Club Med, Noumea, 1979.

Cairns, the objective being to get the skinny on some of our captains of industry at play. (Jackie and I did have a belated honeymoon together, however, a couple of months later when I was offered a freebie at Club Med Noumea.)

Mark didn't stay at *Penthouse* very long. He confided in me that he and Owen Thomson, another News Limited crony, were negotiating to buy the *Melbourne Truth* newspaper, which dealt in anything but, and made a fortune in cash from classified advertising for sex workers. He appointed me deputy editor at *Penthouse* and began to groom me as his replacement.

My ascension to the editor's chair at *Penthouse* came with a dream salary, a company car and a parking spot under the building in Elizabeth Street. But it also brought me into much closer contact with the McWilliam family, who owned the company, and that was a mixed blessing. The patriarch, Old Bruce, was just a nuisance. Young Bruce, who ran the financial side of the business, was a nice guy but a terrible snob. With an increased salary, we had just bought our first home, a very modest cottage in the backblocks of Avalon with a backyard pan dunny, one of the last of its kind. When Young Bruce, who had been weekending at the family's Palm Beach mansion, picked me up for work one Monday, he took a long look at our cute house and then turned to me and said very seriously, 'Oh, we'll have to get you out of there.'

Peter McWilliam, known as 'Mouthy' to his mates, was the magazine's creative director, which mainly meant he got to hang around at the nude photo shoots. He was an ageing Double Bay Lothario who wore his blonde hair in a Robert Redford sweep and favoured cheesy cashmere sweaters, regardless of the weather. Much like everyone in the industry at that time, he was passionate about recreational drugs, and the *Penthouse* boardroom was often in lockdown while Mouthy entertained dubious friends.

When a particularly clinical issue of the magazine was banned in Queensland (not for the first time) and I had to front the censorship board to plead for leniency, Mouthy insisted on coming with me. We met at his room at Brisbane's Lennon's Hotel, where he was drinking champagne and indulging. I helped him out a little with both and we went off to face the board.

I was bad but Mouthy was worse, opening his mouth to speak and collapsing into a sneezing fit. At least he didn't have a nosebleed. The censors banned us for three issues.

I needed some waves in my life. Jackie and I were going to Hawaii, but first we had to go to California, where I was doing some work for Rip Curl, helping their new North American manager, Ron Grimes, form a marketing assault on O'Neill Wetsuits on their home turf. Our arsenal was a range of brightly coloured and brightly named (I hoped) wetsuits that reflected the values of different subsets of surfers. Dawn Patrol, for example, was aimed at adventure surfers and was slightly more subdued than the others. This style was worn by Wayne Lynch, while the near-neon Aggrolite, aimed at young competitive surfers, was worn by tearaways Tom Carroll and Cheyne Horan.

I found myself in California for the second presidential election in a row, this one seeming to have far more dire potential consequences. We were at John Grissim's wine vat for a few days. This is what I wrote:

The naked women in the cedar and redwood hot tub were bawling their eyes out. I wanted to reach across the sea of bubbles and offer a comforting embrace, but I wasn't sure how this would go down with my wife, who was just as naked but not as teary on my side of the tub. I also felt like telling them to get a grip, but I wasn't sure how that would go down either. Instead, we all sipped on long-stemmed glasses of white wine, snorted some cocaine from a silver plate as it did the rounds (being ever so careful not to drip bubbles) and tried to rise above the sheer horror of the moment.

It was about seven in the evening in California, three hours later in Washington DC, and here in the redwood forests of Marin County, north of San Francisco, word was filtering through the airwaves that *Bedtime for Bonzo* star and former California governor Ronald Reagan was going to be the next president of the United States. Although a Reagan victory had never been regarded as a slam dunk, the pundits had been calling it for several weeks as poor old Jimmy Carter got clobbered over the Iran hostage crisis and the fact that he'd told *Playboy* that he had lust in his heart. Shit, who hasn't? But the writing was on the wall when we stopped for beers at the Sand Dollar Inn earlier in the afternoon and saw the exit polls on the TV above the bar.

So the girls had come back to our host's converted wine vat in the hills, pulled out the drugs and the wine, stripped off, jumped in the tub and started wailing. 'Oh my god, there's gonna be a war for sure,' sobbed one of them.

Pets In Paradise cast and crew, Fiji, 1981. (Photo Rennie Ellis)

I couldn't understand the extent of their angst over Reagan—we were living through the Fraser years at the time and surviving—but I liked their style. I wonder how many naked women wailed in their hot tubs over President Trump.

Early season Hawaii was surprisingly mellow for swell, with light Kona winds and occasional showers, and I found myself getting plenty of uncrowded waves on the windward side. Every session spent on those unnamed reefs, peering down at the coral as I rode over it, made me sad that I had succumbed to the suit and tie. I wasn't even much of a weekend warrior anymore. Only when I surfed did I realise how much I missed it.

Something else was concerning me about the direction of my career in the flesh trade. Being the editor of a 'girlie' magazine was a lot different to being a feature writer. I was frequently in the spotlight (which I loved), but for all the wrong reasons. When Kristin Williamson, the journalist wife of playwright David, covered our tawdry 'Pet of the Year' presentation function for the *National Times* I was appalled by what she wrote, yet when I read it now I find it entirely accurate and full of wry wit. Certainly it was kinder to its subjects than most of what I had written in my *Tracks* days.

I think the problem was that I didn't much like what I did or who I was becoming. One day the infamous Northern Beaches bruiser and private detective Tim Bristow (a passing acquaintance) barged into my office without an appointment, flung a couple of black-and-white nude prints onto my desk and suggested, in the nicest possible way, that I might like to make the girl a 'Pet of the Month'. Despite the nature of the photographs we ran, we were trying to attract 'wholesome' girls—TV soapie starlets and junior models, rather than hookers—so I told Tim I'd have to meet the girl and get her to do some test shots before deciding.

The day she came in to see me, we were in the market for a new house (Young Bruce had won that battle). I was concluding a phone conversation with my wife as the prospective Pet walked in. Jackie had found a property she thought was perfect. My final words were, 'Well, let's have a look at it.' By the time I'd swivelled my chair around the girl had stepped out of her dress and stood fully naked in front of me, pouting and projecting her pelvis. I told this true story at dinner parties for years, but despite its relative innocence (she didn't get the photo spread, I didn't get beaten up), it's more sad and desperate than funny, and I don't just mean for the girl.

The truth was, the money was making up for a few ill-advised years, but the toll it was taking on our marriage and our children was clear to everyone but me.

Rennie Ellis had become a major contributor to *Penthouse* and he had flown up from Melbourne to pitch me an idea. Over lunch at Sydney's then 'it' restaurant, You and Me, where you were served a thumbnail of food on a vast white plate and were expected to rave about it, he revealed his cunning plan. We would take the *Penthouse* Pets to a tropical island paradise and make a short feature film. I would produce, while he would direct, and put a camera crew together. Rennie was no longer in the travel game, but as it happened I'd become friendly with Paul Glynn, the principal of an agency called Travel Scene, who was then travel agent to the surf stars. I said I'd ask Glynn to find us a suitable location.

'But there's only one way I'm going to get approval for this,' I told Rennie. 'Mouthy will have to come.'

'He can be a camera assistant,' Rennie said.

Paul Glynn and I flew first class to Fiji a day ahead of the rest of the crew to make sure everything was ready. We drank champagne in the airport lounge and throughout the flight. Somewhere along the way I must have put the brakes on, because when we arrived at Club Natasi Resort I was okay, but Glynn was legless. I looked on in increasing horror as he hit on the resort owner's glamorous wife, picking food off her plate and making fairly graphic sexual suggestions to her. Fortunately the resort owner, a financial adviser to some of Sydney's colourful business identities, had seen it all before. In the morning Glynn's limbs were still intact and there'd been no horse's head in his bed, but he hastily repaired to the airport to catch the plane that was bringing our team in.

The script for our twenty minute short was a bit like Swiss Family Robinson in the nude. It didn't really matter. We had a theatrical distribution deal just on the name—*Pets In Paradise*. We took a couple of resort boats out each morning, found a sand cay where the girls could frolic naked, and the cameras whirred. One day I looked beyond the idyllic cay and thought I could see waves breaking way in the distance. I asked Rennie if he'd heard of surfable waves on the reefs off Fiji. He'd sailed the Pacific years earlier with Peter Troy.

'There are waves on reefs everywhere,' he said. 'Let's go take a look when we've finished shooting.'

In the silvery glare of late afternoon, Rennie and I and our sound guy, 'Hottie', who'd once been a surfer, took one of the boats for a spin out to where I thought I'd seen waves. Our Fijian driver parked up behind a shallow section of reef where swells seemed to crash end to end onto the coral. We watched a few sets break and I asked the driver if he could pull into the protected water in front of the reef. He shook his head. Clearly a damaged boat would mean his job. We sped away from the long reef and the apparently uninhabited island that lay beyond it.

I'm fairly certain the island we saw that afternoon was Tavarua, and the wave shutting down on the low tide reef was the perfect lefthander now known as Restaurants. What a shame my priorities were such at that time that I'd forgotten about the wave by dinner.

The whole time we were in Fiji I was trying to close a secret deal that not even Rennie knew about, drifting away from dinner to make crackly international calls in my room. Kerry Packer had walked away from his license deal with Hugh Hefner's Playboy International, claiming that *Penthouse* had brought the whole sector into disrepute, with sales and advertising revenue falling. My former boss Philip Mason had quickly put his hand up, and with global sales of the original men's magazine in serious decline, he was able to cut a very good deal indeed. And he wanted me to jump ship again and become editor.

Philip wasn't very good at poaching, where the grand gesture gets the quick decision, and the negotiation dragged on increment by increment, night after night. 'Could the company car be secondhand? How about a parking spot nearby?' And so on. But before the shoot had finished we had cut a deal. I planned to go straight from the airport to the *Penthouse* office and hand my resignation to Young Bruce, but Mouthy must have been lurking between the bures in Fiji and picked up a snatch of conversation on the balmy breeze, because Bruce fired me the moment I walked in. *The Australian* newspaper reported on 26 October 1981:

The fur is set to fly in the male entertainment magazine market following the recent change in ownership at *Playboy* and the departure last week of *Penthouse* editor Phil Jarratt ... When news of the *Playboy* deal emerged ... Jarratt was quick to send off telexes to the media boasting that *Penthouse* had emerged as the survivor in the men's magazine market. Now he's changed his view amid increasing speculation that he will be taking over the editor's chair at *Playboy*.

Philip Mason and I had two good years at what was by then Mason Stewart Publishing, with roomy offices in Crown Street that housed us on the ground floor and the 'louts' of *Tracks*, as Philip liked to call them, upstairs. We'd jet off to Chicago each year for the global Playboy International convention (Hefner had gone off to Hollywood to host pyjama parties by this time, but I got to see where he'd once slept), and on the way home I'd stop off in California and do some consulting work for Rip Curl. We had a social cricket team for which the young Cranbrook School cricket coach, Peter Roebuck, sometimes played, and I'd taken up distance running to compensate for my lack of surfing.

Neil Jameson joined our staff as a senior writer, and he and I would pound the pavements several times a week, and do all the big fun runs. But my fitness methodology was quirky, to say the least. I remember finishing the Lane Cove Half Marathon in pretty good time with a mate alongside, and celebrating at the car with two huge lines of coke. Surviving that must have inspired me to seek sponsorship from Pan American Airways to compete in the Honolulu Marathon, but I slipped on the cricket field and pulled my calf a week before the race. I limped onto the plane anyway, started the race but had to pull over at Kahala and submit myself to almost an hour of agonising shiatsu massage. Then I limped back onto the road and finished the race, Jackie meeting me in Kapiolani Park and almost carrying me across the line.

I ran the marathon in four hours and fifty minutes, which would have made me a division winner, had I been an over sixty-five-year-old woman. I was on crutches for my stint on the North Shore for *Surfer*, and decided to stick to fun runs in future.

My time in the skin trade was running out. It just wasn't what I wanted to do. I explained this to Philip and we parted amicably, with me giving him three months' notice, during which time Rennie Ellis and I planned one last major rort in the name of men's magazines.

CHAPTER TWENTY-SEVEN

Villa d' Este on $1000 a day. (Photo Rennie Ellis)

SCAMMERS

Whenever Rennie Ellis and I worked together it was a party. I loved his sense of fun, his energy and vitality. But many of his ideas were wildly impractical, particularly when the man with the purse strings was Philip Mason. The big idea—which I'm crediting to my late friend— was to reverse the old Arthur Frommer Travel Guide concept. Instead of 'doing Europe on five dollars a day' we were going to do it on a thousand a day, at that time a vast amount of money. I thought this would make a good *Playboy* story, but I knew Philip would never approve the expenses. However, one of my running buddies was an Englishman named Neil 'Nellie' Lawrence, who had given up the study of divinity to consult for the luxury French travel group Relais et Châteaux. Nellie thought the story was a splendid promotional idea and would put it to management.

I leased a new model Citroen BX and Rennie and I, accompanied by Jackie, and Rennie's girlfriend Mish Pulling, set off on a totally decadent romp through the most luxurious resort hotels and manor houses of France, Italy and England. There is a photo of us all, sprawled on a meadow high above Lake Como in various states of undress, the detritus of a picnic lunch prepared for us by the kitchen staff at Villa d'Este strewn around us. This was at the halfway point. I don't know how we survived.

But the gig wasn't all beer and skittles. There were real dangers lurking for young players. The French, in particular, were very reluctant to tell you if dinner was on their tab. I remember easing out of the banquette at the signature restaurant of the Hôtel de Crillon in Paris and making a run for it when a cursory glance at the menu revealed that if we had to pay, the bank would be well and truly broken. Invariably though, if we elected to play it safe and eat cheap and cheerful down the road, Nellie would receive an angry telex from the manager, complaining that we had not even tried their fare.

On the other hand, the best times we had were often outside the hotel. We endured two ordinary meals at Villa d'Este and ate like kings at simple waterfront cafes just down the road in Lake Como, which either means we lacked the savoir faire and style for the job, or that in 1983 if you really did do Europe on $1000 a day, you were a bloody idiot. But that's not what I wrote.

Story complete, we went our separate ways. Jackie and I drove south through France to visit friends in the Pays Basque, where I'd first experienced French surf culture a decade earlier. I was also hoping to catch a few waves.

In the middle of the '70s I'd become friends with a former Melbourne journalist named Harry Hodge, who was trying to reinvent himself as a surf filmmaker. I wrote and read the narration script for his first effort, *Liquid Gold*, which didn't set the world on fire, but Harry was nothing if not tenacious. He pulled funding and sponsorship from out of thin air and set off around the world to remake *Endless Summer*, which he would call *Band on the Run*, somehow securing the rights to the Paul McCartney

Debauched picnic lunch, Lake Como, 1983.

song of the same name to use as its theme. I dubbed him 'Hollywood Harry' over this period and lampooned him mercilessly in *Tracks*, but he took it in good spirit and we remained friends.

Band on the Run burnt through everyone's money and never secured proper theatrical release. By most people's measure, it was a career-ending disaster. Harry saw it as a 'future cult classic' and only a minor stumbling block. He repaired to Angourie with his French girlfriend Brigitte Darrigrand to lick his wounds and subsequently re-emerged as a marketing guy at Quiksilver in Torquay. Now he had convinced Quiksilver founder Alan Green to let him try to establish the brand, first in France, then right across Europe.

We stayed in the beautiful old Darrigrand family farmhouse in the rolling hills behind Biarritz. I surfed here, there and everywhere (including a memorable session at Hossegor with Maurice Cole) and we spent the afternoons and evenings drinking good wine, laughing and talking.

Deborah Kerr's husband, the screenwriter Peter Viertel, had introduced surfing to the Pays Basque in the '50s and nothing much had changed since then. At least not in terms of surfwear. French surfers still favoured boxer bathers with undershort lining—it was hard to see them embracing hip-hugging Quiksilvers. But I'd been wrong about the surf industry twice already, so I was not about to burst Harry's bubble. And I had huge admiration for what he and Brigitte were attempting to do.

Even the composition of Harry's executive team had an air of fine madness about it. In 1976 I'd been present at the Torquay pub dining room when Alan Green told Jeff Hakman, that year's Bells Pro champion, that he could have the Quiksilver license for the US if he ate the doily decorating the centre of the table. Hakman hadn't thought twice. He grabbed the ornate table setting, chewed it up and swallowed it. But Hakman's problem was that he often didn't think twice when he should have. Throughout his final two years on the pro tour, Hakman had been a full-time closet junkie, and when the pressures of building the Quiksilver business in America began to escalate, he took to heroin again. In the end his partner, Bob McKnight, had to fire him. Shamed and near-penniless, Hakman took his wife and young family off to Australia to rebuild his life as a surf coach.

There were plenty of sceptics within Quiksilver, but as far as Harry was concerned, a man who had thrown away a potential fortune once would not do it twice. With Jeff, Harry and Brigitte, the fourth musketeer was a laid-back Californian artist/designer named John Winship, who had virtually no experience of business. None of them, except Brigitte, spoke a word of French. Harry was brimming with confidence.

As we left France I realised how much I envied Harry's big adventure. There was no safety net here. His future was totally in his own hands. It was time for me to give the wheels of industry another spin, to push out into the break before dawn, with no idea what awaited me in the black, swirling water, to mix a metaphor or three.

I talked Jamo into going freelance with me and we opened up a little creative agency in a friend's terrace house in Darlinghurst. We became the agents for Rennie Ellis's successful stock photo library, Scoopix, got book contracts from Nine's Wide World of Sports and Apa Insight Guides, and even Mark Day and Owen Thomson hired us to produce lowest common denominator sports books under the *Truth* banner. Working with Wide World of Sports hosts Mike Gibson and Ian Chappell, we produced a giant doorstopper of a thing called *Wide World of Sports Australian Sporting Hall of Fame*. It had to be a big book to fit the title on the cover.

'Gibbo' blew up over a longish lunch one day because Ken Rosewall hadn't made the final cut. 'You blokes couldn't organise a root in a brothel,' he thundered, before storming out of the restaurant.

I was suddenly a busy author, a bad husband and an absentee father. Mark Day phoned me and said he had a 'very big book' for me. He couldn't talk about it on the phone, but he was coming to Sydney and asked me to meet him in a bar in the eastern suburbs. When I walked into the bar, Mark was sitting at a shadowy corner table with what the movie star bios would term a 'ruggedly handsome man' with a deep tan and slick silver hair brushed back. Mark introduced me to Murray Riley, who stood and shook my hand firmly while fixing me with an intense gaze that was softened by a warm smile.

From the moment I met Riley I found it difficult to reconcile the hard man with the piercing eyes and the old school gentleman. Murray was both, and he could switch at the drop of a poorly phrased question. Of course, I knew him by reputation: double Olympic rowing representative, including a shared bronze medal in Melbourne in 1956, good cop gone bad, alleged mastermind of the failed $40 million *Anoa* drug scam of 1978, jailbird for the past six years. Riley's recent release from Long Bay had been headline news, but somehow Mark had got the drop on the rest of the media and signed him up for an exclusive. If Riley liked the cut of my jib, I would author his book.

Murray and I started taping sessions at our Darlinghurst office. If the sun was shining, he liked to take a couple of chairs out into the courtyard, rip off his shirt and work on his tan while he worked on the book. At sixty he was frighteningly fit, and proud of it. We were out in the sun taping one day when Frank Pithers, who'd just done a bit of porridge in Western Australia himself, dropped in. He took me aside in the kitchen. 'That's not who I think it is, is it?' he whispered. I made a zipper across my lips with my fingers and showed him out.

Murray Riley and I were becoming friends. Jackie was highly nervous about this until Murray and his partner, Carol, took us out dining and dancing at the Hunter's Lodge in Double Bay, a famed mobster hangout. The restaurant was fully staffed but we were the only diners. We sat at the best table, dined superbly, then Murray whisked both women around the dance floor like an instructor at Arthur Murray's. He laughed, told stories against himself, and charmed us all with his impeccable manners. As we left he slyly handed the maître d' a very fat envelope of cash.

'Well,' said my wife as we walked to the car, 'that certainly wasn't what I expected. He's gorgeous!'

But Murray couldn't lie straight in bed. He was good on the early years, growing up tough in a Sydney slum, making the Olympic team, even becoming a bent copper. But when we got into serious crime, the stories often didn't add up. He liked to describe himself as a 'scallywag', a slightly naughty boy who bent the rules here and there but did no-one any real harm, but the deeper I dug, the less believable this became. Although he claimed to draw a line between marijuana and heroin, there was compelling evidence that he had been involved in both, and that at certain points in the massive *Anoa* importation, inconvenient people had been 'disappeared', either by his hand or on his orders.

Murray felt I wasn't making enough money to look after our young family. (In fact I was making quite good money, but putting far too much of it up my nose.) He wanted to help out. He introduced me to his circle of dubious acquaintances and through greed, stupidity, or too much drink (or perhaps a combination of all three), I found myself enlisted to write a series of plausible pitches to convince retirees to invest their life savings in dodgy currency futures. Whereas Murray always looked dapper, the guy running the currency futures scam looked like a comic book villain, right down to his pencil thin moustache. We always met on a street somewhere and we'd exchange pitch papers for cash while he reclined against his red Porsche 911. 'Stay with me for a bit and I'll get you one of these,' he said, slapping the bonnet.

I wrote a first draft of a book called *Scammers* but I'd gone way too close to the bone and Riley pulled the pin on his *Truth* newspapers deal. I walked away with a 'kill fee', a publishing term that suddenly seemed a little too close to home. When Murray phoned me at home, if one of the kids answered he would always say, 'Tell him it's Tommy Trickemup.' Years later, after Murray Riley had done time in England over a multi-million dollar fraud conspiracy against British Aerospace and escaped from jail twice, there was a strange message on our house phone one day. 'This is Tommy Trickemup,' a faint voice crackled down the line. 'Just calling to say hello and wish you well.'

Jarratt/Jameson, Darlinghurst, 1984.

On the plane ride back from France in September 1983, I'd started to scribble the outline of a novel based on my passions of the time and the people I'd met in recent years. Perhaps not surprisingly, the main character was a champion marathon runner who also surfed and was a cocaine addict. His nickname, 'Deet', was based on Australia's world champion marathoner Robert 'Deek' de Castella, but there were no other similarities. Another prominent character was a brash but brilliant Aussie sportscaster called Harry Hillsden, who bore a passing resemblance to my friend David Hill,

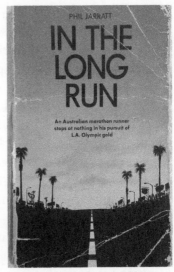

My one and only novel, 1984.

the Nine Network sports boss. The locations were all the places I'd recently been. Deet trains in Hawaii, surfs the North Shore, gets drunk in Milan and thunders through the tunnels to Genoa at warp speed while snorting coke with a spoon. Our hero meets a sticky end at the 1984 Los Angeles Olympics. Oh, and there was lots of sex.

In the Long Run might have required considerable suspension of disbelief, but it had a publisher. While still at *Playboy* I had become friendly with James Fraser, a Penguin executive who had gone out on his own and sublet a small office in the Mason Stewart building. A rascally Scot who enjoyed a drink and a laugh, James agreed to publish my first novel on condition that I sign on to ghostwrite what he described as 'the sports sensation of the century'. Golfer Jan Stephenson, who had made the big time in America as the sex symbol of the LPGA and was seldom out of the tabloids and gossip rags, had agreed to tell all about her wicked, wicked ways. Working title: *Play a Round with Me*.

I was to fly to Cincinatti, Ohio to meet up with Jan and her millionaire Texas oilman boyfriend, Eddie Vossler, at an LPGA tournament, but I stopped off in Los Angeles to spend a night with my old friend Paul Holmes, now the editor of *Surfer*. We drank and snorted until the sun came up. I was concerned that Paul's life was even further off the rails than mine. If I was heading where he'd already arrived, maybe it was time for a reboot. I left for the airport with a shocking, sweaty hangover and a bag of powder big enough to get me through the job ahead.

It didn't take me long to conclude that Jan and Eddie were two of the rudest, most self-obsessed people I had ever encountered. Even now, thirty years later, having met some doozies along the way, they would still be top ten. Close-up and personal, Jan was not quite the glamour queen she was portrayed as. Hard years on the golf course had left her face mottled and dry, but she knew how to hide it, and she wore immaculately tailored sports slacks and open front blouses that highlighted her attractive cleavage. Eddie was a jock heading for slob territory. He wore bright polo shirts tucked into his chinos, creating an unattractive package of soft meat above the belt.

The Cincinatti stop was basically a getting-to-know-you visit, where they laid down the rules of engagement and established that I was being hired help, nothing more. They had the right to veto me as ghost, so I had to bite my lip. A lot.

Jan and Eddie flew to New York in their Citation jet. Despite there being empty seats, I was consigned to the commercial airlines. On arrival at Newark Airport I was shocked to find that they had put me up at an airport hotel overlooking the New Jersey turnpike, about two hours by public transport from the plush Marriott Essex House overlooking Central Park where they were ensconced. Enough was enough. I got Eddie on the phone and told him I had to be nearer to Jan if this was going to work. A secretary phoned me back with the name of a hotel near Times Square. It was sleazy, even by my standards, with no desk and no room for one. This time I phoned James Fraser. I don't know what card he pulled but I was soon moved into the Ritz-Carlton at Central Park, just a couple of blocks from my subject.

Jan was in the Big Apple not to play golf but to film an episode of the appallingly successful reality program *Lifestyles of the Rich and Famous*. As a bit player ('my biographer'), I stood on the sidelines and watched as a camera crew filmed Jan, framed in the window of her penthouse, on the phone making endorsement deals, then issuing orders to a succession of lackeys who would tiptoe into frame and take notes while she bellowed at them. My scene involved me sitting in a chair taking notes and nodding while she paced up and down, bullet-pointing the more triumphant moments in her story.

A few bubbles for the final – Jarratt and Holmes, Bells 1981. (Photo John Ogden)

The caravan moved on to the pretty town of Corning in upstate New York, where Jan was to play a tournament. But first we had to have an important meeting, one that I'd called. In the most tactful way I could phrase it, I told them both that my understanding of the deal with Fraser was that we had to get to the nitty gritty, Jan's crazy tale of love and treachery, greed and stupidity, with her, manager Larry Kolb and Vossler dragging each other through the courts and then kissing and making up, over and over. I've got the sauce, I said, now I need the sizzle.

That night, over dinner in a private room, I got the sizzle. And then some. I switched off my tape recorder after midnight, well satisfied.

CHAPTER TWENTY-EIGHT

AN EVENING WITH DR GONZO

Jackie was pregnant again. We hadn't planned it, but we soon came around to the idea. I had a book to write so we took the kids out of school, flew to Bali and took a two-month lease on one of the first villas to be built in a village called Seminyak, just north of Legian. A walled compound just off the beach, it had two bedrooms downstairs and a sleeping loft upstairs that could double as an office. Between the statuary and the garden ponds a spiral staircase led up to a raised portico from which you could view the ocean. It was perfect for sunset cocktails.

Bali had changed for us over the years, while remaining a constant in our lives. I still made the occasional trip out to the Bukit Peninsula to surf, but the good breaks had been overrun by wave-hungry Japanese and Brazilian surfers, not to mention the first generation of Balinese surfers, young men who had been our board-carriers a decade earlier. Now it was more of a family trip, introducing our kids to the people and culture of this place that was starting to be loved to death.

Kuta now had sports bars on every corner, and hordes of Aussie yobs in Bintang singlets. Our beat now was the relative solitude of the strip of beach between the Blue Ocean bar (where Euro hippies still played racquetball naked in the late afternoon) and our villa, not far from the Oberoi Hotel. But even here, things were beginning to change. A few hundred metres from our place was a club called Chez Gado Gado, where the loud music started at midnight and went until dawn. Further along, Double Six Club was the place to score whatever it took to get you through the night.

I was content to surf somewhere (usually the beach breaks) in the early morning, work on my fancy new Brother WP1 word processor (with the revolutionary flip-up screen) most of the day, then run along the beach to the airport and back through the jungle in the late afternoon before settling in for sunset drinks at Blue Ocean with its owner, Malcolm Williams.

Sometimes we had drinks at home instead. Frank Pithers was in town and he came around an hour before sunset with a bottle of vodka. We laughed and joked through the afternoon, then had the brilliant idea of jumping on the motorbikes and heading along the beach to Blue Ocean for dinner. Frank took off at speed and I followed, Jackie on the back. Somewhere along the way I missed the mound of soft sand ahead and sent us both spinning to the ground in the twilight. My wife was six months pregnant. What had I done? She sat on the sand gasping, and holding a sarong around her stomach. Frank had spun around and come back.

Three-up in Bali with Sophie and Sam, 1984.

We looked at each other in horror. He dropped to his knees and took Jackie's hand, calming her, whispering softly, 'You'll be right old girl, just breathe deeply. You'll be right.'

I realised that night that there was something about this wild, gentle, walking contradiction of a man that I would always love. And he was right. Mother and daughter were fine.

Before we left for Bali, Rennie Ellis and I had submitted a proposal to publisher Kevin Weldon for a kids' guide book to Bali. Rennie had shot the only other Bali book for children, a slim black-and-white volume called *Ketut lives in Bali*, a few years earlier, but now we argued that Australian tourism numbers were growing so fast that a family guide would sell well, and keep selling. Weldon bought the idea and paid us a small advance. Midway through our stay, Rennie, his son Josh and Mish Pulling arrived. We had a cast of four kids, so we rented two Jeepneys and set off on the most wonderful road trip, the kind you simply can't do now, driving from village to village with no real plan, overnighting in simple homestays, visiting temples, watching ceremonies and dances, exploring caves and swimming in mountain streams. Rennie shot everything that moved, while I took copious notes and built a storyline.

Back in Seminyak we drew design roughs and planned the book cover to cover. We thought it was brilliant, but Weldon reneged without even seeing our design concept, never explaining why. I worked on several projects for Weldon in the '80s, and held him in high regard as a publisher and a human, but I think he made a mistake with *Bali for Kids*. It would still be selling today.

Things had gone pear-shaped with James Fraser. We were only weeks away from the 1984 Los Angeles Olympics, at which the climax of my novel was futuristically set, but it was still at the printers. Meanwhile, Jan and Eddie had rejected the first draft chapters of her book, now more modestly titled *Open Season*, as 'too explicit'. Contrary to what he'd originally outlined, Fraser now wanted more golf, less sex. We were engaged in a fax war. Every morning I would ride my bike to the Bali Easyrider Travel Service and send him an angry one-page scribble along the lines of: IF LONG RUN NOT IN STORE BEFORE GAMES DON'T BOTHER, ALL IS LOST. IF JAN DIDN'T WANT EXPLICIT, WHY DID SHE TELL ME ALL THAT STUFF?

The novel came out before Christmas but long after the LA games meant anything to anyone. It scored a couple of positive reviews but sold poorly. James Fraser failed to make Jan Stephenson and Eddie Vossler happy. After the usual threats of litigation from the big swinging dick from Texas, the deal was torn up and *Open Season* disappeared.

Three books in a row unpublished and my novel already in the remainder bins. I was going to need a real job soon.

There was, however, a ray of sunshine at the end of a tough year. Elice Jarratt was born a week before Christmas. I loved her to pieces and nick-named her Pruneface.

I sought some solace from my professional problems at the beach that summer. I dragged my old Brothers Neilsen swallow-tail flyer out of the garage, waxed her up and surfed the Wedge. Yes, I was on a single fin in 1985. My Bali board was a single too, the beautiful black and yellow Hot Buttered that Terry Fitzgerald had won the Om Bali Pro on in 1980, a gift from the man himself. When it came to thrusters, I was a very late adopter, not that it really mattered because my surfing standard had dropped away alarmingly. But I still loved the glide.

Enter Pruneface! Mona Vale Hospital, December 1984.

Cocaine seemed to be locked in a battle with surfing to capture my fullest attention, and the drug was winning. It had become a problem on so many fronts that in hindsight, I'm amazed I couldn't see it. Regardless of our financial situation, I couldn't face a weekend's social commitments without a healthy stash. Drug deals make strange bedfellows, and we found ourselves socialising with people with whom we had nothing in common but drugs. Then there was the aftermath of a coke binge to contend with in a house with young kids and a new baby. The teeth-grinding, sleepless nights that were the major benefit of the drug were bad enough, but a coke bender was always an alcohol binge too, and the double whammy hangovers were so bad that entire days were written off for recovery.

I suppose I was searching for a way out, but not hard enough.

We were going to America on a family holiday. Some ships had come in—more like tugboats—and I hadn't put the money up my nose. I think it was that John Witzig and I had partnered up to produce a couple of highly paid corporate vanity books. Anyway, I had enough dough to cover the mortgage for a couple of months and pay for the airline tickets. Jackie had recently done a photography course and showed some promise, so our plan was to rent a Winnebago, travel around America and sell our stories and photos.

Just before our departure we attended David Hill's fortieth birthday party, billed as 'The Night of Boring Speeches'. I was one of the lesser lights on a star-studded bill and I played to the brief beautifully, boring the audience rigid with a detailed account of a recent trout fishing holiday Hilly and I had in Tasmania until Channel Nine's veteran music director Geoff Harvey gonged me off. Before we all got too drunk, I was approached by Packer henchman Trevor Kennedy, who said, 'Hilly tells me you're looking for a job?'

Kennedy offered me a job as a senior writer on *The Bulletin*, then Australia's most respected news magazine, starting immediately. 'I'll take it,' I said, 'but Trev, there's just one thing ...'

Trevor Kennedy was a laconic kind of guy, quite likeable, but also quick to turn. I half expected him to say start Monday or don't start at all, but he listened as I explained that I'd already bought airline tickets, made commitments, but that I would happily send back features from the States. I'd lined up an interview with John 'Strop' Cornell, who was based at the Bel Air Hotel trying to sell *Crocodile Dundee* to Hollywood. Kennedy sparked on that one. 'Okay, have your holiday, send us some pieces, start September.'

Our family holiday got off to a rocky start in San Francisco. I checked us in to the budget Alfa Inn motel on Lombard Street and phoned a number I had for Hunter S. Thompson. Looking back, I can see that it probably wasn't the smartest thing I've ever done, but the gonzo guru and I had been passing each other in corridors for too long, and I happened to know that he was installed at the Cathedral Hill Hotel for two nights each week while he fantasised his column for the *San Francisco Examiner*. If necessary, the paper would dispatch a copy boy to grab each typed page as Hunter pushed them under the door.

'Uh, yeah, what? Who the fuck is this?' Hunter sounded more confused than angry. I explained who I was, how I was connected, and he agreed to meet me in the bar for breakfast at eight that night.

I kissed the family goodbye, leaving them money for pizza, and told them I'd be back in a few hours. Jackie gave me a knowing look as I fled.

I found a stool at the lobby bar of the Cathedral Hill, drank a beer and waited half an hour before using a house phone to call Dr Thompson in his room. He cut loose. 'Crazy motherfuckers, can't wait for a work of genius so they get shit and that's all they deserve. Be down in fifteen.'

It was well after nine-thirty in the evening when Dr Hunter S. Thompson shuffled into the bar for breakfast, wearing similar apparel to Bill Murray all those years before, and smoking a long, thin cigarette in a holder. He looked athletic and dissipated at the same time. When he sat down beside me I noticed lines of sweat on his lip and forehead. 'Goddamn deadlines,' he said by way of greeting, then ordered four bloody marys. When they came he placed two in front of me, and by the time I took my first sip he'd already drained one. After the second he started to relax. We chatted about politics, mutual friends, his ill-fated 'lecture tour' of Australia, and his plan to spend Thanksgiving boating on the Hudson with Bill Murray, firing sky rockets at passing vessels. 'You should come. It'll be a fucking hoot.'

The more we drank the more frequent Hunter's bathroom visits became, but it had nothing to do with his bladder. About every third time he'd fling me the bag of coke and I'd go load my nose while he ordered more drinks. My hunger had long since passed when he decided we should go eat. 'You like Mexican?' I nodded. 'I'll get Maria to drive us.'

Hunter's girlfriend was far more normal than he deserved, but she too was partial to the devil's dandruff. He sat next to her in front, nursing a beer and feeding Maria spoons of coke as she drove out through the Haight towards Seacliff. We pulled up at a scruffy little diner called Tommy's Mex next to a twenty-four-hour supermarket. The restaurant was about half-full, even at this late hour, and everyone seemed to know Hunter. The patron, Tommy, ran out to hug him and kiss Maria. Tommy guided us to a booth, where Hunter immediately built a wall of menus and started chopping up lines. We drank Dos Equis beers and jugs of margaritas and pushed tamales around on our plates until they got cold.

Hunter was fired up now, telling the most outrageous stories about politicians having sex with wild beasts, and so on. He was mostly hilarious, occasionally disturbing. He saved his best trick for last. We stood up to leave, but he was immediately cornered by a well-dressed couple who peppered him with questions about a recent column. Clearly bored, Hunter did a lightning fast pirouette, pulling a vial from his pocket and snorting deeply from it as he turned. Then, wiping his nose with the back of his hand, he answered the woman's question.

On the way to the car, Hunter picked up a case of beer and a bottle of Jack Daniels. 'We can have a drink back at the hotel,' he said. I begged off and got Maria to drop me at the motel on Lombard. As I got out of the car and shook his hand, Hunter said, 'Next time you're in town, let's do this properly.' My mind boggled at what that might entail.

The next morning we drove south to Santa Cruz in sullen silence, my head pounding. My big night with Hunter had not been appreciated. A surf at Pleasure Point helped clear the head and by the time I came in, the kids had forgiven me, if my wife hadn't. Pruneface would forgive me anything.

Jackie and I had fun working together on stories. We failed in an attempt to interview the new mayor of Carmel, Clint Eastwood, but we snared Strop Cornell poolside at the Bel Air, spotted the ancient Hollywood heartthrob Tony Curtis trying to chat up young girls, and scored the added bonus of meeting Linda Kozlowski, Paul Hogan's *Dundee* co-star and secret squeeze.

With Evonne Goolagong Cawley, 1986.

We drove to Dallas and swapped our rented car for a monstrous Winnebago. Then the fun began. I had no idea how to operate it, but I found that in RV parks all over America there were more than enough retired mechanics and handymen with time on their hands and the desire to make you look small in the eyes of your family. We found we could put the kids to bed in the van after dinner, mix up cocktails in big travel mugs and drive a few hours into the night. A friend had given me a copy of William Least Heat-Moon's wonderful *Blue Highways* and we used that as our guide through the Deep South, though we took a detour and drove north to Hilton Head Island to spend some time with Evonne and Roger Cawley on their beachfront estate.

David Hill had introduced us to the legendary tennis player and her urbane English husband a year or so earlier in Sydney, and we had become friends. Over a leisurely few days at Hilton Head, and a not-so-leisurely kids' trip to Disney World, Evonne and I began to discuss her idea to get back in touch with her Aboriginal roots and write a book about the journey. I loved the symmetry of returning to her origins and finding true happiness after all the fame and fortune. We would call the book *Home*. We shook hands on a deal. All she had to do was convince her family to move back to Australia.

CHAPTER TWENTY-NINE

Bush basher. (Photo Paul Wright)

BUSH BASHING FOR *THE BULLY*

Life at *The Bulletin* was good. I wasn't expected to be in the office every day so I had time to surf again, and the assignments I was given (or that I put to the editor) were varied and usually interesting. Space was at a premium in the Park Street office so reporters at large often had to share desk space. This was how I came to share a cubicle with a loud former seminarian named Tony Abbott. I quite liked Tony, but often I would arrive to find him bellowing into the phone, his feet up on our shared desk, no intention of moving them.

Bob Carr, a former *Bulletin* industrial relations reporter who was now environment minister in Neville Wran's NSW government, was a frequent visitor. He and Tony would heatedly argue about politics before going out for a beer. Often a group of us would lunch together. Tony was always the life of the party, an enthusiastic drinker who could move seamlessly from a bawdy yarn to a philosophical discussion no matter how many drinks he'd had. But he was also fiery-tempered and a bit of a maddie.

In fact, we all thought he'd gone completely mad when he announced that he was leaving to become a plant manager at the Pioneer Concrete company. He was ragged about this career move repeatedly as we drank the afternoon away at his farewell lunch at a Spanish restaurant in Sussex Street. I remember him chugalugging a 'cleansing ale' and saying, 'There's method in my madness.' Indeed there was. Pioneer Concrete's owner was Sir Tristan Antico, who also happened to be a major benefactor of the NSW Liberal Party. Sir Tris had suggested Tony needed some management experience before entering politics.

As a freelancer I had covered President Reagan's visit to Bali in 1985 for the *Bulletin*, so Kennedy and his successor as editor, my old friend and Canberra colleague Ian Frykberg, thought me well suited to covering regional politics. I was sent to Papua New Guinea and, memorably, to Vanuatu to cover a story about a Libyan terrorist training camp that didn't exist. (We still got a cover story out of it!) But both Kennedy and Frykberg had a firm belief that the magazine needed to get back to its roots. When the *Bulletin* was founded in the 1880s its motto was 'Australia for the white man' and its heart was in rural Australia. No-one wanted to reintroduce the racism, but the bosses could see value in going back to the bush. And I was seen as the man for the job.

For the next few years I crisscrossed the most remote parts of Australia, gathering material for numerous cover stories, three special double editions of the *Bulletin* and two books. Photographer Jan Whiting and I rode vast lengths of the Bicentennial National Trail on horseback, and with *Bulletin* staff photographer Paul Wright I followed the overland routes of explorers like Ludwig Leichardt, Burke and Wills, Hume and Hovell and Edward John Eyre, and rediscovered 'Australia's forgotten islands'.

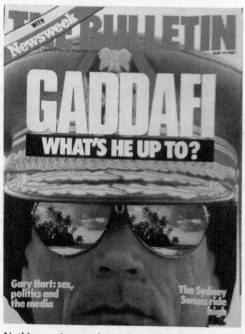

Nothing, as it turned out. Cover story, 1987.

In the Deep North with Paul Wright, 1989.

In those days before mobile phones, we would disappear out of contact for weeks on end. In 1985 I had helped Dick Smith launch *Australian Geographic*, and although he was one of the most difficult bosses I'd ever had, we became friends. On sleepless nights while I was off on my adventures, Jackie clung to the plan that if I did go missing, she would phone Dick and he would jump in his helicopter and find me.

Until this point the closest I'd ever come to remote Australia was surf exploring up and down the coast, but I found I loved the wide landscapes and big skies, and meeting the people who made their lives in these harsh environments. Being in the bush seemed to simplify my life. Sitting by a campfire at a billabong in the desert with a mug of billy tea, writing up my day's notes in a spiral-bound pad, I had no need of cocaine (or champagne, for that matter). I was at peace with myself, and I felt I could re-order my priorities. There were many binges and benders still to come, but I remain convinced that my years in the bush made me a better person. Others have called it the 'church of the open sky'. I wouldn't go that far, but something definitely happened.

Ian Frykberg had kept on his executive role at Channel Nine while editing the *Bulletin*, dividing his week between Willoughby and Park Street, and he encouraged me to do the same. I started spending two days a week at the Wide World of Sports cottage writing scripts for former Test cricketer Max Walker. Max was a big, affable goofball of a guy, and I got along well with him. His fellow presenter, Ian Chappell, on the other hand, regarded him as a buffoon and wouldn't give him the time of day. I was at the Ansett lounge at Sydney Airport one afternoon chatting to Max until his flight was called. As Max went out one door, Chappell came in the other. 'You just missed Tangles,' I said.

'Jarratt,' said the former Test captain, 'timing is everything.'

Frykberg's role at the Nine Network eventually forced him to give up the editor's chair at the *Bulletin* and he was replaced by another former *Sydney Morning Herald* colleague, David Dale. David was an urbane, witty bon vivant who had the disconcerting habit of reaching over and helping himself to food off your plate. He loved lunching and we did a lot of it. One day Trevor Kennedy had dropped by to see him at three thirty or four in the afternoon and was shocked to find that the editor and the entire editorial staff were out to lunch. Somehow he tracked Dale down at the restaurant and got him to the phone.

'Don't you think you'd better get back to the office?' Kennedy enquired.

'Just one more course,' said Dale.

Dale brought an entirely fresh approach to editing the *Bulletin*. While critics of the new look dubbed it 'metrosexual', I thought it was a lot more humorous and confronting than it had been in recent years, particularly the special annual survey David introduced in 1988, 'Australia's Most Appalling People'. Kerry Packer was out of the country when the first survey appeared, lambasting many of his rich and powerful friends. But when the second one appeared the following year, he blew up, giving Dale a comprehensive and expletive-riddled character reading. The editor was told he was on his last chance—he was never to publish anything like this again.

Dale liked to take chances. He couldn't stand Packer but he thought that Richard Walsh, the publisher at Australian Consolidated Press, would offer him some protection. So I was one of three writers briefed to prepare 'The Great Australian Balance Sheet', which would list fifty human assets and fifty liabilities. It was great fun writing the liabilities, taking a long stick to the likes of John Laws, Alan Jones, Derryn Hinch and Alan Bond, but I couldn't help thinking that my friend the editor was on a suicide mission.

The day after the Balance Sheet issue appeared, Packer called Dale into his office, abused him and fired him on the spot. He was marched out the Castlereagh Street exit by a security guard.

A few weeks earlier, Dale and I had been walking in the Blue Mountains (I was tracing the route of Blaxland, Wentworth and Lawson; he had decided to walk off a few of those lunches) when he mentioned that he was having difficulty replacing the magazine's Queensland correspondent, Quentin Dempster, who had come to Sydney for a plum job at the ABC. I said, 'Why didn't you ask me?'

Dale couldn't understand why I'd want to live in Brisbane. I said I didn't. In fact, I'd only take the job if I could live anywhere within a 200 kilometre radius of the city. We had a deal. Just like that. We'd been considering a relocation for a couple of years—the idea of a fresh start in a place where I didn't know any drug dealers had quite a strong appeal— but it wasn't that easy. I was making good money in Sydney, the kids were settled in their schools, we had a strong network of friends. But a professional posting was like an order. You couldn't refuse. That was what I planned to tell the kids.

Jackie and I drove north and scouted every beach town between the Tweed and Mary Rivers, but it was all a hoax. As soon as I drove down the hill into Noosa Heads and saw perfect little lines marching around the points, I knew there was only one place I wanted to live. We'd been coming to Noosa regularly in recent years, camping on the river at Munna Point with the kids en route to Fraser Island. It wasn't the Noosa I'd fallen in love with twenty years earlier, but we liked the whole package—a cosmopolitan village surrounded by parks and waterways. And we found a house. I wrote in my newspaper column:

> We looked at houses on the beach, houses on mountaintops, houses of stone and houses on stilts. We looked at houses with lime green wallpaper and mauve drapes. We looked at houses not even Nick Scali could love. Then, on a rainy morning last week, we drove into a little railway town just back off the coast and paused to look in the window of Toby Brown's estate agency and tackle shop. In it there was a photo of a lovely old Queenslander with ornate verandas along three sides, standing on an acre or so of bush at the edge of town. Don Brown, a retired bank manager who was minding the store for Toby, drove us out to look at the property. 'Good spot this,' Don said.

'Eight minutes to Tewantin Golf Club, five minutes to the Pomona pub and there's a good RSL right here in town. Can't go wrong, really.'

He didn't mention that it was fourteen minutes to First Point, but I'd already worked that out. We bought the house that day.

One of the last things I did before leaving Sydney was to co-host Quiksilver's twentieth anniversary party with Shirley Strachan. (Skyhooks were no longer, but Shirl had reinvented himself as a TV star.) It was a huge affair at a Mexican restaurant in The Rocks, and the Quiksilver team had gathered from around the world. Harry Hodge had flown in from France, Bob McKnight from California. The company was awash with money and the booze flowed all night. It was great to see my old mates so flushed with success, but perhaps my feelings were also tempered with just a little envy. I got over it. There was no future for me in the surf industry. That bird had flown.

Sophie, now a spirited teenager, hated everything about Queensland (including us for bringing her). She hid in her bedroom with her cat and sobbed for about three weeks. But life in Noosa Shire was all kinds of good and she slowly came to realise it. I surfed or ran through the national

Hosting the Quiksilver 20th anniversary. (L to R): Shirl, Harry Hodge, Bruce Raymond, Bob McKnight, me.

park or along the rainforest tracks behind our property most days. Once or twice a week I would take the early morning fast train to Brisbane and hang out at Parliament House, where my old Canberra friend and colleague John Stubbs had introduced me to the new Labor government of Wayne Goss. I became good mates with Labor Party secretary Wayne Swan and later with Goss himself, a decent, honest man with a good line in self-deprecatory humour. The only member of the team none of us could stand was the nerdy policy advisor who we called 'Dr Death'. His real name was Kevin Rudd.

It was an exciting time in Queensland politics, with Goss and his young team (all the key players were my age or younger) bringing new energy to the state after decades of corruption and conservatism under Joh Bjelke-Petersen and his successors. I had plenty to write about.

During that first mild winter in Noosa we were called south by tragedy. Dad had dropped dead of a heart attack while fundraising for Rotary. He was only seventy-four, but he'd had open heart surgery eight years earlier and we knew he was fragile. It's a cliché to say he died doing what he loved, but he really did. Presciently, just weeks earlier his number one Rotary project, our Japanese sister Toshiko had visited him. When it was Mum's turn decades later, Toshiko did the same thing, flying in to be at her bedside just hours before she passed.

Back in Noosa I was approached by a young man named Matthew Rees Jones who wanted to publish a magazine called *Noosa Tatler* but didn't quite know how to go about it. 'Have you got permission from *London Tatler*?' was my first question. 'Ah, yes,' Matt fibbed. I told him if he sold enough advertising to cover the print bill, I'd consider becoming a partner. He came back a week later with the contracts and I was in. A good photographer came on board and Robert, our European art director, carried our first edition in progress from house to house in a battered Globite school case.

We rented a funky old house by the river and turned it into a publishing office. There was no money in it but I was having fun. Our launch party at the river house was such a hit we decided to have a party to celebrate every issue. Noosa seemed to love the new magazine, but *London Tatler* didn't. The cease and desist letter arrived as we were laying out the second issue. We had to come up with another name, fast. 'What about *Noosa Blue*?' said Robert. We looked at him blankly. '*Billy Blue, Noosa Blue*. Why not?'

We were running out of time. It was *Noosa Blue*.

For some years now, Jackie's son Sol had been living mostly with his father, Jim, in Byron Bay, visiting us during school holidays. He had developed into a handsome, athletic young man who also had a dreamy, artistic side. Growing up, he had often exhibited steely determination in the face of all opposition. On a big day at Snapper Rocks, for example, I could not convince him that it was too dangerous to surf. We compromised by jumping off the rocks at Greenmount, where conditions were more mellow, but a large set approached as we hit the water. I made it over the first but Sol didn't. I couldn't see him anywhere. I panicked and rode the first wave that came along all the way in and scanned the shoreline. Eventually I saw him walking along the beach from Kirra, where he'd been swept. He was sobbing quietly. He was eleven years old.

But after his graduation from Mullumbimby High we began to see changes in Sol, subtle at first, then radical. He seemed unable to settle to anything, jobs, hobbies or even the sports he had loved. He smoked all the time, cigarettes and joints. He still drew and painted but the subject matter began to get dark and grisly. Once quite a snappy dresser, he now wore bandanas or tied strings to his clothes. His behaviour and conversation became quite strange. After many months of increasing parental concern, Sol was diagnosed with paranoid schizophrenia.

Jackie struggled to deal with it, barely able to cope with seeing her firstborn in a cloud of confusion at an age when other young men are just embarking on the adventure of life. It was unutterably sad. I took him tailor fishing on the Noosa north shore one afternoon. We camped on the beach and drank beers while we hauled fish out of an inshore gutter. While I grilled our dinner on the campfire, Sol sat in the dark and smoked. Eventually he said, 'So they reckon I'm mad. What do you think? Do you think I'm mad?'

Choking back tears, I took a long time to answer. Eventually I said, 'No, mate, I don't, but you've got an illness that makes you do some odd things, so we've just got to get that under control.' But Sol never could. He was the sweetest guy—he loved his sisters so much and they reciprocated—but his unpredictable behaviour and mood swings made him difficult to be around.

Sol continued to divide his time between Byron Bay and Noosa. In Byron on the sixth day of July, 1992, less than a week since his twenty-first birthday, he sat down in a quiet spot under a tree, smoked a cigarette and drank a Coke, then took his own life.

Jackie and Sol, mid-1980s.

There are no words that can do justice to the agony of the loss of a child. The days became a blur—one minute you're dealing with it, the next minute you're not. I had interviewed a Japanese Buddhist priest who had a retreat near Mullumbimby, and had been impressed by the peace and tranquillity he exuded. I phoned him and asked a favour, and he took us in. There were no prayers or incantations that could take away our hurt, but the simplicity and serenity of that brief time gave us the strength to see our way through the grief—as much as you can. Look at a photo or write a paragraph, as I'm now doing, and you're right back there at rock bottom.

CHAPTER THIRTY

GHOSTWRITER

We threw ourselves into our work. *Noosa Blue* became The Blue Group, with a house and garden magazine joining the lifestyle magazine. Shirl Strachan, now presenting a homes show on TV, came up to launch it for us, alongside socialite Lady Sonia McMahon, widow of Australia's least-accomplished prime minister. (This was a favour for a major advertiser. Sonia drank her own weight in champagne and posed for photos.)

We published photo books and cookbooks. I had to quit the *Bulletin* to devote myself to the rapidly expanding business, as well as to my own book projects. Evonne and Roger Cawley had moved to Noosa so we could start our book, *Home*, and we were negotiating a publishing contract. Goolagong Productions moved into an office at the newly painted Blue Group house.

These were exciting times but we could never escape the shadow of Sol's death. We took too much solace in alcohol and the anger would reach flashpoint night after night, in the workplace and at home. Our friend John Witzig, who had come up from Mullumbimby to help design a cookbook, said he doubted he could ever work with us again. I couldn't blame him.

Jackie developed her own ways of dealing with her grief, and things slowly began to improve. For me, surfing again proved to be my salvation. I had started riding a longboard, the perfect craft for Noosa's peeling point waves, and *Noosa Blue* became a sponsor of the Noosa Longboard Classic, one of a handful of events along the coast that was propelling a longboard revival, particularly popular among baby boomers like myself,

for whom shortboards were becoming more challenging as age and grav-
ity took their toll. I even started competing in age division events for the
first time since the '60s.

Simon & Schuster published *Home: The Evonne Goolagong Story* and
sent us on a round-Australia author tour. We played to packed houses
and Evonne signed books for hours. Introducing her at book lunches, I
developed a routine in which I would talk about our travels in the bush,
reconnecting with her Aboriginality, and her marvelling at the simple
things she found important, like a smooth pebble plucked from the
Murrumbidgee. Miraculously pulling said rock from my pocket, I would
conclude, 'Ladies and gentlemen, this pebble meant more to her than
her two Wimbledon trophies, or all the fame and fortune. Please make
welcome Evonne Goolagong Cawley!' Cue standing ovation as she made
her way to the podium, not a dry eye in the house as she beamed out at
the audience.

60 Minutes flew us all up to Cape York so they could film Evonne's
quest against a picturesque backdrop of ancient rock art. Sales spiked
again. SBS were talking about a television series. Suddenly I had publishing contracts for other prominent biographies, including solo yachtsman
and environmental crusader Ian Kiernan, and the late Reverend Ted
Noffs, founder of Sydney's Wayside Chapel. Business was thriving! We
decided to take a vacation.

Bali was temporarily on our shit list, largely because we had been
ripped off on a land deal that Rennie Ellis and I had entered into with
local sponsors. Cowboy deals abounded in those days, but they left a
bitter taste for a while, so we headed for France instead, taking up a standing invitation to summer with Harry Hodge and his wife Sandee, staying
in the guest house attached to their estate in Bidart. It was a wonderful
summer, days spent chasing surf from Hossegor to the Spanish border,
lazy lunches at the old port or in the rustic setting of La Ferme Ostalapia,
long evenings sipping wine on the terrace and watching the sun set over
the Bay of Biscay.

We did a lot of talking, too. Since the American licensee for Quiksilver
had gone public in 1986, it had embarked on a policy of 'buying back
the farm', even though the farm wasn't theirs in the first place. One of
its first acquisitions was Quiksilver Europe, which in less than a decade
had grown from nothing to a hundred million dollar company. Its sale had
made Harry Hodge a very rich man. Now he wanted to celebrate the life

Competing in my own event. Still lucky to make the final!

Home, 1994.

Launch of *Home*, Sydney, 1994.

Ghostwriter

and career of the man he regarded as key to the company's success—Jeff Hakman. Harry envisaged a best-selling book (written by me) that would become a major Hollywood movie, not only immortalising Hakman but also propelling the Quiksilver brand into new stratospheres of profitability.

It was a typically ambitious plan, but Harry also had a secret agenda. Hakman had started to backslide into heroin. Indeed, he had only recently been discharged from an expensive rehabilitation program in London. Harry felt that putting the spotlight on Jeff's long battle with addiction would be insurance against further lapses. Everyone would know his story; everyone would be watching.

Cruising towards fifty years of age, Hakman was also now cruising on a longboard, and we interspersed chats about the book with enjoyable sessions at the reef break of Guéthary, below the prettiest village in the Pays Basque. I liked Jeff a lot, but despite his fearlessness in big waves, in many ways he was a weak man, and I wondered if he would have the courage to reveal all of his often murky story. I would find out soon enough, but first I had a few projects to clean up back in Australia.

Like most of my book subjects (with the notable exception of Jan Stephenson), I became good friends with Ian Kiernan, and enjoyed putting together the story of the rapacious developer, pulling down heritage buildings to erect ugly blocks of flats, who sees the light and turns into an environmental crusader, all the while sailing solo endlessly around the world. As a rollicking adventure, it had all the elements. Kiernan was a notorious womaniser, but to spare the innocent we rolled all of his transgressions into one, and named her 'Leilani'.

Ian was an entrant in the Sydney to Hobart yacht race, so to finish our taping sessions I flew to Hobart and helped crew the *Maris* back to Sydney. We loaded up on steak, eggs and 'dog beer' (Cascade) and hit foul weather and high seas the minute we cleared the Derwent. Being useless at deck chores in a gale, I was assigned to galley duties, quickly learning to fry eggs and open beers at forty-five degrees. When the skies finally cleared, we tacked into a nor'easter for days, sitting at the wheel taping stories and drinking beer.

Prime Minister Paul Keating launched *Coming Clean* at the Bathers Pavilion in Balmoral Beach with one of the most compelling and spellbinding speeches I have ever heard. For some reason Keating threw away his notes and spoke off the cuff about his boyhood adventures jumping off

Keirnan, PM Keating and me at the Coming Clean launch, 1995.

the Manly ferry and swimming ashore. This might not have been in the league of Kiernan's epic solo crossings, but it perfectly captured a Sydney boyhood that both men had shared, and that no longer existed.

The following northern summer Jeff Hakman and I put together the primary interviews and the structure for *Mr Sunset* in France before I did a quick loop of the world, picking up interviews with friends, family, colleagues, rival surfers and even a few who'd shared his darkest moments. I'd been wrong about Jeff's courage—he laid himself bare, trusting me to humanise him where he needed it. It was an incredible story of a surfer who was addicted not only to heroin, but also to adrenaline and to risk-taking. From a very early age, Jeff had put everything on the line, in every possible way. Maybe Harry was right. Maybe this *was* a Hollywood movie.

In October we reconvened at Hakman's house in Hanalei Bay, Kauai, to put the finishing touches on the manuscript, and surf our brains out on the Hanalei bowl. It was the perfect place to tie up the loose ends. Hawaii was where it had begun for Jeff, when he won the Duke Kahanamoku Invitational in 1965 at just seventeen, and in many ways the hippie town of Hanalei had paused the clock about then. We celebrated the completion of this part of the project at the Tahiti Nui, the down-at-heel Tiki bar you see in the movie *The Descendants*. Then I jumped on a plane and went off to sell it to publishers in America and England.

There'd never been a book tour like the *Mr Sunset* tour. We started in France, then took it to London, Cornwall and Jersey. Everything Quiksilver organised turned into a huge party with boxes of books being given away to guests. Some of the promotions organised by the book trade were less successful. Jeff and I spent a lonely afternoon in London sitting in a West End bookstore called Sportspages. Not one punter bought a book or even acknowledged our presence. We had a similar reaction when we took our roadshow to the Quiksilver Pro G-Land, on a remote jungle coast of Java. The pro surfers were not particularly interested in books, it seemed. On the other hand, my youngest daughter, Ellie, had a ball playing pool with a young Kelly Slater.

From there we toured Australia, stopped off in Hawaii and finished in California with a roadshow from San Diego to Santa Cruz. By the time we finished, word reached us that a company called October Films wanted to option the rights to the book, with Sean Penn slated as director and star. In my wild naivety, I thought I already had one foot in Hollywood.

Harry Hodge, Jeff Hakman and me, launching *Mr Sunset*, Long Beach, CA, 1997.

I was having the time of my life, but I'd taken my eye off the ball with our business back home, which was unfortunate because everywhere I looked I saw opportunities to expand it. Jackie and our daughter Sam, who'd just joined the business straight out of school, stared at me in disbelief when I explained that I'd negotiated a deal with *Surfers Journal* founder Steve Pezman in California to publish an Australian edition of what was fast becoming recognised as the best surf magazine in the world. 'Who's going to run it while you're traipsing around the world?' they asked. Then I told them about the phenomenal growth in girls' surfing, and that I wanted to start a magazine for them and call it *Shred Betty*.

My only ally in the office (we'd moved out of the Blue house and bought a proper one) was John Brasen, an Australian surfing friend of Hakman's who had invested in the business and come to work with us. JB thought anything to do with surfing was a good idea. He was good to have around. You could argue that all of my ideas were good ones, just not all at the same time. We were still a tiny operation with just a handful of staff, but we moved ahead with publication dates for both new magazines. And then another idea emerged.

For the past couple of years I'd been enjoying the Biarritz Surf Festival, which, in typically French fashion, added a cultural framework to a longboard contest, in most years consisting of the idolisation of all things Hawaiian. It was a two-way street because the invited Hawaiian legendary surfers idolised all things French. JB had also been to the BSF and loved it, so together we plotted to transpose the concept to Noosa and tack it onto the existing Noosa Longboard Classic. We crafted a business plan and a program that we thought would have wide appeal, and presented it to the organising committee of the Noosa Malibu Club. We won a close vote and held the first Noosa Festival of Surfing in March 1998, flying in special guests like big wave guru Greg Noll and Hawaiian world champion Rusty Keaulana, and scraping together enough world champions to stage a 'champion of champions' exhibition, which proved a huge hit.

We were away. A small sponsor the first year, Breaka Flavoured Milk signed up and threw big money at us for the next one.

In July we were back in France for the BSF, sponsored this time by Quiksilver. I had been asked by Harry Hodge to chaperone the Australian VIPs, paying particular attention to 1964 world champion Midget Farrelly and his wife Bev, first-timers in France. Jackie and Bev had been friendly for decades, but my relationship with Midget was more complex. Since the mid-'60s Midget had harboured a grudge against Nat Young, the world champion who followed him, and the elements of the surf media that he felt had embraced Nat and the drug culture, which he saw as one and the same. When I was the editor of *Tracks* I was in this camp. Since then, I had been in and out of favour, but in France that summer Midget was in a sunny mood and seemed prepared to put any grievances to one side.

(As I wrote the words above, I received word that Midget had died of cancer, aged just seventy-one. I knew he'd been sick for a year, but it still hit me harder than I could ever have imagined, because while he remained a hero to me, we were mostly at loggerheads during the final two decades of his life.)

Midget was the star turn at the festival and seemed to enjoy the attention. When he wasn't required at the site, we showed him and Bev the countryside and introduced them to French friends. He was enchanted by the identical twins Max and Manu Berque, surfers who also built tiny yachts at their farmhouse near Contis-Plage and sailed them across oceans without instruments. We spent a day at Contis, surfing, inspecting their latest hull and, inevitably, enjoying a red wine lunch.

On the way back to Biarritz that night, I proposed to Midget that he spearhead a re-enactment of the final of the 1964 world title, thirty-five years later, at the 1999 Noosa Festival of Surfing, and he agreed to do it. There were conditions, of course—there were always conditions with Midget—but he agreed. I was ecstatic. I bought us nightcaps at Le Surfing Bar next to Midget's hotel and we toasted the success of the '64 Rematch'.

The Nine Network had TV rights for the Commonwealth Games in Kuala Lumpur that year and I got hauled out of television retirement to join the writing team with Jamo. Jamo had been paired with the eminent face of the network, Ray Martin, while I had drawn the new kid on the block, Eddie McGuire. Being neither from Melbourne nor an AFL fan, I didn't know who Eddie was, which Eddie found unfathomable. The relationship didn't get off to a good start, which made life difficult for both of us, since much of scriptwriting for major live sport involves crawling under desks out of camera view to press hand-written updates into the sweaty palms of the presenters. And heaven help the writer if the information is wrong, or even incomplete.

It was a tough gig, but for me, the real pay-off from being in KL began the day the games finished, when I grabbed the surfboard bag from my room and flew to Padang, Sumatra, to join Jeff Hakman, JB and other friends for my first surf trip on skipper Martin Daly's *Indies Trader*.

Since Daly had acquired an old salvage vessel, cut it in half and extended it by two cabins a few years earlier, the *Trader* and her skipper had attained legendary status in the world of surf adventure. A lot of surfers had begun to tire of Bali's crowded Bukit Peninsula and look further afield along the Indonesian Archipelago, or even beyond it to the islands and atolls of the Indian and Pacific oceans. They discovered that there was surf everywhere, but by far the most glittering jewel in the crown was Martin Daly's discovery of a seemingly endless string of perfect reef waves along the Mentawai, Telo and Hinako island groups off the west coast of Sumatra. By now the island treasures were no longer a secret, but Daly, a mostly affable Aussie, kept his charts hidden and refused to answer questions about locations as we steamed out of Padang for the overnight crossing.

That trip was one of the most magical experiences of my surfing life, just a handful of friends sharing perfect waves in impossibly exotic locations, day in, day out. Although my business life had already begun to revolve around surfing again, this put the heart and soul back into it. I was approaching fifty and I wanted to ride as many perfect waves as possible while I still could.

CHAPTER THIRTY-ONE

Surfing's Don King with Layne Beachley.

THE DON KING OF SURFING

Some old salts still recall the 1999 Breaka Noosa Festival of Surfing as the best ever. We had more surf legends than you could poke a stick at, a huge contingent of Hawaiians for the world tandem surfing championships, and California's young stylemaster Joel Tudor battling Hawaii's Bonga Perkins for the professional title. But the thing the old salts remember is Midget Farrelly appearing from out of their pasts, surfing like the champion he always was and defeating all the living finalists from 1964 all over again.

For organisers John Brasen, John Lee and myself, it was a nightmare from start to finish, at which point the Breaka executive team, having seen not one wave ridden at the heavily branded First Point site, went home in high dudgeon, saying never again. Lack of surf on the points meant we'd had to construct a makeshift event site miles away at Castaway's Beach every morning and take it down every night—but that was a piece of cake compared to the high drama unfolding behind the scenes.

Following our agreement in France the previous July, Midget Farrelly and I had sparred by phone and fax for months over the conditions attached to his appearance, for which he was to be paid two return airline tickets to Los Angeles. Most of the conditions related to who could attend and who could not. Reluctantly, I had to ask his old foes Nat Young and Bob McTavish to stay away until after the '64 Rematch, then give Midget assurances in writing. But it all fell apart a few days before the festival when an article in the *Sydney Morning Herald* described the reunion as 'surfing's grudge match of the century' and claimed that Hawaii's

With John Brasen, 1999.

Joey Cabell would have won surfing's first official world title, had he not been penalised for interfering with other surfers' waves.

I had not spoken to the journalist and had no prior knowledge of the line his story would take, but Farrelly held me responsible, and he was furious. Under no circumstances would he come to Noosa. When I pointed out that the three overseas finalists from 1964 were already on their way, he took a different tack. He would come, but he would take no part in any official or media functions and accept no accommodation, hospitality or appearance fee. He hung up. In a follow-up newspaper article he described me as 'the Don King of surfing', an unflattering reference to the unscrupulous boxing promoter.

I'd heard rumours that Midget was in town, but with ten minutes to go before the appointed start time, he hadn't appeared and my fingernails were chewed to the bone. The other four competitors (the fifth, Bobby Brown, had died in 1967) had checked in and were posing for photos when someone spotted the familiar figure, way up the beach, ambling towards the contest site. Midget was fifty-four at the time. Most of the people in the massive crowd on the beach had never seen him surf, but as he approached they started to mob him. Long minutes ticked by as he signed autographs on magazines and T-shirts and posed for group pictures. Finally, I had the beach marshal run down and give him his contest jersey. We hit the hooter and got underway.

Midget surfed superbly in the windblown but long-walling waves, carving off the bottom, stalling in the pocket, leaning on the accelerator and walking casually to the nose. It was a masterful exhibition, for which he received a standing ovation as he disappeared into the crowd.

We had barely recovered from the festival and started to look for a new lead sponsor when Harry Hodge phoned me. Was I available to come to France for the month of May to write and help design a new 'look book' (trade jargon for a magazine-style catalogue)? There must have been some doubt in my response because he weighed in quickly. 'Fifteen thousand Euros and business-class flights.' I was on board.

Harry picked me up at Biarritz airport on a Thursday afternoon. I started chatting about ideas for the look book, but Harry cut me short. 'We can start working on that on Monday. In the morning we're going to Monaco for the Grand Prix.' It was a weekend of high octane indulgence,

With Peter Crawford and Rennie Ellis, 1998.

The Don King of surfing

but what I didn't realise was that it was also a test for two of us in the party, which was an odd mix of Quiksilver Europe executives and friends of Harry. I was being tested for compatibility with the group, since Harry had a proposal to put to me. Bernard Mariette, the young French president of the company, was being tested for his organisational skills, which were often found to be lacking. Bernard was a big-picture guy; he didn't take well to booking cabs and making dinner reservations.

We first met Bernard in 1995, less than a year after he'd been hired away from Timberland. He and his young family had settled in the Basque country and he was renovating a beautiful old stone farmhouse in the hills. We sat in the construction debris while Bernard taught me the ancient art of 'sabre-ing' a bottle of champagne. For this you need a heavy knife and a good champagne. We had both. Bernard ran the knife along the neck of the bottle a couple of times and then lightly chipped the ridge. The top fell off and the champagne bubbled forth, hopefully taking any shards of glass with it. (I became quite good at this, but Bernard was the master.) Bernard was smart, funny and a good party guy. We became good friends—right up until I found myself working for him.

This, of course, was Harry's proposal, revealed as we worked our way through the look book production with his young marketing team. Harry wanted to bring me in over the heads of the current young marketing bosses, get them back on budget and try to merge their good but undisciplined ideas into a cohesive marketing strategy across all European markets. I knew it would be a huge challenge, particularly with my schoolboy French only slightly improved through recent contact, but the idea excited me. It would create huge upheaval in our lives, but the money was very good, and living in a village in France was something we had always talked about. When I got back to Noosa I sabred a bottle of Moët et Chandon and Jackie and I drank it on the patio while we talked. The second bottle was surplus to requirements. We were moving to France!

But it wasn't that simple. Ellie, our youngest daughter, was still in school, so Jackie would have to commute quite a bit, and there was still the small matter of the family business. After almost a decade, regional publishing had begun to grind us down. We'd already closed the house and garden magazine, and *Noosa Blue* was starting to struggle, with advertising revenue now being shared with newer rivals. On the surf front, *Shred Betty*, our girls' title, had folded after a handful of issues. I was committed to *Australian Surfers Journal* but we were paying printing bills and royalties in US dollars and the exchange rate wasn't doing us any favours. And, of course, the new and critically acclaimed Noosa Festival of Surfing was not yet making any money.

Even as I pondered these fairly significant problems, Harry was pounding me by phone and fax. I was needed back in France. I had an event to run!

Professional surfing was now almost twenty-five years old, so the Association of Surfing Professionals (ASP) had decided to tap into its own history by creating a masters event, similar to golf and tennis. The first two ASP World Masters had been sponsored by French company Oxbow and held successfully in Fiji and Mexico, but when Oxbow walked away from the sponsorship in 1999, Harry Hodge grabbed it for Quiksilver Europe. It was decided that we would stage the Quiksilver Masters in our own backyard, at a break called Lafitenia about five minutes from the sprawling Quiksilver campus, and that Quiksilver International's Rod Brooks and I would run it on behalf of the brand, with ASP judges and administrators.

The invited field included a handful of world champions and most of pro surfing's biggest stars from the pioneer years. It was like old home week for me. I'd kept in touch with quite a few, but there were many more that I hadn't seen since the '70s. Some had grown paunchy, others had lost their hair, but none had lost the fierce competitive spirit that had got them to the top of the rankings in the first place. And the fiercest of the fierce was Gary 'Kong' Elkerton, the beefy son of a Queensland fisherman who had finished runner-up for the world title three times in the '80s and '90s. Elkerton was an energetic conversationalist who would bail you up at any time and complain bitterly about how he'd been robbed of the championship, but he was likeable, despite his brashness.

Early in his career I'd called him 'Kong' throughout a profile I'd written for *Surfer*. He'd just starred in a short film called *Kong's Island* so I thought I was on fairly safe ground, but he phoned me one evening, perhaps after a few beers, and roundly abused me for insulting him. It seemed he was okay with Kong again now, and when he became one of our sponsored surfers we became friends. He frequently called me 'Komodo' after the dragon—getting me back, I suppose. Kong finished runner up once more in that first Quiksilver Masters, but he more than made up for it by winning the next three, in France, Ireland and Hawaii. I'll never forget him theatrically kissing the sand at Lafitenia when his final wave score was announced, giving him the title. He was a world champion at last!

At the end of December 1999, Jackie, our youngest daughter Ellie and I were invited to celebrate the Millennium with the Quiksilver family at the first place past the International Date Line—Fiji. Harry Hodge booked out Namotu resort, while Bob McKnight took over Tavarua. It was an extraordinary week of surfing and partying even enjoyed by Miki Dora, the mysterious and usually elusive 'black knight of Malibu', who was on the Quiksilver Europe payroll as a sponsored surfer despite being sixty-five years old, and who was also my new neighbour in the village of Guéthary.

But as the dawn of the new millennium approached, Miki grew more introspective. People around the world had been taken in by the idea of the 'Millenium bug', but Miki's fears were far darker. He confided in several people his absolute belief that the world would end at midnight on New Year's Eve. When it didn't, he still wasn't happy. We were on the edge of the planet in Fiji, he said. In New York and London the shit would have hit the fan, computers blowing up, people rioting in the streets, cops and militia gunning them down like dogs. Chile was the only safe place to be, he said.

Harry Hodge and Bernard Mariette, Quiksilver campus, St Jean de Luz.

Partying in Paris with Gibus de Soultrait, Martin Potter, Nat and Ty Young.
(Photo Jason Mccallum)

And indeed, in the first week of 2000 he lit out for Chile, not returning to France for several months. 'Well, we're still here,' I said on his
return when we met for coffee in the *bar tabac* downstairs from our flats.
Miki just scowled.

Life in Guéthary was good, and I enjoyed most aspects of my
work as head of marketing at Quiksilver, although my position on
the management committee had begun to bring me into conflict with
Bernard Mariette. Part of the problem was that committee meetings were
conducted in French, and mine wasn't quite up to the task. The French
had a way of saying one thing and meaning another, and I often felt frozen
out. On the other hand, my job took me around Europe constantly, travelling at the pointy end of the plane and staying at the best hotels. I liked
playing the high-rolling executive.

But as the months went by I began to realise that I was heading
into dangerous and largely uncharted waters, both professionally and
personally.

CHAPTER THIRTY-TWO

Harry Hodge and Bernie Mariette at the Quiksilver Masters, 2000.

ZORRO DOES EUROPE

With our youngest daughter Ellie still in school, Jackie spent a lot of time in Noosa in 2000 and 2001, while I was on the road in Europe living out my high-flyer fantasies. A friend got me membership at Soho House, a trendy London club. I took to wearing black from head to toe, with matching black horn-rimmed glasses. I was turning fifty, and I suppose this was my mid-life crisis. I couldn't afford a Porsche, so poncing around the great cities of Europe looking like Zorro would have to suffice.

The more involved I became in my fantasy world, the worse I treated my wife, and the deeper my web of deceit became, the more I found myself lying to people I trusted and who trusted me. Friends came from all over to celebrate my fiftieth birthday at Dan's Bar in Contis-Plage, a funky beach town halfway between Biarritz and Bordeaux, and many of them could see that something was wrong with our marriage, a fact that I thought was well hidden. My two closest friends, Rennie Ellis and Neil Jameson, saw right through me. Not a word was spoken, but I knew they knew, and I could feel their disapproval.

A couple of weeks later I flew to Ireland to prepare for the Quiksilver Masters World Championships in Bundoran, County Donegal. The slower pace of life there gave me some time to reflect on what I was doing, and surfing the many good waves in that beautiful part of the world made me feel more in control of my life. But as soon as Jackie arrived for the contest week, we were at each other's throats again. The forced separation was turning us into strangers.

We flew back via Paris for a reception, and I was sleeping off a hangover in our Guéthary apartment when our daughter Sophie called and advised me to switch on the television. 'A plane has just flown into the Twin Towers in New York,' she said. 'Probably an off-course crop duster,' I responded sleepily, then switched on the set just in time to see the second plane strike its target. It was horrific beyond my comprehension. It seemed like the world had gone mad.

With airports shutting down in major cities all over the world, the ASP made a hasty decision to call off the upcoming European leg of the World Championship Tour, meaning that our Quiksilver Pro France would not be held. I decided that as soon as the dust had settled I would take some time out, fly home to Noosa and work on my marriage.

In February 2001, Jeff Hakman, 1989 world surfing champion Martin Potter and myself were at Biarritz airport on a bright, clear morning waiting to catch a flight to Munich. As it turned out, Biarritz was experiencing weather at the other end of the spectrum. With snow blocking the runways, no flights were expected to land all day. Given this reprieve, we decided to drive across the border to San Sebastián and take a leisurely lunch with surfboard shaper Peter Daniels. We reconvened at the *bar tabac* below my place at noon for a beer in the sunshine. As we sat drinking, Miki Dora joined us for a coffee.

On a whim, I said, 'Miki, would you like to come out to Australia next month as the guest of a surf festival?'

With Miki, Bill Hamilton and Susan McNeil, Surf Hut, Guéthary, 2000.

Jeff Hakman, Mark Richards and me, Bundoran, Ireland, 2001.

He pondered this for a while, which was a good sign. 'There'd have to be a contract,' he said. 'I'm not a frickin' sideshow.'

So began one of the more interesting chapters of my personal association with Miki Dora. I'd already decided that I couldn't go on running the Noosa Festival of Surfing by remote control, and my partner John Brasen agreed. This would be my last year. What better way to go out than to land the elusive Miki Dora as a special guest. It would never happen, I was told over and over again. 'Oh, he'll take the ticket and the hotel room,' people said, 'but you'll never see him.'

Since Miki had mentioned it first, I drew up a contract that required his attendance at several social events during the course of the week-long festival, and stipulated exactly what we would pay for and what was to be Miki's responsibility. It couldn't have been more precise. I should have known better. For some years, Miki's life in France had been funded by Quiksilver through a 'team rider' contract that basically spelt out his obligations to his sponsor—none. This was the kind of contract that Miki liked. He still surfed regularly, and beautifully for a man of his age, but if anyone attempted to photograph him, he would paddle in.

Zorro does Europe

The legends and VIP guests were ensconced at the South Pacific Resort, a couple of kilometres back from the surf. It was a beautifully landscaped place with poolside gardens and cabanas. Miki was apparently quite happy here—we rarely saw him at the beach. But he did honour his social obligations. It was only on the who-pays-for-what issue that we ran into trouble. One day surfers Robert August, Mark Martinson and Wingnut Weaver asked Miki to make up a foursome for golf. Late in the afternoon I got a phone call from Wingnut at the country club. 'Miki says you're paying for him.'

'Jesus, Wingy ... what are we talking about here? Fifty bucks? You pay and I'll fix you later.'

'Ah, it's actually a bit more than that.'

Miki, it transpired, had gone berserk in the pro shop and run up a very large bill, which he insisted that I would pay. I gave them my credit card details and bit my lip.

On the morning of Miki's departure, I had a call from the front desk. 'Mr Dora is checking out and he refuses to pay his phone bill. He's getting very abusive.' I jumped in my car and drove to the resort, where I found Miki pacing around the lobby, muttering at the staff and making theatrical gestures with his hands.

'Mr Dora,' said the duty manager, 'has made twenty-nine international phone calls and refuses to pay.' Miki exploded. 'I never touched my room phone.'

'Mr Dora,' said the exasperated manager, 'every day you've come down here, asked us to get numbers for you, then spent hours talking to people on that phone there.'

'Oh, *that* phone,' said Miki, pointing to the lobby phone. 'That's not *my* phone.'

Of course there was only one way out. Friends later said, almost admiringly, that Miki had got me on a technicality. But at the time I was furious. Nat Young was supposed to be driving him to Angourie, but they'd had an argument and now Miki needed a ride to the airport, which was where I too was bound. I fumed all the way, my wife and I in the front, Miki in the back with our bags. He kept muttering about the 'public phone' in the lobby. I badly wanted to hit the bastard.

As it turned out, Miki and I were on the same flight to Singapore. I was on a Quiksilver-paid-for business-class ticket. Miki was on the economy ticket I'd bought him. I knew this was going to get ugly.

'I'm with him,' he told the check-in clerk. 'We want to sit together.'

'I'm sorry sir, this is an economy ticket.'

'No, no ... I'm with him, goddammit!' I made a hasty exit through the gates while Miki hurled abuse over the counter. At Changi Airport I found him in the transit area and took him with me to the Qantas Club Lounge, where he availed himself of the buffet bar and sat down opposite me on the comfortable chairs. Relaxed, after a good sleep and a few glasses of wine, I suddenly saw the funny side of it all. We sat there chuckling quietly, like old sparring partners.

As offensive and unfair as he could be, it was difficult to stay mad at Miki. Besides, the worse he stung you, the better the dinner party stories later on.

A couple of months after his return from Australia, Miki had an annoying tumour removed from his neck and a biopsy revealed that it was cancerous. Further tests showed that the cancer had spread to several organs. Miki took the news in typical fashion. It simply wasn't possible. These doctors knew nothing. After several disappointments, Miki even made a trip to Germany, where some quack diagnosed it as 'Bavarian werewolf cancer'. The prognosis was no different, but it suited Miki's self-image a lot better.

On 11 August 2001, a group of about twenty friends celebrated Miki's sixty-seventh birthday at the Chez Francois restaurant in the village of Biriatou on the Spanish border. It was the kind of social event Miki had pretended to loathe for much of his life, yet on this warm evening on the terrace overlooking the Bidasoa River, he played the tables like a politician, moving from one group to the next, full of smiles and funny stories. It was a particularly poignant occasion because all of us knew that for Miki, there would be no more birthdays.

When I returned from Ireland a month later I was shocked to see how much Miki had aged. His weight was slipping away and he had developed a stoop. As the summer faded, Miki kept on surfing as much as he could, although he no longer really had the strength to push himself onto the face at Guéthary. I ran into him on the stairs one evening, dripping wet in the gloom, leaning on the railing gasping for air. I asked if I could help. 'It's okay, I got oxygen inside,' he said, nodding in the direction of his apartment.

The morning I left Guéthary to return to Australia, I slipped a note under Miki's door, telling him to contact me if there was anything he needed. It was a pointless gesture but I knew as I pushed it across the floor that it would be my last contact with Miki Dora. A couple of weeks later he too left Guéthary, returning to the care of his father and stepmother in Montecito, California, where he died peacefully just after New Year.

Back in France after the Christmas break, Jackie and I helped Harry Hodge pack up Miki's belongings. There wasn't much to document such a famous life, but then Miki's stock in trade had been his mystery. Among the papers we found uncashed cheques from the Screen Actors Guild for his bit part roles in the *Gidget* movies nearly forty years earlier, and letters he'd supposedly saved from a house fire in South Africa, which were burnt evenly around the edges so that they could still be read.

In April Harry organised a memorial for Miki on the terrace overlooking Guéthary. His father, Miklos, (a sprightly and dapper ninety-year-old) travelled from California, and several of Miki's oldest friends and one-time lovers came from around the world. Local surfers Christophe Reinhardt and François Lartigau paddled Miki's ashes out to the break, the mayor of Guéthary unveiled a memorial plaque, and we all went off and had a few drinks, a few tears and a lot of laughs.

Two days later I walked down to the terrace to check the surf and discovered that two of the screws holding Miki's plaque in place had been removed in an attempt to steal the memorial as private memorabilia. I replaced the screws but within a week the plaque was gone. Ah, Miki, your memorial, now a prized trophy on some shithead's wall. Exploited to the end.

Jackie and I were picking up the pieces of our marriage. We both knew it was going to be a long, hard road, but we were committed to the journey. We flew down to Marrakech and spent a few days wandering around the souks, sleeping and eating in superb riads, marvelling at the mansions of the Palmerie, trying to reclaim what we'd once had. It was a start, a promising start.

As it turned out, Morocco was also the venue for my next big project, one that would place me in direct conflict not just with Bernard Mariette but with the entire Quiksilver board of directors. A French–Moroccan surfer named Laurent Miramon, who ran a Quiksilver-sponsored surf camp not far from Casablanca, had been filling our ears with stories of big, challenging right-hand barrels at the mouth of the port of Safi. Jeff Hakman and I went down to investigate, along with my project manager for events, an Australian called Barry McGrath. Safi didn't quite turn it on for our visit, but we got an idea of its potential. Laurent and his family switched on the hospitality and introduced us to all the local dignitaries. When the Wali (governor) of the prefecture of Safi promised to seek royal sanction for the event, to renovate a well-worn but beautiful cliff-top hotel for our exclusive use, and to regrade and seal the dirt track that led from the hotel to the surf break, we were sold.

Since the best month for swell in Safi was February, it was decided that we would forego running the 2002 Quiksilver Masters and bring the first ever world surfing titles to Morocco early in the new year. Over the next six months Barry and I made several trips to Safi to oversee the construction and hire all the necessary tents and equipment. Safi was a diamond in the rough, a seedy port town with hidden treasures, not least of which were its citizens, who could never do enough for us. We were invited into homes for fabulous tagine dinners, and feted whenever we appeared in the town square. But in Washington, President George W. Bush had started to rattle sabres about 'weapons of mass destruction' in Iraq, and in these post-9/11 times, the entire Muslim world was becoming the enemy.

Maroc Masters poster, 2003.

Zorro does Europe

Early one December morning at the 'Serpent's Head', the surfside car park that would soon become our event site, I received a call on my mobile from Bernard Mariette's secretary informing me that I needed to get back to France by that evening to take a conference call from the Quiksilver board. In the flat at Guéthary I chucked back a couple of glasses of wine to settle my nerves before the call came through just before midnight. Global CEO Bob McKnight spoke first, and cut to the chase fairly briskly.

'We've decided that we are not going to conduct a Quiksilver event in a Muslim country at this time,' he said. I started to protest that Morocco was a kingdom of free religious choice and that Safi was as far from Baghdad as Paris was. Charlie Exon, the company counsel, cut in. 'Phil, I think you'd better shut the fuck up and just listen.'

Then they all weighed in. The Safi Masters was dead in the water, and if I wanted to argue the toss, so was I. Emotions were running high. Realising that I was just giving them reasons to fire me on the spot, I bit my lip and listened to the tirade. Then I hung up and opened another bottle of wine.

Two days later, on a bitterly cold Paris morning, Bernard Mariette and I visited the Moroccan Ambassador to France to apologise to him, and through him, to the Wali of Safi and to the King for Quiksilver's withdrawal from the deal. It was a brief meeting. The Ambassador was gracious and eloquent in both French and English. 'Your decision is noted and your apologies will be conveyed,' he assured us. His impeccable manners matched those of the vast majority of Moroccans I had encountered, and only made me feel worse. I'd put heart and soul into this event and my heart was almost breaking. It's only a surf comp, I told myself.

And now we had another one to run. The Americans had opened the door for us to run the Masters at Mākaha, so I was off to Hawaii.

Thanks largely to the patronage of Richard 'Buffalo' Keaulana, the big kahuna of Mākaha, and to his extended family, the Mākaha Masters was a huge success, with good waves and good vibes. To punish myself, I kept track of what was happening in Safi that week and it was flat. Obviously God, not Allah, rules the waves.

But this was to be the last of the Quiksilver Masters World Championships. Bernard Mariette had become global president of the company, and his growth objectives were more about acquiring companies than spending on marketing initiatives. But Mariette found plenty of money to spend on his charm offensive, convincing the board and the executive that Quiksilver should buy the venerable but ailing French ski company Rossignol.

At increasingly lavish company conferences around the world the message was drummed into us—follow Bernard and the world can be your oyster. When we arrived at the Delano Hotel in Miami Beach for the most extravagant conference yet, we all received a Mont Blanc pen and notebook set, into which was folded a note from the boss—'Thank you for your hard work'—and a cheque for $5000.

I took the money but I honestly didn't know how long I'd keep my job, particularly that northern summer after I'd incurred the wrath of the company's new European president, Pierre Agnes. Jackie and I were taking a well-earned vacation in the Algarve when my phone lit up with messages from Australia. Our dear friend Rennie Ellis had died from a stroke at only sixty-two. Grief-stricken, we bolted for the airport. I emailed

Rennie and I celebrate What A Nuisance's Melbourne Cup, 1985.

Zorro does Europe

Waxed up and ready to surf, Guéthary. (Photo Jeff Divine)

Agnes to say I needed a few extra days off then flew to Melbourne, where I delivered one of the many eulogies at a packed memorial for this special man at Prahran Town Hall.

On my return to France, Agnes read me the riot act about my unauthorised absence. Incensed, I reacted badly.

'We are not working well together,' he said as he dismissed me from his office.

CHAPTER THIRTY-THREE

With Surfer of the Year 2016, Matt Wilkinson, at the Surfing Australia Awards.

MASTERS OF THE UNIVERSE

At the Delano conference in Miami I had taken a few quiet drinks with Charlie Exon, who I'd known since before his days on the Quiksilver board. Despite our difference of opinion over Morocco's role in the 'axis of evil', I liked Charlie. I also knew he harboured literary ambitions.

I said, 'Quiksilver's got such a rich and colourful history, and only parts of it have been told. With Bernard taking the company into a whole new realm, this would be the perfect time to do a big fat book.' He looked interested, so I continued my pitch. 'I'd write it, you could oversee the project on behalf of the management.'

Charlie leaned back and took a long sip of his martini. 'Big project,' he said. 'How much do you estimate?'

'It's such a good story I know I can sell it to a publisher, which not only authenticates it but also takes care of the print bill. Quiksilver just does the marketing.' Charlie nodded as he called the waitress over and ordered another round. He said he'd put it to McKnight and Mariette.

A few months later I'd signed a contract with Chronicle Books in San Francisco, we'd packed up in France and were heading to California, albeit only for as long as it took to produce the book. This was a mixed blessing, for a few reasons. One, despite my acrimonious relationship with Pierre Agnes, we loved France and didn't really want to leave. Two, we'd spent enough time in Southern California to know we didn't really want to live there. Three, the move was putting me back in Bernard Mariette's direct orbit, and we too were on a collision course.

On the other hand, the money was good, I had the freedom to set up an office and hire my own team, and we found a cute clapboard cottage to rent in Laguna Beach, with lovely views of the sun setting behind Catalina Island. And our friends Paul Holmes (and new partner Kiku Terasaki) and Peter Townend were in the 'hood.

Although the Quiksilver history project was to be directly managed by CEO Bob McKnight and Charlie Exon, it fell under the auspices of the new Quiksilver Entertainment division, which meant I also had to report to its co-directors Danny Kwock and Matt Jacobsen.

The two directors were like chalk and cheese. Pint-sized Kwock was a great surfer who got his break with Quiksilver when McKnight caught him stealing board shorts from the warehouse and gave him a work program rather than turn him in to the cops. Within a decade he had become Quiksilver's marketing director, and a secret major partner in rival startup Volcom (a move that would later make him a multi-millionaire, although not very popular with the Quiksilver board). Kwock was bouncy and full of ideas. Jacobsen was a sports TV producer wannabe who sent emails on his Blackberry throughout meetings and seldom made eye contact.

Internal meetings about the project were a nightmare, but I managed to get everyone to sign off on a format and chapter plan. It was to be a monster coffee table book that told the gritty but inspiring story of Quiksilver's creation, while showcasing its position as the biggest and most successful surf company in the world.

We were about a year into the project, with maybe another six months required to get it to the printer when, unusually, I took a call from Bob McKnight on a Sunday morning. Sundays were all about surfing and beach volleyball for Bob. He didn't do meetings unless there was a good reason, and he was calling me to one that afternoon at Bernard Mariette's estate house on the Newport Coast. I guessed it was more likely to be for a slap on the face than a slap on the back.

The two leaders of the company were already in Bernard's home office when I arrived. There were no preliminaries, no drinks offered. Mariette took the lead, throwing my work-in-progress manuscript on the desk.

'What is the meaning of this?' he asked angrily. 'We are a public company, we can't publish this bullshit.'

I protested that we had already published most of the controversial bits, to great acclaim, almost a decade earlier in *Mr Sunset*, and that Mariette himself had been at several of the launches, cheering us on. But it was the Moroccan Masters all over again. The more I protested, the worse my position became.

Mariette said, 'You have two choices. You start again and tell the story of what Quiksilver has become, not some fairy story about what you think it was, or you leave the company tomorrow. Take your time, think about it overnight.'

So I put all the good bits on a disk for another day, commissioned puff pieces from various presidents and sales executives and stitched it all together with the worst hagiography I'd ever written. Horrified, Chronicle Books pulled out of the deal and Quiksilver footed the bill for producing, printing and distributing tens of thousands of copies of *The Mountain and the Wave* that to this day sit rotting in cardboard boxes around the world.

But strangely, my career at Quiksilver was not yet over. Although Chronicle had run a mile from a corporate vanity book, I had proposed a multi-book partnership and they were very interested in the second and third books. The second was a pretty picture book featuring the young surfer girls who represented the Roxy brand, in which my role was relatively minor, liaising between the brand's marketing team and the publisher. The third was a book suggested to me by Peter Townend, a look inside the head and lifestyle of the greatest surfer the world had ever seen, Kelly Slater.

Slater, then in his early thirties, had already published a ghosted auto-biography that told of his tough early life with an alcoholic father and his salvation through surfing. But anyone who had known Slater through his emerging years as a world champion surfer, myself included, knew there was much more to the man than just a rags-to-riches tale. The problem was, I was pretty sure Kelly regarded me as the enemy.

By the time I met Slater for the first time at the Quiksilver Pro at G-Land in 1997, he had already equalled Mark Richards' long-standing record of four world titles and had his sights set on a fifth that year. Whereas most of the pro surfers at the remote camp were entirely focused on their performance, Kelly was a congenial dinner partner, a good conversationalist and obviously intelligent. I also liked the way he related to the kids at the camp, playing pool into the night or watching cartoon videos with Alan Green's young daughter and mine. And his surfing blew my mind. I paddled out on a contest lay day with Tom Carroll and tried to catch a few left-overs in a building swell, but I was completely mesmerised by the view from the shoulder as Slater carved backhand tracks down the line. As always, it was fascinating and mildly depressing to watch a master surfer describe emphatically the yawning gulf between that small elite and the rest of us.

But when I went to work at Quiksilver Europe a couple of years later, I found that my encounters with the greatest surfer in the world were less congenial, mainly because Kelly's sponsorship obligations were almost as loose as Miki Dora's, and in Europe I was invariably the one whose job it was to drag him off to a press conference or a filming obligation. Once, in Munich, I waited in the lobby of his hotel with an increasingly impatient German television crew. I sent him a text and got no answer. I tried phoning but the line was engaged. I went up to the room and knocked firmly. No answer. I started back down to the lobby, then turned and went back and pounded on the door until a sniffling, tearful superstar opened the door with a phone at his ear, looked daggers at me, then held up five fingers and slammed the door in my face. Kelly didn't speak to me for much of the day, but I slowly got the story. He and girlfriend Pamela Anderson were breaking up.

Now, with nothing to lose, I contacted Kelly's manager and publicist and arranged for a meeting at Venice Beach in Los Angeles. I asked them to emphasise to Kelly that I was happy to stand aside for the author of his choice, but would edit the book and work with him on the photo selection. When we sat down for the meeting, Kelly was all smiles, but seemed fidgety, like he wanted to be somewhere else. I reiterated my offer to step aside if he'd prefer to work with someone else. 'Hell no,' he said. 'You're the author, so why don't you, ah, auth?' Cracking himself up, he stood up to leave, calling over his shoulder, 'Give me a call when you want to start.'

For the next year or so I tracked Kelly Slater around the globe, vying for his attention in a world full of distractions. We taped sessions in Hawaii, Fiji, France, all over Australia and up and down the California coast. He provided access to dozens of high-flying friends, including Eddie Vedder and Pamela Anderson, who was utterly charming over breakfast at her Malibu home. But at times he was the most frustrating, infuriating working partner. I titled my introduction, 'Waiting For Kelly'. When he read it, Kelly said, 'Wow, that's giving it to me straight!'

One of his closest friends later told me, 'When Kelly keeps you waiting a long time, it's not that he's being rude to you, it's just that he's being super nice to the person before you.'

The book, *Kelly Slater: For The Love* (his title) was a success in most markets. I think that together we succeeded in depicting a champion in the prime of life, a man of many talents and even more interests, a man who would have succeeded in whatever he decided to pursue. Kelly could be a flake at times, but the man I discovered underneath that was one I feel privileged to know, a man of ideas as well as action, a man of warmth as well as steely determination.

Surfing's only true superstar, he had never forgotten that he grew up tough on Florida's Space Coast. He treasured ordinary moments. Once I arrived at his new apartment on the Gold Coast to find that he had borrowed a friend's ute. "Come on," he said, "we have to go buy a fridge." We drove to a bargain warehouse in South Tweed where he haggled over the price for twenty minutes before signing autographs for another twenty. Then four of us carried the fridge to the carpark. At the other end we enlisted the help of some neighbours to get it up three flights of stairs. I was ready for a beer but Kelly had only coconut water. He sat at his kitchen bench beaming at his whitegoods wonder.

With Kelly in Spain, 2008.

Masters of the universe

Cloudbreak, 2007. Same session, different wave. (Photo Tom Servais)

One of my fondest memories of the long interview process is of a night at the Tantina de la Playa in Bidart, France. The Billabong Pro Mundaka had finished that afternoon, and after the long drive back to France, Kelly was in a relaxed and expansive mood. Over several bottles of good red wine, we covered everything, from the existence and nature of God to an insider's view (Kelly is of Syrian descent) of the Palestine situation. Suddenly it was two in the morning. We had been the only customers for several hours. The waiters stood by discreetly, smiling when we looked at them. When I switched off the recorder and called it a night, Kelly signed memorabilia for the staff, then we sat back down and drank rounds of apple manzana with them before staggering into the morning.

My most embarrassing memory is of a surf session at Cloudbreak in Fiji, when I showed my intent by paddling hard for a set wave. Slater and his pal Shane Dorian paddled aside and let me have it. I took the drop and turned hard before hearing a piercing whistle. The young free-surfing prodigy Clay Marzo had been lurking up the line and whistling at anyone who started to take off on him. I presumed he was somewhere in this pit behind me and turned the board harder to push through the lip and off the back. Slater and Dorian were shaking their heads and thumping their boards in frustration. 'You just don't fuckin' do that!' an exasperated Slater shouted at me. I looked up the reef and saw Clay Marzo, still sitting on his board.

I learned later that a lot better surfers than me had been yelled at in the line-up by Kelly Slater, who is human after all. His rage was momentary and the incident was never mentioned again, but it still haunts me. As I wrote this, nearly ten years after that incident, I had one eye on the keyboard and the other on another screen, where Slater, then forty-four and still, on his day, the greatest surfer in the world, had just thrashed John Florence, his heir-apparent, in the final of the Billabong Pro Tahiti. It was his fifty-fifth tour victory, which put him in contention to win a twelfth world title. My friend Peter Townend, the first world professional champion forty years ago, had one tour victory in his career.

But it isn't the staggering weight of his achievements that make me such a huge Kelly Slater fan. It is the fact that surfing is not the whole man. By being so much more than just a surfer, he has elevated our sport, our culture, more than anyone else since Duke Kahanamoku, and I have the deepest respect for him for that.

In the course of working on the Kelly book, Jackie and I had moved back to Australia, from which base it was agreed I would work out my Quiksilver contract. It was an amicable agreement. There were no hard feelings ... yet.

In 2004 we had celebrated our twenty-fifth wedding anniversary by renewing our marriage vows in front of an Elvis Presley impersonator in Las Vegas. Despite the comical and somewhat tawdry setting, there was serious intent. We felt we had overcome our problems and were ready to move on with the rest of our lives. In that same year, Sam and her husband Clinton blessed us with our first grandchild. It took another three years to extricate ourselves from America, by which time another grandson had been added to the brood, and we were ready to go home to Noosa to become slightly respectable grandparents.

I didn't have a clear plan as to what to do when the Quiksilver pay cheques stopped coming, but we had some property in Noosa and, after nine years in the corporate jungle, I was reasonably cashed up. In the back

Older, wiser, happier, in a warm place, 2010.

The whole damn, wonderful clan, Noosa 2015. (Photo Jason Mccallum)

of my mind I kept hearing a conversation I'd had decades earlier with the writer Craig McGregor, when Peter Crawford and I dropped in to see him in the hills behind Byron Bay. I had told Craig that I wanted to write a novel, but that paid work kept getting in the way. 'Take a chance,' he'd said. 'Don't worry about the money, put your faith in your talent, and if you've got any, the money will come.'

Maybe the time had finally come to take that chance.

Back Beach publicity shot, 2008. (Photo Jason Mccallum)

EPILOGUE

In our last year or so in California, Jackie and I had been frequently amused by the hard-sell television advertising for housing loan sharks. 'Been declared bankrupt? No problem. Criminal record? No problem.' It seemed insane to us that seemingly reputable banks could offer relatively low-interest loans to people who had little hope of repaying them. We had no idea that this was merely the tip of an iceberg that was about to sink the world financial system.

So back in Australia we put a chunk of money into high-risk shares and the rest into creating my dream surf shop. Well, it wasn't exactly a 'surf' shop, but an emporium devoted to all the stuff that I would put into my ideal beach house—collector surfboards, primitive islander paddles, surf art and photography, Hawaiian-influenced furniture and furnishings, rare books about the beach, fabrics and artefacts from all the places in my surfing memory bank. Then the global financial crisis kicked in, the shares tanked and the retail market dried up. Most of the beach houses that could have used our stuff were on the market at a fraction of their value.

It appeared I'd taken the wrong chance.

But it was not all bad news. I published a well-received book called *Salts and Suits*, which told the inside story not only of Quiksilver's fall from grace but of the virtual disintegration of the once-thriving surf industry. This did not endear me to several surf industry executives, but it did create a lucrative sideline for a few years as a consultant to investment groups who wanted to understand how the surf industry worked, and apparently thought that I knew. A string of other books followed, including an official history of Australian surfing and a best-selling book about Bali.

The real game, however, the project that drained me of time and energy year in, year out, was the Noosa Festival of Surfing, which had been labouring for a few years and which I took control of again in 2009, dragging the entire family kicking and screaming into the hellfire with me. It was, and remains, an economic basket case, with little hope of ever making any real money, although now that it is run by my efficient and cool-headed daughters, Sam and Ellie, perhaps that will change.

But when it comes to the festival, money has never been the point for me. It has kept me in touch with not only the big names, but so many common or garden variety surfers that I've met over half a century on one coast or another. Inevitably, our lives have moved down different paths, some easy, some less so. Some have dropped off the vine, others threaten to. But surfing remains a constant, and I treasure every moment I spend with real surfers, the ones who share the love and pass on the spirit of what we have—what we still have, despite the overloaded beach car parks and the weekend log jams on the water.

It was my search for that spirit that led me into one of the most enjoyable and gratifying projects of my latter career, documenting the story of the original Sydney surfboard manufacturers for television, in collaboration with my friend Shaun Cairns. Still active in their eighties and nineties, these gentlemen helped me put a human face on the industry and culture that had been my bedrock for more than half a century. Barry Bennett, still 'blowing foam' at his Brookvale factory at eighty-five, told me he'd be there 'until they carry me out'. Scott Dillon, a legendary surfboard craftsman and big wave rider of the '50s and '60s, now eighty-eight, told me at his nursing home, 'I think I'll go back to Hawaii and just catch a few more before I go, soon as they let me out of here.'

I've got a little way to go yet, but I think I'll be like Barry and Scotty. They'll have to carry me out, too.

With Bob McTavish at Back Beach, 2009.

I wrote in the introduction to this book about the wake-up call that is a heart attack, and how it fundamentally changes how you view your life. I consider myself very lucky that two years on, my heart is strong again and I am able, within reason, to enjoy life much as before. I consider myself even luckier that I have a wonderful, loving family to share these years with—Jackie, my wife of thirty-seven years; daughters Sophie, Sam and Ellie; sons-in-law Clint and Jay; grandsons Jackson, Beau, Hunter and Hamish.

Most of all now, I treasure every moment I spend in the ocean, every wave I paddle into and feel that surge of power behind as I slowly get to my feet and steer my way through the obstacles. My surf sessions get shorter and recovery takes longer, but as long as the passion remains, every day you catch a wave is a good one.

I love to watch my grandsons surf, and to surf with them. I'd like to show them how to stand parallel on your board and push through a wave, like Bobby Brown showed me when I was their age, but alas that's beyond me these days. Two are already surfers, and I hope that in time all four will feel the stoke, if only so that I can see that wondrous expression in their eyes when they catch a good one.

It's an expression that captures what they know and what I still hope—that the best rides are still to come.

Family team event with grandson Jack at Noosa Festival 2017.
(Photo Kim Molnar)

Hunter's first surfing lesson, 2012. (Photo Jason Mccallum)

ACKNOWLEDGEMENTS

This memoir is dedicated to the memory of all the people who have been an important part of my life and are no longer with us: Dad, Mum, Sol, Derek Brand, Rennie Ellis, Peter Crawford, Albie Thoms, Richard Neville, John Stubbs, Brian Johns, Ian Frykberg, Ron Saw, Max Walker, Michael Peterson, Miki Dora, Shirley Strachan, Peter Troy, Lester Brien, Wayne Goss, Barry McGuigan, François Lartigau ... the list is long, but not forgotten.

Among the many people who have helped me unlock the vaults of memory, I particularly want to acknowledge my sisters, Wyverne Smith and Robyn Leaver, whose insights into our childhood years were invaluable, and who will possibly read some of this with mixed feelings. But one

Still out there! Noosa Logger comp, May 2017. (Photo Ian Borland)

of the joys of getting older—and there aren't that many—is that we grow more tolerant of those we love. Despite our very different paths in life, my sisters and I are closer now than ever before, and I am grateful for their non-judgemental and unconditional love.

I am also grateful to my publishers, Hardie Grant Books, for their continued support in this, my seventh book in as many years with them. Fran Berry has been my rock at HG, and she will be missed. Thanks also to Pam Brewster, Meelee Soorkia, Vanessa Lanaway and Jane Grant.

Many of the photos used in this book have been retrieved from archive boxes and I have no idea who shot them, so a heartfelt thanks to all my photographer friends (credited and uncredited) who shared the ride for a time.

I am indebted to current *Tracks* editor Luke Kennedy for commissioning a column called 'The Wonder Years', which necessitated me digging up old material I'd almost forgotten I wrote, and to all-time *Tracks* tragic Ray Henderson for providing scans of old pages. Neil Jameson also has a far better memory for detail than mine, and generously substituted his fact for my fantasy, while taking the sting out of my tail where necessary.

Now that we are grey nomads much of the year, chunks of this book were written in boltholes all over the place, for which I have to thank: Sue Cummings and Bliss Swift at Umah Kembar, Bali; Patrick Burgess and Galuh Wandita at Berawa, Bali; Paul Holmes and Kiku Terasaki at Laguna Beach, California; David and Joan Hill in Pacific Palisades, California; Jeff and Denise Bradburn in Bidart, France, and at Mahanga Beach, New Zealand; John and Sharon Brasen at Nerang, Queensland; Rod and Andrea Brooks and Paul and Karen Neilsen at Tugan, Queensland; John and Di Pickering at Southport, Queensland; Judy Bray and Graham McConnell in Waitui and Sydney, NSW; Harry Hodge and Louise Wallace at Newport Beach, NSW; Tilly Heppel and Simon Dibbs in Mosman, NSW; and Rob and Allan Leaver at Farmborough Heights, NSW.

Finally, I thank my family for being, well, family. Particularly Jackie, who has stayed the course despite some bumpy patches, and knows that things always get better when there's surf. Love yez all.

Phil Jarratt
Noosaville, November 2016

Me at the Salton Sea, California, 2005. (Photo Jason Mccallum)

Phil Jarratt has worked in surf publishing and the surf industry for more than forty years, and is regarded as one of the sport's foremost authorities. The editor of *Tracks* and *Australian Surfer's Journal* and an associate editor of *Surfer*, outside of surfing Phil has been a staff writer for *The Sydney Morning Herald* and *The Bulletin*, the editor of *Playboy* and *Penthouse* during the eighties, and in sports television has worked on two Commonwealth and one Olympic Games.

He has authored thirty-five books including award-winning surf histories and bestselling biographies. Phil has received the Australian Surfing Hall of Fame Media Award four times and has won numerous other awards for his work as an author and film-maker.

Selected publications
The Wave Game (1977): The first book about professional surfing.
Home: The Evonne Goolagong Story (1993): Best-selling collaboration.
Mr Sunset (1997): Best-selling biography of surfer Jeff Hakman.
The Mountain & The Wave (2006): Official history of Quiksilver.
Kelly Slater For The Love (2008): Collaboration with the greatest surfer ever.
Salts & Suits (2010): The unofficial history of the surf industry.
Surfing Australia (2012): The official history of surfing in Australia.
That Summer At Boomerang (2014): Duke Kahanamoku's 1914 visit to Australia.
Bali Heaven And Hell (2014): Best-selling cultural history of surfers in Bali.